REALITY
of your
ASCENSION

I0805774

REALITY of your ASCENSION

Teachings of Serapis Bey

Elizabeth Clare Prophet

Summit University Press®
Gardiner, Montana

REALITY OF YOUR ASCENSION
Teachings of Serapis Bey
by Elizabeth Clare Prophet

For information, contact
The Summit Lighthouse, 63 Summit Way, Gardiner, MT 59030 USA
Tel: 1-800-245-5445 or 1 406-848-9500
info@SummitUniversityPress.com
SummitLighthouse.org

Library of Congress Control Number: 2022935297
ISBN: 978-1-60988-400-0 (softbound)
ISBN: 978-1-60988-401-7 (eBook)

SUMMIT UNIVERSITY PRESS®

25 24 23 22 1 2 3 4

Contents

Foreword

At some point, most of us ponder the purpose of our life—or lifetimes—on planet Earth. Hopefully we will do this while there is still time to make a difference in how we choose to live that life.

The question is not new, of course. Through all of recorded history, people have sought the answer to life's ultimate question.

For millennia, the mystics of East and West have known the answer: the goal of life is to ascend back to the source from which we came. Sometimes stated plainly, sometimes veiled in mystic symbolism—even recorded in the very stones of the Great Pyramid—they have left us keys to the path of the ascension.

Yet even when the principles of that path were plainly set forth, hierarchies who saw themselves as the inheritors of the world's religious traditions have sought to obscure the real meaning and power of the spiritual keys the mystics revealed—and even the reality of the goal itself. They would keep people bound in orthodoxy rather than allow them to find their ultimate freedom.

At the turning of the age, as at the turning of the last age two thousand years ago, people are once more awakening to the goal of the ascension. And the Masters of Wisdom are once more engaging in the world scene to reveal the reality of the goal of life and how to attain it.

In 1979, Elizabeth Clare Prophet came to San Francisco—an ancient focus of light known today, as on ancient Lemuria, as the city of seven hills—to hold a seminar titled *A Retreat on the Ascension.* The seminar was sponsored by Serapis Bey and the Brotherhood of the Ascension Temple, the etheric retreat of the ascended masters at Luxor, Egypt.

The masters and their messenger spoke about the violet flame as the practical means to soul liberation in the Aquarian age, of the ritual of exorcism as an essential tool for the spiritual seeker, of the calling of the initiate to be active in world affairs, of how to apply the eternal truths of the path to the challenges of the modern world. In short, the Brotherhood revealed the most practical and essential keys for all who seek ultimate liberation from the wheel of rebirth. The book you hold in your hands is the record of those teachings.

We invite you to enter into the experience of this retreat. Experiment with the spiritual exercises. Make your attunement with the ascended masters and cosmic beings whose words you will read, and receive the transfer of light they offer. Gain a glimpse of the reality of *your* destiny to be an ascended master.

The doors of the Ascension Temple are opened. The Brotherhood of Luxor bids you enter. Dare to cross the threshold and experience the reality of your life as it is meant to be.

THE EDITORS

CHAPTER ONE

The Path of Reunion with God

Good evening, everyone. I am so grateful to be gathered with you in the presence of love. We are so fortunate to be able to assemble together on this golden shore to commune in the love that is our individual keynote of victory.

We are grateful for the sponsorship of beloved Serapis Bey, son of Sanat Kumara, light of the Brotherhood of Luxor. He has called us together in celebration of the ascension of the Mother. The feast of the Assumption of the Virgin Mary is celebrated on August 15. It is the sign of the white flame that rises within us as our own ascension light as we magnetize that flame by love. And so it is to love we go to understand the goal and the victory of life.

As I come to a retreat called by the hierarchy, I come as a little child excited to know what is the great marriage feast that the ascended masters have prepared for us together. And as I muse in my heart and exercise all of the notes of the teachings that they have given to us, I know that it is more than in the words of the teaching or in the books they have written. It is in the very essence of the transfer of light that they come.

And I remember when I was in college how bored I used to be with a professor that would take up the textbook and read it in class, and that would be the sum of the course. And I would say, "Give us more, give us more; we can read the books at home. Tell us what you know, tell us what you are, tell us what you have become." But unfortunately, some of those professors, though professing to know, have not become their subject and so they can only rehearse and still rehearse the textbooks.

And we seek a living flame and we seek a living experience and we go to the churches and we go here and there, and somehow we hear the repetition of the same old words, when we are really seeking not words but the living Word. The Word is our goal, and to understand the Word we must understand the incarnation of God. We have feared to contemplate that God comes as an indwelling light, a light that exists as potential until we rise to meet it.

This *Retreat on the Ascension* is inspired by Serapis Bey in celebration of the release of his paperback book, *Dossier on the Ascension,* which was dictated to Mark Prophet, my late husband, and written down and treasured in our hearts all of these years. It is the body and the essence of Serapis that he imparts. It is like the stones of the Great Pyramid, which he inspired.

That teaching is something for you to read and study and review. It is not only I who must exercise those scales on the piano of the teaching, but you also must exercise your minds, and I cannot do it for you. I have assimilated that body and that blood of that teaching, and so I have come to be the vessel of the transfer of the light of which the teaching is a cup.

The *Dossier* is a cup, and we drink of that cup. And the essence of the contents of the cup is the essence of the Word. The Word is the Word that Serapis Bey has become. Becoming the Word is the path of all those who seek the ascension as the goal of life. The sublime climax of the mission of Jesus Christ was the reunion in the white cloud that received him out of their sight.[1] That cloud is the I AM THAT I AM, and the ascension is the return to the God from whence he descended by the flame that is the white light.

We are gathered here for two days to explore the meaning of that light, to experience that light, to know its cleansing power, its intrinsic wisdom and the love that we share because of its presence.

In the Footsteps of the Avatars

Elijah ascended in a chariot of fire.[2] Gautama Buddha ascended. Moses ultimately ascended. And so the great avatars known and those not so well known have achieved that goal of life. Yet somehow the knowledge of this goal is withheld from us. Or if we come to believe that we will attain it, we believe somehow it will miraculously happen in an unknowing or an unconscious way simply because we have followed certain rituals of religion.

Elijah Taken Up in a Chariot of Fire, Giuseppe Angeli

But, in fact, the ascension is the process of many lifetimes. Jesus had many incarnations, as did Gautama and Moses, and the life we know of Jesus Christ is the culmination of the raising up of that light in many episodes of service to God and man. The penetration of your own lifestream, if you dare to look, will reveal a process of the soul's putting on more and more of the inner light, coming into a greater and greater awareness of the Real Self who is God, coming into that awareness, magnetizing that light into this vessel, using the light for service, for giving the gift of love upon the altar of humanity. And the greatest gift of love is the gift of the self—the giving of our self as an instrument of whatever we are called to do that raises every other part of life to a higher awareness of self.

The Buddhists call it the dharma. It is the path of Christ, of Zoroaster, the path of putting on and fulfilling the divine plan and the inner blueprint. Essentially, this is the path of the ascension, and that path is written individually for every one of you.

How marvelous to consider that by the Holy Spirit within us we can come to know that path. We can discover through the indwelling Christ the way to walk. We can pursue the divine plan and know that each one of us is a tender flower—very special, very different, very unique, but having the one common light, the Real Self who is the person of Christ.

This is the great teaching of the Lord Jesus, who came to save us for that individual path of self-mastery and self-realization and came to quicken us to know that that which is in him exists within us when we determine to become humble—humble before the one God diversifying himself in all.

Serapis Bey speaks of the great garment of humility that is worn like an undergarment—something we are never without, something we never forget. And so, the path of reunion with God begins with that first step of humility before the awesome Presence of the Lord, who is I AM THAT I AM.

Recognizing that light, that Person of God the Father who sends his Son, the Mediator, to be our teacher, our guru, we enter into that sublime relationship of the Father and the Son. The Son exists as the Self toward which we reach. The soul is the potential that decides whether to rise into that higher Self or whether to exist as a quasi-self or a not-self.

So we begin as the soul that determines to be, that has the courage to awaken in the name of Gautama, that has the courage to put on its inner reality, knowing that with that responsibility comes the responsibility not only for this life but for every part of life. For we are seized with that magnificent conception that we are one, that within each other we experience the love that is God, that we are cells in the body of God if we choose to be. And when we choose to be, we become a part of the stars and the suns and the galaxies. We become a part of each one's heart. We become a part of the joy and the pain of a whole creation groaning and travailing to give birth to this conception of reality.

The Seven Chohans of the Rays

The ascended masters are those who have gone before us on the path. They have discovered the light. They have determined to become one with it. They have lovingly become the disciples of that light wherever that Word has been embodied. They have followed the Lamb, as John wrote, "whithersoever he goeth."[3] They follow the Person of the Son of God.

The ascended masters, whom we know so dearly, so intimately, define for us how individual is the path. There are seven chohans (lords) of the seven rays that come out of the Holy Spirit. And they are almost as different as night and day.

Take El Morya, the turbaned one from Darjeeling. He was embodied as Saint Thomas More, and in his presence one feels the scintillating blue lightning of the will of God. One contemplates the ultimate sacrifice he made—lifetime after lifetime loving the will of God more than life itself, and thereby becoming that will. No one could understand why he would not spare his life when a simple word of retraction would have sufficed. But he would not. He would rather have his head removed by the edict of Henry VIII than move one moment apart from his devotion to that will of God as the Christ gave to him the gift to see it.

Thomas More

El Morya

And so the tremendous power of the lord of the first ray is something that we follow for an understanding of energy, power in ourselves, power in government and in the economy. We learn from him the path of individual Christhood through service in organization and the administration of life itself.

We move on to the second ray of wisdom and the lord of that ray, Lord Lanto. He serves in the Royal Teton Retreat, and he embodies the tremendous peace of the wisdom masters, the tremendous wisdom that comes out of ancient China. The path of wisdom is the quiet knowing of God that becomes a stupendous power for change in an entirely different way than the way of El Morya.

And then we come to know love through the person of

Paul the Venetian, the Italian artist who perfected works depicting the Trinity. Paul the Venetian depicts the beauty of the soul and he teaches us the love of the Holy Spirit.

The fourth ray is served by Serapis Bey. It is the white light of the Mother. Out of it comes architecture, the principles of mathematics, the foundations of the building of the matter temple. In the presence of Serapis, one knows an entirely different conception of what we call the Christ, the real person of us all.

And then we come to Hilarion, who was embodied as the apostle Paul, who gives to us the green ray of precipitation of that architectural blueprint that Serapis holds in the Great Pyramid. And we learn from Hilarion the intensity of a science that becomes a whole civilization by the very rock of truth. We learn the meaning of health and the abundant life. We learn to deal and grapple with the very immediate problems that he dealt with when he expanded the mission of Jesus Christ.

Nada

Saint Germain

Nada is the lord of the sixth ray, the lady master whose teachings of law and of love apply in the ministration and service of that sixth ray, which was the gift of Jesus Christ to us in the Piscean age. This is the path most nearly identified with the path of Jesus—the path of ministering to life and service to life as he taught.

Then we come to the seventh ray and the Aquarian age and Saint Germain, and we see a master alchemist, a diplomat, a statesman, the Wonderman of Europe and the sponsor of the United States. We see an entirely different person—one who has embodied as Saint Joseph and as Samuel the Prophet, one who is very interested in the applications of the seventh ray in terms of freedom. He becomes the heart of freedom to the nations.

All of these seven rays and their seven persons tell us that one of those paths is for us uniquely, that we in many incarnations have served on one or more of those rays, that we are affinitized to those rays and that we identify with one or more of those masters. And ultimately all of the seven rays blending into the white light leads us to the path of the ascension. The ascension path is the white light; it is Joseph's coat of many colors[4] (worn by Jesus in his embodiment as Joseph) now become his seamless garment.

The harmony of the seven rays becomes our keynote in this class. And what is the white light? The white light is the light of the Mother, and it is the base for the building of our individual pyramid.

We are going to commune with that white light and with that white stone through music, through meditation and through the teachings of the ascended masters. I bid you welcome to the retreat and welcome to the *Dossier on the Ascension.* I suggest that you secure a copy and read this book, because it will tell you so much more than I can put into words and give you the chalice to receive the light.

A Practical Path

Your victory *is* your ascension. And the path of the ascension is for sons and daughters of God who understand that you can't make your ascension until you raise a portion of the earth with you. The service you give to life has to leave the world in a better place or you don't qualify for your ascension.

So when the ascended masters call you to the path, they are calling you as friends of freedom to give to the earth that flame of freedom that you feel mounting in your heart in a practical way, with practical solutions in education, in our government, in our money system, in what is happening in Central America, in Nicaragua, in Mexico, what is happening with the energy crisis. All of that you become more involved in because you are on the path. The path isn't retreat from action; it is going into a retreat in the heart, discovering the sacred fire, coming forth with that sacred fire and saying, "O universe, I am *here,* and I am here to win my victory through service to my family, my community, my nation, and my planet."

And so the call of Saint Germain, the chohan of the seventh ray, to all those who come into this embodiment for their ascension is "Friends of freedom, arise, arise." We call to the friend of freedom, the ascended master Jesus Christ. We call to all ascended masters of the Great White Brotherhood, and then we turn our gaze and our eye upon the earth and we say, "Friends of freedom, arise, arise. Souls of light, arise and set the earth free."

In some way, in some manner, because you enter the path of your ascension, you will contribute to earth's freedom. This is the battle cry, and it's a battle that is Armageddon—light swallowing up darkness, light transmuting darkness through the Word. The ascended masters have become the Word. They are here to show us how, so we call to them and their chelas in the inner retreats to gather together with us.

Serapis Bey Receives a Neophyte into His Mystery School,
Norman Thomas Miller

CHAPTER TWO

The Story of Serapis Bey: The Squaring of the Circle

Beloved Serapis Bey is depicted as the hierarch of the Ascension Temple in this painting done by Tom Miller. It illustrates you, the disciple, coming with hands outstretched, asking the master for the transfer of his light and attainment, which you understand will come to you step-by-step as you walk the path.

You notice the long corridor that leads to the King's Chamber, and you see in that chamber the blazing light of the resurrection flame. You see an inner ceremony taking place there. It is the ceremony of the ritual of the resurrection.

Jesus gave a public example of this ritual. First, there is the crucifixion, then the laying of the body in the tomb. You will notice in this illustration the tomb where the initiate is placed. There he must work out the problem of being, which, in the terms of the Brotherhood of Luxor is called the squaring of the circle.

The squaring of the circle means the drawing forth of the flame of God and precipitating that flame within this body temple for the purpose of the resurrection of the soul to eternal life. That initiation Jesus Christ submitted himself to before the

Hierophant of Luxor. In the *Dossier,* Serapis Bey describes Jesus Christ coming to the door of his retreat, being received as the Son of God, and bowing in humility and saying, "I would begin at the very first steps."

Jesus went through the initiations at Luxor, Egypt, in the inner retreat of the temple of Serapis Bey. He emerged after studying there and in the temples of the Brotherhood in India[1] to reveal to the world in three years the steps along the path of the ascension. Each one of his miracles and his healings demonstrate the principle of the squaring of the circle.

The Great Pyramid is the carving in stone of the record of the path of initiation whereby the soul, beginning in matter—the base of the pyramid, the four sides—rises from the center of the pyramid to the apex. The raising up of that flame is the meditation upon the white light that travels in the physical body from the base of the spine to the crown. The Hindus call it the Kundalini fire. It is the white light, the sacred fire that we call the Mother flame. The meditation upon that flame is a very important key to the integration of all of the faculties within your being.

Serapis Bey, then, is a friend of freedom who has arisen in our midst to teach us the way that has been walked by many of the saints that we know and some we do not know.

The Saviour Sanat Kumara and the Establishment of the Mystery Schools

Who is Serapis Bey? First of all, he is the son of Sanat Kumara, the Ancient of Days, who came to earth in her hour of distress to raise up once again the adoration and devotion to the light. Some of you know the concept of the seven root races destined to embody upon earth. Sanat Kumara came in the period of the fall of the fourth root race—after the great rebellion of the archangel Lucifer and his angels when the fourth root race on

Lemuria had gone out of the way of the path of light and they were fulfilling only the law of death.

It was the saviour Sanat Kumara, whom Daniel the prophet saw as the Ancient of Days,[2] who came to earth with one hundred and forty-four thousand volunteers. Together they said: "We will keep the flame of life—the Mother flame and the threefold flame—burning in the retreat of Shamballa. We will keep that flame until the multitudes of the people of earth once again respond to the love of Almighty God."

These voluntary pilgrims and exiles of light journeyed to earth. Among them are sons and daughters of God who today are ascended masters—after all, it was a long time ago. They embodied among earth's evolutions. They ministered to life. And they did not lose the thread of contact with their Source and with the Ancient of Days. And so they walked the earth as adepts and avatars in the various ages that have preceded the very dawn of recorded civilization, ages on Atlantis and Lemuria.

The Last Days of Atlantis

Serapis Bey, then, the son of Sanat Kumara, was embodied on Atlantis in its closing hours, when that continent was to be destroyed because of the people's misuse of love in science and in the manipulation of energy against one another. The sinking of Atlantis, as you know, is recorded in Genesis as the flood of Noah. Prior to its sinking, Sanat Kumara notified certain of his sons that it was time to transfer the flames that they had consecrated on the altars of the temples of Atlantis to other parts of the earth because the continent was about to go down.

Serapis Bey was one who journeyed with devotees of the white light to the place where Luxor, Egypt, is now, for the purpose of setting up of the retreat of the Ascension Temple on the physical plane and the etheric plane.

Serapis Bey was embodied on Atlantis in its closing hours, just before the final sinking of the continent. *Atlantis* by Auriel Bessemer.

Saint Germain was another who left Atlantis in her closing days. He established the flame of freedom in the Transylvanian foothills, now part of Romania. That flame of freedom was to become the foundation of the House of Rakoczy.

Others also went forth from Atlantis, and because they sailed, and because they were willing to dedicate their flames in other parts of the earth, after the Flood passed and civilization began again, there were mystery schools where souls of light who responded by their hearts' devotion to the flame that was kept could go.

Serapis Bey did not take his ascension until about 400 B.C., choosing to remain in embodiment to become the sponsor of some of the greatest architectural feats that have ever been brought forth upon the earth.

The more we study about Serapis Bey, the more we grow in

awe for this son of God who has held steadfast to the disciplines of the white light and has received, year after year, candidates for the ascension. The requirement for earth and her evolutions to keep in the orbit of the sun, to keep open a way of life, the requirement for the planet to continue to exist is that one son of God make his ascension each year. This is the requirement. If it were not for the mystery school of Serapis Bey and the Brotherhood at Luxor, the teachings on the ascension would not have gone forth and therefore earth's evolutions would not have fulfilled the requirement of the law.

One day, because you attended this retreat, you may be the one who meets the requirement for the ascension of a single son of God upon this planetary body. And if there is just one of you out of this audience who becomes that one, then our purpose and our mission in coming to San Francisco this summer will certainly have been fulfilled, and we shall have been rewarded many thousands of times.

Chohan of the Fourth Ray

Serapis Bey occupies the very key position, then, among all of the chohans. He is the chohan of the fourth ray. And if you take the number seven, you see that the fourth ray is midpoint between three on one side and three on the other. The center figure of four is key because it is the merging of the white light, it is the nexus of the figure eight, it is the point of the Mother flame always embodied in the Guru, East or West. The person of the Mother is veritably the person of Sanat Kumara, who moves in and among us and through us by that white light.

The chohan of the fourth ray is also the sponsor of the fourth root race, and it is the fourth root race that fell under the influence of the rebellion of the fallen angels who rebelled against God the Father, God the Son, God the Holy Spirit, and God the Mother. The great degradations that occurred on Lemuria were therefore perversions of the white light.

The white light is the sacred fire of creation itself. It is the fire of creation. And its perversion, of course, becomes black magic. We see, then, in Egypt, the focal point of the ascension flame, the practice of black magic by the Egyptian Black Brotherhood that went on for centuries upon centuries in defiance of the very presence of Serapis Bey within his temple.

We see, then, that the point of redemption of earth goes back to Lemuria, the Motherland, and the Mother flame itself. The Mother flame and the ascension flame are one and the same. Earth has a tremendous karma with this flame, for the multitudes of the earth followed after the fallen ones and the fourth root race. And their perversions of the Mother flame, which took place right here in San Francisco and off the coast of California, ultimately left the way open for the desecration of the temples, priests and priestesses defiling the temples, and ultimately ending in sexual orgies and perversions of the life force. And the last and final act of the fallen one was the murder of the highest representative of the Mother on Lemuria.

The Raising Up of the Mother Flame

The desecration of the person of the Mother and her flame was the real cause for the sinking of Lemuria, and since that hour earth has been slowly, slowly working through all of the ages until the coming of the age of Aquarius, arriving at an age once again when the light of the Mother, the light of the Woman, could be raised up in all, both male and female. And the raising up of that light in you and in me will bring about once again the honoring of the woman and of the Mother, and a reunion of the Mother light rising from the base with the light of the Father that descends out of the I AM Presence.

And so, as we stand on the golden shore of the west gate of the United States and of the City Foursquare, we are standing in time on the golden shore of the age of Aquarius. The next two thousand years is destined to see the raising up of consciousness such as has not occurred since the golden ages of Lemuria.

It is a tremendous joy to live in this moment and to realize that together we are feeling and sharing, as it passes through us, this tremendous love of God for the reunion of Father, Son, Holy Spirit, and Mother—the four pillars in the temple of being within our own consciousness. These are the four sides of the Great Pyramid. These four Persons of the Godhead are the base and foundation of life.

The Path of the Ascension: Alignment with the Inner Light

A resolution of those forces is necessary within our consciousness, and this is the path of the ascension—to make the base of life once again the square that can become the cube. Gautama Buddha's great lesson was that we are out of alignment with the inner light and therefore all of life is suffering—a suffering because of desire, a desire that causes an out of alignment state, nonalignment with the inner will of Being.[3] So getting into alignment is the real teaching of Serapis Bey.

We can see, then, that the Great Pyramid and his teachings are the fulcrum of life. They become the keystone in the arch of hierarchy, the fourth ray, the fourth chohan, the Mother flame. Without the white light we cannot enjoy the integration of selfhood. We may explore all the various paths of psychology or religion or whatever way we may seek in order to establish that basic and essential harmony that we crave, but in reality, through all of these processes, what is really wanting is the resolution of the soul as the jewel centered in the very center of these four pillars of our temple.

Serapis Bey, then, becomes a very important key when more people than ever before are experiencing problems of their psychology, when there is more crime, more murder, more rape, more taking drugs to escape life. All of this is the sign of this coming of the Mother light that is so intense that when it rises from the altars of Lemuria, unless we dive into it and become a part of it, we find that it becomes the rock—as Jesus and Paul spoke of it—that unless we fall upon it and allow our misconceptions to be broken, it breaks us.[4] It is the light that resolves identity—but is so powerful that it can destroy that identity that rebels against it.

We see the whole world in rebellion against the light of God, and yet we see the whole world seeking God. It is the mysteries of the Brotherhood of Luxor that can resolve these questions. But we need to take time and space to meditate upon the teachings, to be alone with our inner self, to not always be the subject of the bombardment of outer stimuli but to be quiet and alone with our inner being, to experience the harmony of that being and then by that harmony to measure within ourselves what are those anxieties, what are those fears, points of selfishness, points of darkness that will easily be dissolved in the light if we will only let the light come into the temple.

Amenhotep III

In the millennia since Serapis Bey transported the flame from Atlantis to Luxor, he continued to incarnate, and the hierophant guarding the retreat until his ascension is one who has gone on before him.

Serapis was embodied between 1414 and 1379 B.C. as Amenhotep III, the Pharaoh of Egypt who preceded Amenhotep IV (Ikhnaton) and Nefertiti. He was the ruler of the Egyptian empire, and during his reign Egypt was at her height of prosperity, peace and splendor.

Knowing he was the adept reincarnated from Atlantis, we realize that the prosperity and peace and splendor of Egypt during his reign was the direct manifestation of his own communion with his heart flame and with the hierarchs behind him, the ascended masters, all the way to the one, the Ancient of Days.

Statue of Amenhotep III in the British Museum

That which appears in community is the direct product of individual communion with God. Civilizations rise on a firm foundation when the people are attuned to the inner light. Civilizations crumble when they no longer have that attunement and a life that is based upon the principles and the person of the Word.

Looking upon Serapis in this life, we can see what is this squaring of the circle, the circle that becomes the square, the flame in the heart that becomes the building of a matter base, or the materialization of the God flame. The word *materialization* comes from the words "matter realization," or to realize in matter what we are one with in spirit.

This is the challenge of the path: Do you know God? Prove it by your action, by the work of your hands, by the love of your heart. What you manifest is what you know. And unless you can manifest what you know, you don't really know it. So this extension of the self—from the inner I AM THAT I AM to the outer manifestation—is the path of the ascension.

The Colossi of Memnon
These twin statues were constructed at the entrance of the funerary temple of Amenhotep III, the largest and most opulent in Egypt at that time, covering a total of 86 acres. Each of these statues, originally carved from a single block of sandstone, is sixty feet in height and estimated to weigh 720 tons.

Serapis Bey in this embodiment was regarded as the greatest ruler on earth. He maintained a high level of peaceful diplomatic relations with all nations during most of his reign of thirty-six years.

Part of the great wealth of his treasury was spent on the construction of magnificent temples and palaces. He enlarged the existing Temple of Karnak, and he built a huge funerary temple on the opposite bank of the Nile. All that remains of this temple today are the Colossi of Memnon, the monolithic seated statues uncovered on the banks of the river.

These very large statues depicted personages. There are only two remaining, but the remains reveal the outpicturing in stone of the understanding by Serapis Bey of the Word incarnate in the hierarchical order of initiates of ascended masters, of rulers of golden ages, of philosopher-kings, if you will, of those who embodied God and who had walked the earth in the earlier golden ages before the fall of the archangel and his angels on Lemuria.

The first three root races did not fall, did not descend. They lived in three golden ages unparalleled, of which we have not even the slightest comprehension. Such civilizations today exist only on the etheric plane. When you think of it, all of those embodied on earth in those three root races graduated and made their ascension in the light. They all returned to the Flaming One and have since become cosmic beings.

These statues brought forth in Amenhotep's reign remind us that on Atlantis and Lemuria they still remembered the golden ages. We also remember the golden ages as the faint dream within our hearts, the very daring to dream that life can be better, the very goal of perfection that we pursue, even though we know not how to pursue it. All of us dream of a more perfect world because a more perfect world really does exist. We have somehow lost the thread of contact, and the ascended masters have come in this conclusion of Pisces and the dawn of Aquarius to tell us what is that thread of contact to our own I AM Presence.

The Grand Colonnade of the Temple of Luxor

With all of this outpicturing from his heart flame in thirty-six years, the three times twelve, the greatest construction was that of the Temple of Luxor, which remains partially intact today. This temple embodied in its geometry and design the physical outpicturing of the esoteric law that had been passed down through the priesthood for generations. It stands today as a thorough textbook of advanced science, art and philosophy.

The Etheric Retreats of the Ascended Masters

The Temple of Luxor is the physical counterpart of the ascension retreat, which is today on the etheric plane. All of these retreats of the Brotherhood were removed from the physical and withdrawn to the etheric octave because of hordes and war and destruction and the defiling of those temples when they were physical.

So the ascended masters teach us in their very early lessons that when we go to sleep at night, we make the call to the I AM Presence and the Christ Self, to the guardian angels, to Archangel Michael to take us to the retreat where we would study the teachings of the Law.

Serapis Bey invites us to that retreat of the Great White Brotherhood, and there he teaches us the path of the ascension. The *Dossier on the Ascension* is given to us as a physical textbook, and he says that this entire textbook is taken from the classes that he conducts at the Ascension Temple. So you can have anchored into your conscious mind through that book what you learn when you are out of the body while you sleep at night.

The most wonderful thing about the soul's journeys to the retreats of the Great White Brotherhood is that the soul in its innocence and its freedom can learn far more of the great mysteries of the Christ than the outer mind dare accept. The outer mind of many people is programmed to an entrenched doctrine and dogma that denies the incarnation of the Word in every child of God, and so the hearing of these mysteries and the hearing of Serapis Bey becomes such a conflict to the outer mind that it cannot begin upon the path of those simple truths where Jesus Christ himself began. But when the guardian angels come and take our souls and we journey on the etheric plane to the etheric retreats, we are free of that programming of our embodiment and we take up the thread of the soul's journey on its pilgrimage to the homeward Source.

And so, often when people pick up the books of the ascended masters and read them, it is like coming home. Everything they read, they instantly know is truth, because they have already been God-taught in the inner retreats.

One of the purposes of this *Retreat on the Ascension* is to connect you with your soul's inner experiences. So often we have flashes and memories and glimpses and feelings, and we know there is more to life and we ourselves know more about life, but we can't quite get to that compartment of consciousness where it all is.

We know that our conscious mind is only the tip of the iceberg. We know there is a vast experience that we have experienced—if only we could contact it, if only we could remember where we were in a recent embodiment or on Atlantis and what we have known through all of our experiences upon earth. Well, this is what Serapis Bey teaches. And this temple at Luxor, which is there today in the physical and you can visit it, has its counterpart on the etheric plane.

What is the etheric plane? Maybe you've heard of your etheric double. The etheric plane is simply the counterpart of you and your life and your consciousness in another frequency of matter. It's still in the earth plane, but it is at another frequency.

We only hear so much sound; we only see so much color; we only have certain radio frequencies; and then it stops.

That's the spectrum of physical experience. Beyond it there are waves and vibrations, the etheric plane. It's where people go when they pass from the screen of life and they don't again return to the physical body.

You have an etheric body that is just as real as your physical body. In fact, it is more real. It is congruent with your physical body when you are waking and working. And the saints who experience bilocation can be in many places at once through that etheric body. At night it becomes the envelope or the sheath of the soul. It's the body in which you travel.

And so to Luxor we go, especially during this retreat when Serapis Bey is welcoming new students on the path and old students who are accelerating.

The Courtyard of Amenhotep III in the Temple of Luxor

The Temple of Luxor

Look at what Serapis knew when was embodied as Amenhotep III. The Temple of Luxor is overshadowed only by the Great Pyramid in its grandeur of conception. It displays the idea of the birth of the Divine Man based on the transformation of the universal Mother principle. Every proportion, angle, carving and hieroglyph is a means to the end of enshrining the process of the ascension of man into the immortal realms.

The temple is actually built to correspond to the outline of the human skeletal framework, traced according to anthropometrical methods and precisely proportioned. Its courtyards and rooms closely correspond to the body.

Egyptologist René Adolphe Schwaller de Lubicz spent fifteen years studying its architecture. His conclusion is:

> The Temple of Luxor is indisputably devoted to the Human Microcosm. This consecration is not merely a simple attribution: the entire temple becomes a book explaining the secret functions of the organs and nerve centers.[5]

The Egyptians considered the organs of the human body to be images of the divine universal organism. In other words, they understood the principle of man, the microcosm, the little universe, against the backdrop of man, the macrocosm, the big universe. They understood the stars and the galaxies corresponding to atoms and molecules and organs in the body temple. And they understood that the path of life was the fusion of this self within this temple with the larger self within the greater temple. Serapis Bey enshrined this conception in the temple at Luxor.

Schwaller de Lubicz remarks that "the Temple of Luxor could be called a Parthenon based on its fundamental kinship with the Parthenon of Athens."[6] It is in fact the true Parthenon, that is to say, the temple devoted to the spiritual conception of man.

Leonidas

The next embodiment of Serapis Bey we are looking at is 480 B.C. You will remember that the Persians sought to conquer the country of Greece at that time. The effort was massive, culminating in King Xerxes leading a huge army to the Greek peninsula. They marched from town to town, collecting Greeks who were willing to join the incoming army and act as traitors to the national cause.

Leonidas, king of Sparta (whose name means "Son of the Lion") was sent by his countrymen to maintain the pass of Thermopylae against the vast invading army. Three hundred Spartan warriors marched with him, expecting the rest of their allies to follow at the conclusion of the Olympic Games, which were taking place simultaneously. Meanwhile, he was joined by six thousand troops—his forces now seven thousand strong as they reached the pass.

By holding this narrow passage between the mountains and the sea, Leonidas was acting to protect the nearby Greek fleet from being outflanked in combat. He and his men faced the Persian hordes, which numbered anywhere from the 250,000 modern scholars have calculated to the 1.7 million the Greek historian Herodotus claimed.

For two days Xerxes suffered heavy losses without breaking Leonidas' resistance. Then a local man, Ephialtes, led Xerxes' forces to a path through the mountains, and a hand-picked force of Persian "Immortals" attacked the Greeks from the rear. Leonidas at once informed the fleet, dismissed all but 1,400 men —700 Thespians, 400 Thebans and his own 300 Spartans—and prepared to die, declaring that he and his Spartans would not abandon their post. Then, with the handful of troops under his command, he charged the myriads of Persian soldiers.

Leonidas fell in the thickest of the fight. "And now there arose," Herodotus records, "a fierce struggle between the Persians and the Lacedaemonians [Spartans] over the body of Leonidas, in which the Greeks four times drove back the enemy, and at last by their great bravery succeeded in bearing off the body."

At the end, the Greeks were left with only a tiny hillock on which to fight. Here "they defended themselves to the last," Herodotus said, "such as still had swords using them, and the

Monument at Thermopylae commemorating the stand of Leonidas and the three hundred Spartans

others resisting with their hands and teeth; till the barbarians . . . overwhelmed and buried the remnant left beneath showers of missile weapons."[7]

The Persians killed every Spartan and Thespian, but the Thebans laid down their arms and surrendered. Afterwards, Xerxes ordered that Leonidas be beheaded and his body crucified. But no such ignominy could mar his image. His heroism and selfless devotion to the flame that was Greece—the greater cause and glory more precious than life itself—had secured him a singular place in history, and in the imagination of his own and succeeding generations. By his superlative discipline and sense of timing, the Greek fleet was able to retreat and later defeat the Persian fleet at the Battle of Salamis.

A monument in the shape of a lion was erected on the spot where the 300 had taken their last stand. A stanza immortalizing them reads, "Go tell the Spartans, thou that passeth by, / That here, obedient to their laws, we lie."

This battle has been held up by historians as a prime example of the character of courage and fearlessness in fighting for a cause against massive odds. The stand of Leonidas helped to carry on the spark of national identity of the Greek nation, and the following year they decisively defeated the Persian forces at the Battle of Plataea.

This embodiment of Serapis Bey is noted as we read the akashic record of the assembling of 300 chelas of Luxor who were in embodiment with him. They were an extraordinary type of manhood. Some of those chelas are today ascended masters; some of them are in embodiment.

The Battle Then and Now

That was a physical war against physical odds. Today it is a battle of Armageddon against spiritual wickedness in high places of Church and State. It is not a battle of flesh and blood but the mind of God consuming the anti-mind, or the greater Self consuming the not-self. And this warfare is the presence of the Spirit in our midst. It is all-consuming love, and in its presence all unlike itself is consumed.

This is what we are witnessing today. In every octave and every plane, we have been called upon to show forth this courage. The mark of the fourth ray is the utter sacrifice of the self for the cause, for the principle, for the devotion to the blueprint of life.

Those initiates knew that the cause for which they stood was the entire cause of Sanat Kumara, the Ancient of Days, the perpetuation of the flame of freedom in the earth. They knew they could lay down their physical life and take it again in another incarnation.[8] But they knew that unless they gave their life, that cause would be lost.

By their devotion they anchored a flame of freedom, and that flame of freedom manifest in Greece has been a focal point of identity ever since. It is a flame that has expanded throughout the Mediterranean and throughout the earth. Jesus said,

"He who seeks to save his life will lose it. And he who loses it for the sake of the Christ in all will find it again."[9]

Today in America and in all nations we have too many people who are seeking to save the life of the physical body and its physical pleasures and willing to pay the price of the very life of the soul for that temporary gain. Why have we become so attached to the temporal, the ephemeral, to the passing fancies of life when all around us decisions are being made that will determine the very fate of freedom in America, in China, in Russia, in Africa, in South America? Freedom itself is not going to be preserved either by World Communism or World Capitalism. Both systems are wanting. The only way it will be preserved is by the flame of Almighty God in our midst in the very practical path of initiation.

We have allowed ourselves to be divided and to seek saviours in Church and State who cannot save us, who are the hirelings. They run when they see the adversary coming. The wolf comes to devour the sheep, and where are our leaders? They are not there. They have not the courage to stand, because they have no flame upon which to stand. They are not standing upon the foundation of the great pyramid of Being, so they have not the courage to be. And therefore, compromise and sell-out, disloyalty and immorality, and the general degeneration of the light within the nations is very evident.

Battles such as Thermopylae are meaningful in that they store virtue in the soul. They lay up treasure in heaven, and that treasure in heaven is light that those individuals can then draw upon. So the building of life is the increase of the aura, the aura of the great causal body above, the aura of the self below.

The path of initiation teaches us how to increase the light of the aura—not alone by meditation or prayer or by dynamic decrees but by works that are done as a sacred labor of the love of the heart for the individual people.

Phidias Showing the Frieze of the Parthenon to His Friends, Lawrence Alma-Tadema (1868)

Phidias

Serapis Bey was embodied as the sculptor Phidias during the fifth century B.C. in Athens. He was regarded as the greatest of all the Greek sculptors. His most famous work was the forty-foot-high statue of Pallas Athena in gold and ivory that stood inside the Parthenon in Athens. He was also the architect of the Parthenon itself and supervised its exquisitely masterful construction.

He created a huge statue of Zeus out of gold and ivory that stood in the temple of Olympia. Phidias was also a painter, engraver, and master of metalwork. His art is characterized by its exalted beauty and spirituality, and he lived as the ultimate personification of the golden age of Grecian master artists who had an enduring influence on all subsequent Western art.

I experienced a most amazing thing about the presence of Pallas Athena within that statue when I was at the Parthenon with Mark and a number of students of the masters when we were there in 1972 as a part of our journey to the Holy Land. Standing in the Parthenon, one stands in the presence of a piece of architecture that is designed by an individual who knows how to use form, symmetry, geometry, angles for the housing of a flame. The forcefield of the Parthenon contains an essential flame. So does the Temple of Luxor. So does the Great Pyramid. This is the tremendous understanding of the squaring of the circle.

And what did he place there? A forty-foot statue of the Mother figure, the Goddess of Truth. Pallas Athena is no mere figure of mythology. She is an ascended lady master who ascended long, long ago. She embodies the flame of truth, the same flame that Hilarion (who was embodied as Saint Paul) embodies on the fifth ray. She did this on Atlantis and earlier on Venus. She, too, came to earth with Sanat Kumara.

I had an interesting experience with Pallas Athena, an experience that you may have had with one or more ascended masters, one which people often have with Jesus Christ. When I was a student in Boston and I first came on the path of the ascended masters, a friend sent to me a card with a picture of that statue of Pallas Athena. It was the first time I had ever seen that statue or had been reminded of her person in this life. And when I saw it, I was so moved that I simply burst into tears. It was as though I was seeing an old friend, and I could not explain why I was crying.

The Parthenon, Athens

This statuette of Athena, found in Athens, is considered to be the truest and best preserved copy of the original statue of Athena in the Parthenon.

I had contacted an inner soul memory. Later when that memory was opened by Saint Germain, I came to realize that I had known Pallas Athena in the Temple of Truth on Crete and I had been there in that civilization. I'm sure that many of you were. Pallas Athena is a Mother flame, a person of the Mother who has chosen to ensoul Truth so that we can understand what is truth through the person of herself.

Serapis Bey, then, showed that he understood form and formlessness. The geometry of the building is the geometry of the principle of the law of God, but the statue tells us that he knew that geometry incarnates in a living flame that is a person, a son of God, a Christed One incarnate, one who is anointed with the inner light. And so he shows us that always there is the balance—Alpha and Omega—Alpha the principle, Omega the person—Alpha the blood of Christ, Omega the body of Christ. These two, when fused in yourself, teach that *you* are the Great Pyramid; *you* are the Parthenon; *you* are the Temple of Luxor, and *you* house a living flame.

Doesn't the Christian Bible record in the words of Paul, "Know ye not that ye are the temple of the living God and the spirit of God dwelleth in you?"[10] And because that spirit dwells in you, you honor it; you love it; it becomes the moving force of your life. You would do nothing to dishonor that living flame, because it is the very Person of God. And in the years and lifetimes of your devotion to that living flame that burns upon the altar of *your* temple, ultimately you become one with the object of your devotion. You love that flame so much that your soul is fused with it. This is precisely what Serapis Bey has sought to teach us in these great monuments.

Architect of the Great Pyramid

Serapis Bey was the architect of the Great Pyramid. We do not know when it was built, but we know that he was its architect. This is a tremendous point of contact with his heart flame.

The Great Pyramid

Scientists have said that no man could build that pyramid, but only God. And yet in the days of these adepts, these sons of Sanat Kumara, there were those in embodiment—some speculate 10,000 B.C., some as far as 78,000 B.C.[11]—who walked the earth who not only had the adeptship but were the living incarnation of the Word to such precision that they knew the science of levitation and the literal transfer of the laws of perfection into stone, stone upon stone, made to the precision of one-thousandth of an inch; stones so heavy they could not be moved by current standards; stones so perfectly wrought that no craftsman today could imitate them.

Obviously the individuals who were responsible for that pyramid had a superior attunement with the God flame and knew the science of its use in matter. They determined to leave in stone the mystery of your self.

In the book of the *Dossier,* in many of the teachings of Serapis Bey, you will learn many more mysteries than you would ever dream you could find in the outer world today. But they are only keys to greater mysteries that you learn as you commune with those words, as you commune with Serapis.

Serapis in the Hellenistic Age

I think many of you are not aware that in the Hellenistic age (from the death of Alexander the Great in 323 B.C. to the rise of Augustus in Rome in 31 B.C.), Serapis became one of the most important gods of the Egyptian and Greco-Roman pantheons. He was revered as the patron of Ptolemy, kings of Egypt and as the founding deity of the great city of Alexandria.

There are numerous historical records from that time of the intimate contact of Serapis with men throughout Egypt and Asia Minor, and there are over 1,080 statues, temples, and monuments dedicated to Serapis Bey erected during that era.

Head of Serapis found at Carthage, North Africa

Demetrius of Phalarum, the founder of the Alexandrian library under Ptolemy I, was miraculously cured of blindness by Serapis and wrote hymns of thanksgiving to him. Serapis often spoke through oracles and gave counsel as well as personal, miraculous healings to many people.

There is a famous historical account involving Serapis that marked an important era in his establishment as the most prominent deity of Egypt and Greece. King Ptolemy I, ruler of Egypt, was visited in a dream by Serapis, who commanded the king to bring the god's statue to Alexandria. After vacillation and a second dream with Serapis, the king had the statue brought with the blessings of the Delphic Oracle and installed it in the Serapeum, the great temple of Alexandria. This temple contained part of the famous Alexandrian library of three hundred thousand volumes.

There are many legends involving Serapis. It is recorded that the great Grecian King Apis, the ruler of Argos, settled in Memphis, Egypt. He was a famous physician, seer and hero. Upon his death he is said to have become the immortal adept, known afterwards to the Egyptians and Greeks as Serapis.

Archaeologists believe that these subterranean galleries beneath the Serapeum of Alexandria were most likely the place where the mysteries of Serapis were enacted.

Many epithets are ascribed to Serapis, including "Father," "Saviour," and "the greatest of the deities." He was regarded as the sponsor of intimate contact between the gods and mortals.

Serapis is regarded in the annals of the esoteric tradition as the hierophant of the secret Egyptian initiatory rites. There were basically two schools of philosophy in Egypt: the lesser mysteries, dedicated to Isis and intended for the layman, and the greater mysteries, which were dedicated to Serapis and Osiris and which were transmitted only to initiated priests who underwent severe rites of trial and initiation in the temple of Serapis.

Serapis was known to the early post-Christian Gnostics and regarded highly by early Christian bishops. The Emperor Hadrian traveled through Egypt in A.D. 134 and reported that the bishops of the Church worshiped at the shrine of Serapis.

Over a period of six to seven hundred years, Serapis became the supreme deity of Egypt and Greece. But in A.D. 385, Theodosius, the exterminator of so-called pagan religion, issued his edict: *De Idalo Serapadis Dirvendo,* "Tear Down the Idol of Serapis."

"Tear Down the Idol of Serapis" The Luciferians Then and Now Reject the Incarnate Word

In obedience to this edict, Christian soldiers destroyed the ancient statue of Serapis and the Serapian temple, along with the famous Alexandrian library housed within its walls. This particular tearing down of the Word incarnate was accomplished, as it has always been accomplished, by those fallen ones, the Luciferians who have embodied in every religion, every nation and every age.

They, in their great rebellion, have rejected the Word incarnate, the Christ who is the real person of every son and daughter of God. They have come in the name of their religion or their philosophy, and each time there has been a son of God who raised up that person of Christ within himself, they have torn it down.

So we find the rabbis and the high priests tearing down the image of that Word incarnate in Jesus. Jesus came to teach us the great living truth of the pyramid, which had been taught before him. And so among those three hundred thousand volumes in the Alexandrian library were great mysteries written by great adepts on the real path of the soul's reunion with God.

Those individuals who destroyed the temple of Serapis were not the real followers of the Spirit of the Word. They were idolators who worshiped the flesh and blood man of Jesus Christ, and they could not tolerate the idea that any other son of God had ever become the incarnation of the Word. And those same fallen ones, as the wolves in sheep's clothing, are among Christians today, denying that any child of God can truly choose, as Paul the Apostle directed them to choose, to become the joint heir with Christ[12] and to experience that sonship coming into the temple.

The apostle Paul understood it and taught it, and yet those same wolves in sheep's clothing have sought to tear down the image of the Word in the great avatars and leaders of the past so that they could then deny it in the little children today who must be raised up to understand the supremeness of self-worth because God lives in them and because they may elect by free will to become one with that God.

This is the battle of Armageddon. It begins right there with the great rebellion of Lucifer, denying the supremacy of the only begotten Son of God and denying that God's own children were vested with that image and every one of his children was created out of that image and likeness, having that image sealed in the heart.

God the Father said to the archangel and his angels, "Bow down before the living Christ and serve that Christ in my children." And Lucifer and his angels said, "We will not serve the Christ. We were here before his creation. We are superior. We do not need to worship God the Father in the person of God the Son."[13] That was the nature of their rebellion. They not only denied the Son, the Word, in Jesus, they denied that Son in every one of you, and they do so to the present hour.

This is the sickness of religion in America and the world today. It is the disease of their cancerous philosophy that makes religion of non-effect. Unless you contact that inner light, the intensity of that flame and that person, you can do nothing. "I can do all things through Christ which strengtheneth me,"[14] and without him I can do nothing—not a thing. And therefore if we do not accept that real person and living Word in all of us —Jew, Gentile, Muslim, Buddhist—we don't understand that real person of the Godhead; we have not begun to live and we cannot begin to conquer ourself or our society.

This is what this retreat is all about—to go back to the very fundamentals of life that have been denied lifetime after lifetime, millennium after millennium since that original fall on Lemuria. And if I had the hours to do so, I could show you in the scriptures themselves that every word I speak to you was taught by the personages of the Old Testament and the New Testament and has been taught in the religions of the East. This is the fulfillment of the Word and not its denial, and it is not some new religion I have invented.

I speak as I hear, and I hear by the Holy Spirit, and by the Holy Spirit I stand. And I come by that love for one reason, because I love you intensely and I love the soul in you and I love the God in you and I love what you are right now—sinner, saint, believer, nonbeliever, it doesn't matter. I love you because God made you to be a part of himself, and I see so many crosscurrents in our society today attempting to take from you that essential knowledge of your self-worth.

Let them tear down the statues. Let them burn the libraries. God has placed the real and living Word in a place where it cannot be touched. He has said, "I will write my law in their inward parts."[15] God has written his name in the secret chamber of your heart, in the inner place of communion, in the closet where you go to pray. Right in that inner chamber, which is a real and tangible place, God has given to you the person of himself, that inner Christed One, that inner image. There, you go to pray and you go to worship and you find your inner teacher. And no one can take from you the law written in every cell and atom of the physical temple and the spiritual temple.

The Word Incarnate in You

The ascended masters come to remind us, by the power of the Holy Spirit, what they have attempted to leave recorded for us in stone. And so, though the remains are there, we need them to teach us what our outer teachers are not teaching.

The most amazing thing about Serapis is that in the designing of the Parthenon a thousand years later, he has fulfilled the Temple of Luxor. And hear the remark of de Lubicz that

Luxor itself is a Parthenon. We see the same flame, the same soul repeating again and again.

What does this tell us? It says that the eternal flame that burns on within us can raise up again and again the fulfillment of the inner purpose. What does it tell us about the Word who lives in us? God sent forth the Word and he said, "My Word shall not return unto me void. It will accomplish the thing which I please."[16] It goes forth and it returns. And Jesus said, "Heaven and earth may pass away, but my Words shall not pass away."[17] The Word is not merely the spoken Word. The Word is the person of the Christ that cannot pass away.

It is the goal of your soul to unite with that Word so that you are in the Word, "hid with Christ in God."[18] That is your freewill election. The Luciferians elected a long time ago to live outside the Word, to denounce it, to deny it, to defile it, to create their philosophies whereby you or I could not figure out again how we could contact the Word. There is a freewill choice on the path of the ascension. It is the choice to be or not to be in that Word. Your soul can decide to be in the Word, or it can rebel against it and live outside of it.

That is what we are all about in this century. We are at the end of the age. We may elect to enter the path of the ascension, or we may be continuing on our outer rounds and go the way, ultimately, of those fallen ones who would lead us astray. The way they go leads to the final judgment and the second death, and they stalk the earth seeking what souls they may devour[19] and take with them to that second death.

The ascended masters come to show us that we do not have to follow the false Christs, the false teachers, the false prophets. We can follow the living spirit of prophecy, the Holy Spirit, reunite with God and live forevermore.

The Triumphal March from *Aïda:* "Why, I Have to Make My Ascension in This Life!"

The path of the ascension is the path of eternal life at the conclusion of your lifetime, after a service to your family, to your community, to your nation and to your earth. You have a life to live. How you live it is your choice. In this retreat we're going to talk about that choice and its practical consequences, what we can do to walk in the footsteps of a Jesus or a Moses or a Gautama or a Serapis Bey.

When you come to Luxor and you have fulfilled the requirements of the ascension—and I will tell you what those requirements are—after you have taken all of your instruction and you stand to receive the transfer of that living flame, you will hear the keynote of the ascension flame itself.

Every flame of God has the sound of the music of the spheres contained within it. Some of earth's great composers have captured the flames and their keynotes. Giuseppe Verdi captured the music of the ascension flame in the "Triumphal March" from *Aïda.*

The story of *Aïda* is the story of Serapis Bey and his twin flame, the account of a lifetime when the situations of karma and dharma did not allow the union of those twin souls. The story ends with the death of the hero and his twin flame, who must yet undergo other disciplines and initiations before the fulfillment of love.

But in the "Triumphal March" from *Aïda,* the triumphal march of the victor, is felt the intensity of the ascension flame. I know that in my childhood, whenever I heard that music, long before I ever knew what it was, it would carry me to the heights of my God consciousness. And the stirring of that music of the fire of victory translated to me the promise of something that I did not yet know or understand—the path of the ascension.

But one day when I was about to graduate from high school, I was standing on the steps of a church in my hometown that I used to attend. I was standing in the bright sunlight, and I felt the fire of God come upon me, and I heard the voice of God say, "You must make your ascension in this life." I heard it and I said out loud, "Why, I have to make my ascension in this life." Much later I learned that the angel who announces to you and to me our ascension is the angel of the annunciation, Archangel Gabriel.

I have talked to other people who have told me of experiences at various points in their life, even as little children, when they suddenly had an all-consuming awareness that this life was the life of reunion with God. That passion seized them and they have gone here and there and everywhere seeking the understanding of that path of reunion.

That was a tremendous day for me. It gave me hope and a sense of the heavenly hosts. And when I finally met Saint Germain and he put all the pieces of the puzzle together, I remembered that day and how God is never failing to contact each one of us to let us know the moment and the hour of that integration of the flame.

CHAPTER THREE

Serapis Bey and the Founders of the Theosophical Society

The ascended masters and their Brotherhood have been attempting to contact us since the nineteenth century. It's the dispensation of the end of the age of Pisces and the beginning of Aquarius—the end of an age when there is a release of light for the new dispensation. And so the Master M. and the Master K.H., Morya and Kuthumi, in 1875 contacted their amanuensis, Helena P. Blavatsky, and began the unveiling of the Secret Doctrine.

Unknown to most modern religious historians, Serapis Bey played a vital role in the initial thrust and direction of the endeavors of the Brotherhood during that century. Among the earliest letters from the adepts and masters to the founders of the Theosophical Society were those of Serapis Bey and the Brotherhood of Luxor.

It was the intention of Serapis that the Theosophical movement should, as its initial work, engage itself in an explanation of the ancient truths to be gleaned from the then popular spiritualist movement in Europe and America. Spiritualism is not considered by the Brotherhood today as a valid avenue for the dispensation of their teachings. But at that time it was for some the hope and reminder that life after death is continuous.

Helena Petrovna Blavatsky and Henry Steel Olcott, founders of the Theosophical Society

The dispensation was misused and became unfortunately subject to psychicism and all kinds of phoniness and fraud, and so it lost its purpose. But the ascended masters went on. Serapis took personal charge of the direction and chelaship of the amanuensis Helena Blavatsky and of Colonel Henry Steel Olcott, who was the co-founder and the president of the Theosophical Society.

During the six months preceding the formation of the society in 1875, Serapis sent many letters of encouragement and instruction to Colonel Olcott. The letters were written mostly on thick green parchment in gold ink, signed by Serapis in script, and inscribed with an esoteric symbol of the Brotherhood of Luxor. It is characteristic of the letters written to Henry Olcott that he continually gave the exhortation to him, "TRY." And those of you who have studied Saint Germain's course in alchemy know that he has used the word *TRY* as a key to the understanding of the law of the Logos within the heart of the chela.* The master Serapis stressed the need for courage and fearlessness, the same strong traits he outpictured as Leonidas.

*In *Saint Germain On Alchemy,* the master says: "Alchemists of the sacred fire, here is the sacred cosmic formula: Theos = God; Rule = Law; You = Being; *Theos + Rule + You = God's law active as Principle within your being (TRY).*"

These letters make for very quaint reading. They show to us the experiments of Serapis Bey, the ascended master. M. and K.H. did not ascend till about 1898; they were adepts in the unascended state. So there is the ascended Brotherhood of Luxor contacting their successors, Morya and K.H., and they contacting the amanuensis. It was the first attempt in many centuries. They met with Christian fanaticism as well as stubbornness and human pride, and their letters are often rebukes of those conditions. They even had problems with Blavatsky herself.

Once Blavatsky wrote in her diary, "M. came to me with orders from the chief to establish a society." Serapis was known as the chief in those days.

Here is an example of a letter that he wrote to Henry Olcott:

> Brother Henry—Greeting!
>
> *"Be courageous and hopeful."* Blessed words! The divine, ever working Law of Compensation whose humble ministry we are has not overlooked the tiny seed, cast by the charitable hand of our brother on the soil of the future harvests—of good and evil.[1]

Another letter, "From the Brotherhood of Luxor, Section the Vth, to Henry S. Olcott":

> Brother Neophyte, we greet thee.
>
> He who seeks us finds us. TRY. Rest thy mind—banish all foul doubt. We keep watch over our faithful soldiers. Sister Helen is a valiant, trustworthy servant. Open thy Spirit to conviction, have faith and she will lead thee to the Golden Gate of truth. She neither fears sword nor fire, but her soul is sensitive to dishonor and she hath reason to mistrust the future. Our good brother "John" hath verily acted rashly, but he meant well.

Is that not often what is said of the chela?

> Son of the World, if thou dost hear them both, TRY.[2]

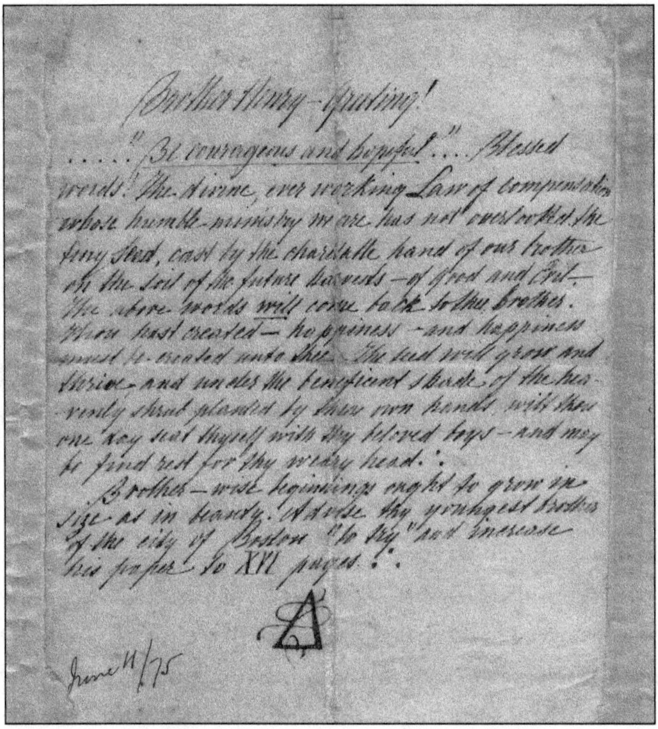

Brother Henry—Greeting!

...."Be courageous and hopeful"... Blessed words! The divine, ever working Law of compensation whose humble ministry we are, has not overlooked the tiny seed, cast by the charitable hand of our brother on the soil of the future harvests—of Good and Evil. The above words will come back to the brother. Thou hast created—happiness—and happiness must be created unto thee. The seed will grow and thrive—and under the beneficent shade of the heavenly shrub planted by thine own hands will thou one day seat thyself with thy beloved boys—and may be find rest for thy weary head.

Brother—wise beginnings ought to grow in size as in beauty. Advise thy youngest brother of the city of Boston "to try" and increase his paper to XVI pages!

June 11/75

Letter from Serapis to Colonel Olcott, 1875

The letter speaks of three masters of the Brotherhood of Luxor—Serapis Bey, Polydorus Isurenus, and Robert More—and it is signed by Tuitit Bey. And the return address on that letter reads "Observatory of Luxor." (Obviously Serapis would have an observatory!)

Now, the Master Morya, Kuthumi and the Indian section of the Brotherhood regarded Serapis as their chief, as I said, and this is depicted in a letter from Morya to Olcott.

> Once that you had determined to make of India your new home, it was in compliance with the direct orders of our beloved Lord and Chief—him who you know under the name of Serapis—the Maha Sahib that you sailed not sooner but later than you ought to.[3]

The personal love and intimacy of the master for the chela is seen in Serapis' letter to Olcott in 1875 when he writes,

> The Lodge is well acquainted with our Brother's qualities, and it is those higher faculties of analytical reasoning and our Brother's powerful gift of extracting spiritual truths from the dead letter of seeming contradictions that compel us thus to trust his spiritual intuitions for the accomplishment of this delicate mission. . . .
>
> God lead thee, Brother mine, and may He crown thy noble efforts with success.[4]

The Masters and Their Chelas

That type of communication teaches us much: it teaches us that the ascended master valued the virtues that we have externalized; the discipline of our consciousness, our scholarship, our education, or whatever is our path makes us useful to the Brotherhood in implementing their plans.

The plan of Serapis Bey was to set forth the ancient wisdom through Blavatsky, and Olcott played a very important role in setting forth that teaching. And so this expression of gratitude to an unascended chela was genuine. And in it we see that the ascended masters can do no more than their chelas allow them to do. If they find willing hearts and hands to carry their message and their mission, they move forward in a particular century. And if those chelas are not there, they are not allowed to come forth and do it because they are ascended masters.

So we see Jesus Christ totally dependent upon his apostles. What became of Christianity was directly the result of the work of those apostles and disciples. So it is with every dispensation. And so the teachings of the path of the ascension are not merely something for your private benefit. They become an opportunity to anchor in the earth the dispensation of the Brotherhood for Aquarius. This awareness makes us want to merit the attention, the discipline, the love of the Brotherhood. We feel like striving when we have a chief or a coach who is appreciating our overcoming, who understands the trials and tribulations we go through, and who welcomes our victories.

When we have no one to be beautiful for, no one to be victorious for, no one to work for or accomplish for, we kind of lose interest—even lose interest in life itself. That's why we need to love and be loved. But when we understand that there is a higher order of evolution—there are ascended masters who are watching us and working with us; they need us, humanity needs us—we become that point of the fourth ray. We become the keystone in the arch, key to the ascended masters' work, key to other people, discovering the great light. So when you have usefulness and meaning in life, you strive more to perfect yourself, to do a better job of being useful.

Serapis writes to Olcott:

> Upon returning from the office know the Brotherhood will be assembled in her [HPB's] room, and seven pairs of ears will listen to your reports and judge of the progress your Atma does in relation to intuitional perceptions. Heed her not when she will tell you that your words do not interest her; go on, and know you are talking in the presence of your Brethren. When needed they will answer you through her. God's blessing on thee, brother mine.[5]
>
> SERAPIS

That is a very cute letter that is written directly to Olcott without the knowledge of HPB. Serapis is well aware of the cantankerous nature of HPB, and he foresees that when Olcott will be called upon to present certain facts and teachings, she will put him down for bringing forth these teachings. And so Serapis is saying, "Never mind. Go on and present your teaching, because seven pairs of ears will be listening"—no doubt among them the ascended masters. So I thought that it was very interesting that the regard for the chela was supreme in the heart of Serapis.

In another letter to him we read:

> I followed you, Brother mine, all the day of yesterday. My sympathy was with you and you have the approval of the Brotherhood. As I have said before, the rules of the Lodge are positive. . . . You must not part with Helena if you desire your initiation. But through her you may be enabled to conquer the trials of initiation. They are hard and you may yet despair more than once, but do not, *I pray thee*. Remember, some men have toiled for years for the knowledge you have obtained in a few months. Fear not, immortal man, scorn the evil whispers of the double-visaged Janus called public opinion.[6]

Public opinion has always been against the contact of the soul with the ascended masters. Why? Because the mass consciousness is dominated by the factors of its enslavement to the fallen ones and their philosophy, whereas when the soul contacts the ascended masters, it begins the path of its soul liberation.

The entrenched forces of the world today do not want the individual to be free to become one with God within the sanctuary of his own being. So public opinion has not much to say for the bringing forth of the messages of the ascended masters. They are for those souls who have the light within themselves and who recognize it in the teachings of the masters.

Dossier on the Ascension consists of letters dictated by Serapis Bey through Mark Prophet. These letters in the days of Theosophy were precipitated. There they were, found on the table written in gold ink on green paper, or whatever it was. There they were signed and sealed. That was the dispensation of a century ago.

Today we receive those letters by the full power of the

Holy Spirit. The dictations come forth and they are precipitated not on paper but by the heart flame itself, the master's heart contacting the heart of the messenger. And when the Word is spoken, it reaches into your heart and so you become the third person of this trinity.

Morya, the Master M., would sign his name with three dots; and in those three dots he was teaching that law. There is the ascended master releasing the energy through the messenger and there is the point of its goal, the great multitude. The great multitude of people figured in the Book of Revelation[7] are those who are to receive the teachings.

The letters in the *Dossier* are much like these letters. You can hear the directness, almost the abruptness, of Serapis. He tells you immediately the sort of school he runs. He runs a tight ship. He runs a disciplined place. He says he's not interested in people who are still crying after their earthly mothers. And he talks about people who say that it is too hard at Luxor and they must go home and they cannot take the disciplines.

So the teaching is there for you to read, and you do not need to fear to read it. It's placed in a book so that you can make contact with it, and you can make your freewill decision whether to apply that teaching.

Twelve Paths of Initiation under the Twelve Solar Hierarchies

At this moment I would like to invite you to sing, because the singing is the intoning of the flame through your chakras. And in this retreat we're going to experience the joy of the white flame of the Mother passing through our chakras for the integration of the self.

One of the sons of Serapis Bey is known as Djwal Kul. Djwal Kul also released his teachings in the past hundred years. He has released them again in his *Intermediate Studies of the*

Human Aura.[8] Those teachings give us the meditation on the secret chamber of the heart, the interior temple of illumination. Teresa of Avila records in her works going into this interior castle. She has the mystical experiences of the saints.

The teachings of Djwal Kul are on the twelve lines of the cosmic clock. Twelve points of that clock are for the twelve paths of initiation under the twelve solar hierarchies. This is not worldly astrology; it is the great astrology of the ascended masters—and the two are miles apart. The ascended masters teach us how to invoke the flame for the mastery of our daily astrology, which is our daily karma. Day by day the karma, positive and negative, that comes to your life can be met and mastered by these twelve paths and twelve flames.

Djwal Kul had earlier prophesied that he would release his work once again in 1975. He contacted me to write down his *Intermediate Studies* on that schedule, and the affirmation that we will give contains the key to all of the teaching in the book. It becomes an affirmation of the principles, the teaching, the geometry that he has desired to transfer to our seven chakras for the acceleration of our being in this dispensation. So it's very exciting to me to now hear the affirmation that contains the twelve paths of initiation in this music.

I would like to make an invocation to God invoking the light of Djwal Kul to initiate you and all of us and all of the lightbearers on the earth on this very special path of love by the heart. The flame of love in the heart is his path. He was the third wise man. Morya, Kuthumi and Djwal Kul were the three who came out of the East. By the inner flame of the heart and by their certain knowledge of astronomy, they knew the hour and the moment of the birth of Jesus. They came to give adoration to the incarnate Word. They themselves were adepts. Djwal Kul, then, is the third, and he teaches the path of love. And love is the key to the ascension.

So if you'll meditate with me now, I'm going to make an invocation. The music accompanying the invocation is by Beethoven [the second movement from Symphony no. 2], as Saint Germain has asked us to use the nine symphonies this summer. The symphonies of Beethoven are the greatest music of freedom that has ever been lowered into this octave by an initiate in physical embodiment, and we'll meditate with that music for our invocation now. Won't you go into the secret chamber of your heart.

Djwal Kul, Come!
Initiate Us in the Secret Chamber of Our Hearts

O mighty light of freedom, come forth from out the Great Central Sun. O mighty light of freedom, stir the hearts of souls of light everywhere. O Spirit of the Great White Brotherhood, I call thee forth upon this altar. In the name of the Father, in the name of the Son, in the name of the Holy Spirit, in the name of the Mother, on behalf of these souls of light and souls of light everywhere, come forth now with thy quickening love.

Djwal Kul, come with Morya El and Kuthumi. Come forth, Saint Germain, Serapis Bey, Hilarion, and Nada. Open the way of the seven-fold path of initiation. Open the way to the twelve solar hierarchies and the Elohim. Release now the sacred fire of the heart into those who open their hearts gladly to the Christ and the Buddha for the fusion of the light of East and West.

Lo, I AM come to do thy will, O God, in the very center of life. Lo, each one who partakes of thy body and thy blood would also assimilate thy living Word.

Alpha and Omega, in the name of the living Christ, in the name of the Christ Self of each one, come forth and open the way made plain. Sanat Kumara, let thy dispensations reign. Living Word of the Brotherhood of Luxor, of the Royal Teton, of Darjeeling, of Lake Titicaca, come forth now. We present ourselves, O God, the instrument of thy light.

In the name of the entire Spirit of the Great White Brotherhood, the I AM THAT I AM, Djwal Kul, come! Djwal Kul, come! Come into our hearts and initiate us now in the secret chamber there. The love of the ruby ray is thine own. We take up the ruby cross. We take up the ruby ray and we march with the legions of light. Amen.

Let us sing together Djwal Kul's meditation.*

Djwal Kul, Come!

Djwal Kul, come!
In the center of the One,
Anchor now thy radiant sun,
Magnet of the threefold flame,
Expand God's aura in God's name!

Djwal Kul, come!
Threefold fountain, fill my heart;
Let thy angel now impart
The name of God—I AM THAT I AM,
I AM THAT I AM, I AM THAT I AM,
I AM THAT I AM!

Djwal Kul, come!
Flame of gold, pink, blue, and white,
Seal thy victory star of Light;
Renew my vows to God's own name;
Come, O Christ, in me now reign!

Djwal Kul, come!
Expand the fire of the Sun;
Alpha 'n Omega, make us one,
Seal my energies in Christ,
Raise my energies in Light!

*These words may also be given as a decree.

Djwal Kul, come!
Align my consciousness with thee,
Make us one, O make me free!
Seal my heart and hand in thine,
In God's mind I AM divine!

Djwal Kul, come!
Blaze the action of the Whole,
With light of victory fill my soul;
Return me to the Flaming One,
I AM begotten of the Son!

Coda: I AM God Power, I AM God Love,
I AM THAT I AM, I AM THAT I AM,
I AM THAT I AM!

I AM God Mastery and God Control,
I AM THAT I AM—
AUM (chant)
I AM THAT I AM—
AUM (chant)

I AM God Obedience now,
To thy Law I vow,
I AM THAT I AM, I AM THAT I AM,
I AM THAT I AM!

God Wisdom flame I AM,
God Wisdom flame I AM,
God Wisdom flame I AM!
AUM—God Har-mo-ny (chant)
AUM—God Har-mo-ny (chant)
AUM—God Har-mo-ny! (chant)

God Gratitude, God Gratitude, God Gratitude!
I AM God Justice in full view,
I AM God Justice in full view,
I AM God Justice in full view!

God Re-al-i-ty! (chant)
I AM God Vision, God Victory won,
I AM God Vision, God Victory won,
I AM God Vision, God Victory won!

We are grateful to the ascended masters for inspiring upon us and releasing the music of the spheres for this dispensation. We feel in it the new light. And when we hear it and sing it and meditate upon it, we actually feel the light of the Lamb sounding the tone that summons all of our forces and energies into an inner alignment in the inner spiral that rises in the temple.

We remember it is written in the Book of Revelation that those 144,000 that gather with the Lamb, those ones who came with Sanat Kumara, the Ancient of Days, sing a new song.[9] They sing a new song because they express a new vibration. The new vibration is the ancient vibration.

The Light of the Ancient Motherland

Some of you remember at Mount Shasta in 1975 that an ascended master by the name of Ra Mu spoke to us from the Brotherhood of Mount Shasta and from the ancient temples of Lemuria. *Ra Mu* means "ray of Mu" or "ray of the Mother," and he came to anchor the light of the Motherland and to anchor the light of the ancient religion of devotion to the eternal Mother as the white light.

The seven Holy Kumaras spoke in a conference in Hawaii of the raising up of the Mother flame of Lemuria. The flame was upon a central altar, and around it, on what is known as the fire ring of the lands that border the Pacific Ocean today, there were twelve other temples all dedicated to the Mother light. Those twelve temples were for the solar initiations of the twelve hierarchies, and those initiations each had their tone and their flame. It was to those hierarchies and those flames that we just meditated and sang, as Djwal Kul has taught us.

Ra Mu has kindled in us the light of the ancient teaching of Lemuria, the light of that fourth ray that we had before the sinking of the continent. So out of his dictation has come a dispensation of that ascended master and his causal body and the Brotherhood of Mount Shasta, who also sponsored Godfré Ray King and his initiations with Saint Germain.

Let us sing our meditation to Ra Mu.

Harpstrings of Lemuria

I AM Ra Mu

1. Hear the music, hear the AUM
Intonation of the AUM
From Mount Shasta anchoring the sound
Memories of the Motherland.

Devotees of ancient Mu
Masters and their chelas, too
Sound the music of the Motherland
Calling, calling, calling you.

2. Hail, children of Lemuria
Children of my heart
I AM Ra Mu.

Hail, children of the Motherland
Children of the Mother
I AM Ra Mu.

3. From Mount Shasta hear the chant,
O hear the chant of love
We are one, we are one, we are one.
Invoke the light of Mu,
invoke the light of Mu
We are one, we are one, we are one.

Gentle waters flowing still,
the cooing of the Dove
We are one, we are one, we are one.
Invoke the light of Mu,
invoke the light of Mu
We are one, we are one, we are one.

(Repeat verse 1)

As you know, the ascended masters teach the science of the invocation of the Word. Currently the ascended masters in their *Pearls of Wisdom*[10] are delivering to us the teachings of Sanat Kumara, and he is delivering the teachings on the ruby ray. He speaks of the science of the invocation as that by which the light of the Presence is drawn into the temple of being, and he said it was the science whereby the future becomes the now.[11]

Religion has procrastinated the incarnation of the light. Messiah is always coming, the resurrection is in the future, the meeting of the master is in the future. But the science of the Word draws a portion of the Higher Self into the heart in the now, the now that is the only accepted time and space.

Our beloved Paul the Venetian opens this retreat with a dictation that he desires to give to us in this moment. We always give before our dictations the invocation of the Word for the alignment of our being with the ascended master who is speaking.

The most important dynamic decrees that you can learn and take with you this evening are the *Heart, Head and Hand Decrees*. We are going to give them now. And instead of teaching the science, we will demonstrate the science. It is another way of singing a new song.

Heart, Head, and Hand Decrees

by El Morya

Violet Fire

Heart

Violet fire, thou love divine,
Blaze within this heart of mine!
Thou art mercy forever true,
Keep me always in tune with you. (3x)

Head

I AM light, thou Christ in me,
Set my mind forever free;
Violet fire, forever shine
Deep within this mind of mine.

God who gives my daily bread,
With violet fire fill my head
Till thy radiance heavenlike
Makes my mind a mind of light. (3x)

Hand

I AM the hand of God in action,
Gaining victory every day;
My pure soul's great satisfaction
Is to walk the Middle Way. (3x)

Tube of Light

Beloved I AM Presence bright,
Round me seal your tube of light
From ascended master flame
Called forth now in God's own name.
Let it keep my temple free
From all discord sent to me.

I AM calling forth violet fire
To blaze and transmute all desire,
Keeping on in freedom's name
Till I AM one with the violet flame. (3x)

Forgiveness

I AM forgiveness acting here,
Casting out all doubt and fear,
Setting men forever free
With wings of cosmic victory.

I AM calling in full power
For forgiveness every hour;
To all life in every place
I flood forth forgiving grace. (3x)

Supply

I AM free from fear and doubt,
Casting want and misery out,
Knowing now all good supply
Ever comes from realms on high.

I AM the hand of God's own fortune
Flooding forth the treasures of light,
Now receiving full abundance
To supply each need of life. (3x)

Perfection

I AM life of God-direction
Blaze thy light of truth in me.
Focus here all God's perfection,
From all discord set me free.

Make and keep me anchored ever
In the justice of thy plan—
I AM the presence of perfection
Living the life of God in man! (3x)

Transfiguration

I AM changing all my garments,
Old ones for the bright new day;
With the sun of understanding
I AM shining all the way.

I AM light within, without;
I AM light is all about.
Fill me, free me, glorify me!
Seal me, heal me, purify me!
Until transfigured they describe me:
I AM shining like the Son,
I AM shining like the sun! (3x)

Resurrection

I AM the flame of resurrection
Blazing God's pure light through me.
Now I AM raising every atom,
From every shadow I AM free.

I AM the light of God's full Presence,
I AM living ever free.
Now the flame of life eternal
Rises up to victory. (3x)

Ascension

I AM ascension light,
Victory flowing free,
All of good won at last
For all eternity.

I AM light, all weights are gone.
Into the air I raise;
To all I pour with full God-power
My wondrous song of praise.

All hail! I AM the living Christ,
The ever-loving One.
Ascended now with full God-power,
I AM a blazing sun! (3x)

We will prepare for beloved Paul the Venetian and his dictation with mediations from Beethoven. I'd like to ask you to prepare by uncrossing your legs, placing your feet flat on the floor, your spines erect and yet comfortable. Hold your hands cupped in your lap and take a deep breath, expel the air, and go into meditation on your heart. Through the flame of your own I AM Presence is the transfer of the Word.

CHAPTER FOUR

The Call of Serapis

Paul the Venetian

Most gracious children of the Sun, Serapis Bey has called and I have answered and so have you. And we have come to meet in the dot of the center of the circle within and without the square. And within that dot, behold, I AM there, you are there and we are one.

And we have come to begin the rising spiral of being whereby ascended adepts call chelas near and far. For we would set a flame and a fire here in the heart of San Francisco. We come to ignite an ancient spark within the souls of devotees who have lived and served here within these seven hills that were the seven temples of the seven Holy Kumaras.[1] We come in the service of the Mother light, guarded for aeons by the Goddess of Purity.

You have seen the dissipation of mass elements of human karma in the recent earthquake,[2] all of this in preparation for the release of a greater light. For certain elements of the human consciousness were required by law to be dissipated before we could release those initiations to any and all who would respond to the call of Serapis.

Understand, then, when mankind themselves do not dissipate their human karma, by ignorance and for want of the use of the violet flame, then it is elemental life who, themselves bearers of the cross of planetary karma, must expiate in physical conditions those ancient discords that prevent the race from accelerating to the higher place of God consciousness toward which you aspire.

Because you aspire to that place, you have come. And because we aspire to lead you there, we have come. And therefore, the Brotherhood welcomes you in the flame of love to service, to sacrifice, to surrender, and the path of selflessness.

There Is a Price for Eternity

Is there a price for eternity? Indeed there is. It is the price of the exchange of the lesser self for the Greater Self. And who do you think it is, my beloved, who gets the greater bargain? Why, of course, it is the soul who comes, who must surrender that which appears to be the only thing that it can surrender. But in reality, the thing surrendered is not the Real Self but the temporary portion, the temporary self. Thereby, in having that self to give, one can receive the initiation of the descent of the Higher Self.

Is there any other path? Is there any other goal? Believe it not. For some have offered an easier way, the way of indulgence or formulas or this or that mantra as being the all and the end and the everything of life. Well, my beloved, if it were so, then many, many would have joined the ranks of the candidates for the ascension at the Temple of Luxor. But as a matter of fact, they have not.

And therefore the many byways offered today, coming with the allure of making life easier and exalting the outer personality, have detoured souls of light to endless, endless labyrinthian passages. But all this must end.

When does it end? It ends when the individual soul declares, "*Enough!* I have had enough! I will find my freedom and I will find it lawfully, lovingly, God's way, the way of the eternal Logos, the way that the doves have flown, the way that the stars glow."

O my beloved, yes, there are innocent sheep trapped in the false teachings, but there are also many who are the goats who enjoy the false teachings because they enjoy the perpetuation of unreality. Therefore this is the question you must ask yourself, "Do I desire to know the truth even when the truth hurts? Or do I desire to continue hearing only what the lesser self desires to hear?" By and by the real souls of God tire of the half-baked half-truths. By and by the souls who are real come to the door of Luxor.

The Love of Serapis

My brother Serapis and El Morya have called upon me to speak to you, for they would give to you through me the essence of love that is the true heart of the initiations of Luxor, though many there have been who have denied that there is any love in Serapis or in the brothers of his retreat because of the appearance of sternness. Indeed, they are one-pointed and sure-footed. Indeed, they know the way and its pitfalls, and they must uphold a light of discipline for the purest light, the whitest way on the great white way.

I AM come to assure you that the core of that teaching is nevertheless love—a love that loves your soul far more than you know and far more, indeed, than your carnal mind, a love that does not pamper but compels you by the most immense compassion to rise to the Greater Self even when fear assails and demons and discarnates berail you, the soul, rising with Christ upon that cross.

Do you think that any soul is exempt from the path of the cross? Nay, if it were so, he would have told you. But he said that the cross must be borne, it must be taken up.[3] It is a cross of light. Remember that the burden is light.[4] The appearance is of burden, but that burden is light. When you carry light as light is given to you by the hierarch of Luxor, know that that light is for a purpose and not for the glorying of yourself but for the mission. It is for the bearing of personal and planetary karma.

Wherever there is a vortex of light as the person of the Word, there the darkness goes to be transmuted. For even the darkness is God misqualified. It is his energy misqualified that longs to be realigned with the Word. Where there is light, there is a vortex of transmutation. When you draw forth light in your meditation, then you must know the path of preparedness to deal with the darkness that is exposed within the subconscious of the self, within previous incarnations, and within the planetary collective unconscious.

What for the path, if not to assist the way of a brother, a sister? What for the path, if not to raise up an entire evolution?

A Path of Joy

We are the real and the living Brotherhood of light and we show you a path of joy. It is not a path of sorrow or deprivation, save for those who are not of the light in the first instance. For them the path is drudgery. They soon weary of it and they are no more. But the soul of light who knows who he is and why he is born seeks the way out, not for selfish reasons but because by love he senses the plight of a humanity that by God must be enlightened in this age if it is ever to be enlightened! And by God, it must be enlightened by those of you who have taken embodiment determined to effect change.

Why, some of you have recently spent other lifetimes squandering energy, and you have come before the Lords of Karma[5] and you have seen Serapis Bey and me and Morya and you have said, "Let me go back. Let me now take up my life in earnestness and contribute something of worth, for I have spent, lo, this and other lifetimes here and there. And now, with the vision of inner levels, let me go forth. Let me go forth with a light to lighten my way and the way of others." And you have pleaded with Serapis Bey himself to contact you in this your present incarnation and to not leave you bereft of the memory of the Ancient of Days.

Dare to Be Different

Therefore we come to touch your heart with love and to tell you that if you would do something about your present plight and that of this planet, then you must dare to be different than you were when you entered this forcefield. For, could you change the earth when you entered the hall this night?

I say to you, beloved, if you could not, then, is it not obvious that something must change. Is it the Brotherhood of Luxor, or is it perhaps your own soul's understanding of life itself? Changes come and by those changes you rise in new dimensions of your own Selfhood. And by the gradual process of love, you come to know more expedient methods for contacting the multitudes of souls who are waiting to be fed.

Would you become a shepherd, feeding the sheep on the hillsides who know not the way to go? Is this not the real longing of yourself, rather than to follow the fashions of the times and this or that interesting book or show or even some new teacher offering some new way of rearranging energy, perhaps?

Well, we are not content merely to rearrange energy. We come to challenge energy to rise. And the matrix of the rising of the flame in you is ascension's flame, ascension's pyramid.

My beloved, the Brotherhood of Luxor knocks on the door of the heart of the chelas of any and all gurus and those who have not yet entered the path of chelaship. Our purpose in this year 1979 is to work with the World Teachers, Jesus and Kuthumi, to instruct, to initiate, to bless and prepare you who know that you have a more-than-ordinary mission and a very special life to live in the giving of the Word to souls who need both the teacher and the teaching—souls who need love and someone who cares enough to sit down with them and break the bread of life.

We come, then, in search of those who have vowed recently before the Lords of Karma and those who have vowed thousands of years ago to strike a blow for the LORD in the beginning of that Aquarian age. It is an age that can commence a spiral of freedom and lead the earth back to those inner golden ages that once she knew.

It is also an age when, by the absence of free will, children of the light may postpone for untold aeons the coming into the physical octave of that which is destined to be. No psychic predictions can secure for the United States or Russia a victory of light, a breaking down of the engines of war and of manipulation and of the abuses of the people for the gain of money and power and blood.

The Tie to Hierarchy Is Necessary

Yes, indeed, there are initiates of the left-handed path walking the earth, manipulating the governments and the fates of the people. Indeed, there are initiates of Satan. Mark my word well. Therefore, let the initiates of light come forth and understand that if you would be a match for those fallen ones who have seized their positions of power in your very government, you yourself must learn to increase the light in the sacred centers of being.

You must know that not you but God in you can save a life that is your own and a life that is a planet and a people. You must know that it is by the eternal chain of hierarchy and your tie to it that mighty works are wrought. You must know that when you go forth to challenge those who are the deceivers and destroyers of the people, it will require the extraordinary arm of the hosts of the LORD and of our Brotherhood to effect those changes that are desired.

Well, tell me, then, if in the last decade all of the discussions and all of the demonstrations and all of the wars and all of the grabs for power have netted any light for the children of this earth or any greater vision of freedom? I do not see it. Perhaps you do.

I only see the futility of the outer self by a scientific humanism, by Marxism,[6] by a perverted capitalism, by manipulations of monopolies, national and international. By all of this, I see only the lessening of light in the total civilization side by side with the increase of light in the few who have understood the path and pursued it to the best of their ability.

Thus, side by side, in this age is the degeneration spiral of death in the midst of those who have gone astray, destroying their sacred centers by chemical means and drugs and pollutants and thereby closing the door to the higher contact. We have seen those souls who have been tempted by the fallen ones to take the initiations of the left-handed path through the drug culture. We have seen these pass through the treacherous waters of the allure of the astral plane, losing hold on reality, the flower of youth passing into some psychic unreality while the demand of the hour is to feed my sheep![7]

Have you not heard the Saviour's cry? And do you not know the allure of the fallen ones who promise salvation is, in reality, unto death, not the mere death of the body but the death of the soul? This is a battle for ultimate survival. And therefore, we come.

The Path of the Ruby Ray

We are gratified that there are so many souls of light in this nation alone who uphold the standard of freedom. Now we would introduce to you the shortest distance between two points outlined in the Great Pyramid. It is the path of the ascension by the initiation of the ruby ray. The ruby ray is the intensity of the blood of Christ that is the true essence of love in such concentration, as the rose pink of the third ray becomes an intensity that is a sword that is able to divide, as a laser beam, the Real from the unreal and to judge error and the path of error. The path of the ruby ray is being revealed by my father Sanat Kumara, your father and my own.[8]

The path of the ascension is the path of the white light of the body of Christ. The body is the temple. The body is the Word. The body is the teaching. And the body is the Mother, and the Mother light within you is the light of Omega.

Thus by the ruby ray and the white light, the blood and the body, the Alpha, the Omega of being, there is the fusion within you of a path of acceleration that is for the sincere and the determined ones who recognize that they can no longer dally the centuries away, waiting, waiting, procrastinating their own self-mastery. But indeed the fate of civilization hangs in the balance of the decision of the few.

There are other paths, lesser paths and slower paths that wind up the mountain, allowing greater passages of time and space between initiations, further incarnations and, of course, not the great demands of the self for sacrifice and service. But, my beloved, consider—consider the prolonging of that surgery that must one day come if your soul is to become the fullness of the Christ that is in you. Consider, then, why not now? Why not remember the ancient vow? Why not?

You say, "Why?" And I say, "Look with me upon the suffering masses. Look upon world hunger and the displacement of persons and the boat people and war and look upon those fallen ones and their treachery and their cruelty and their torture of human life mercilessly. Who will call forth the judgment for the binding of those fallen ones? It must come by the science of the Word within you. And it will come when you decide to make your throat chakra the instrument of the seven chohans of the rays, and your heart chakra and your third eye and the crown."

These are gifts of life that we have long ago given to Almighty God. And he has come into those centers and he has worked a work through us whereby many have walked through the door to eternal life. This is the joy of the path. It is knowing that you become the indispensable link in the chain of universal Being when you love enough to live and to give of yourself that another self might become the fullness of itself.

Thus, the goal of the path is your ascension. But the path of the ascension includes all of life. It is the infusion by the light that flows through you of the body of humanity with the light of the living Lord.

I Would Impart the Sacred Fire Breath

My beloved, I embrace you. For I, Paul the Venetian, have stood with the Maha Chohan, with each one of you as that representative of the Holy Spirit breathed into your nostrils the breath of life in this incarnation. Aye, 'tis the cry of the Manchild. Aye, it is the breath of life that I long to hear.

And now I would impart to you the sacred fire breath of the Holy Spirit, that when you speak the children will listen and the demons will tremble and the gifts of that Spirit might be yours to bind these fallen ones that are, to put it in the vernacular, messing up things on this planet, messing up the cities and the homes and the lives and the souls and the hearts of souls whom I love and know as my brothers and sisters.

I lift the veil for a moment that you might see me as I AM. For you know me and you know our band. And I AM determined that the decay and rot of a diet that is fed this generation shall no longer block your brains or your chakras, that you shall fast and pray and eliminate those toxins polluting your bodies that make you dense and not able to contact our light or recognize us.

Yes, I come in the name of the Holy Spirit. And I feel in my very being the intensity of the Maha Chohan, the intensity of the challenge of all those purveyors of a synthetic civilization that has served to stand between the children of light and the angelic hosts. Why, angels walk and talk with you today, but you do not answer. In olden days, the children answered. The only difference was the absence of pollutants. Do you know that that substance and all of those chemicals in the atmosphere actually cut off the outer senses from the inner senses of the soul?

My beloved, I know you feel that intensity as you look upon the bodies and the faces, so many of them blank and the eyes so burdened with an inner sadness, of people who are truly of the light and yet are so beset by the burdens of this life.

Wake Up!

I pray to you in the name of Gautama Buddha. In his name, in the name of the Lord of the World, in the name of Maitreya: Wake up! *Wake up! Wake up* and live for a cause greater than the feeding of your mouth and the clothing of your temple and the enjoyment of paltry gain. *Wake up* and see life who needs you and needs your love.

Be not concerned about this messenger. Be concerned about your own relationship to the Great White Brotherhood. That is what counts. It is the teaching that counts and it is your application of the teaching. Messengers have come and gone, but it is the Word they bear that lives on. It is the Word that we transfer to you and we must have a physical messenger and a physical temple. But your relationship with us must be sought and won on your own merit and your own love.

Take, then, the gift freely given and know that in the community of Camelot* we have called forth the sangha of the Buddha and the community of Christ and his disciples. We have prepared a home and a school for children and a place for retreat and study. It is our cradle for you to give birth to the Manchild within you. Won't you come as the wise men of old and attend your own birth in this lifetime, the Mother's giving birth within you of the eternal Christ.

We have come to celebrate your own Christ Mass. Welcome, my beloved. I pour forth my love to you and I breathe a breath for that transfer of the Spirit.

[The master breathes the holy breath.]

Purusha.

Be sealed in the love of the Brotherhood and your own God Presence.

I love thee, I love but thee,
With a love that shall not die
Till the sun grows cold,
And the stars are old,
And the leaves of the judgment book unfold![9]

Yes, I quote one of your bards to express the intensity of the love of the Brotherhood for our unascended devotees. It shall not die but it shall quicken you to life.

I touch you with a kiss of peace upon the brow.

---

*Camelot was the name of the community founded by the ascended masters in California's Santa Monica Mountains near Malibu. It was a unique experiment in community life, where parents, children, and people of all ages could come together to share in the joys and challenges of the spiritual path. Camelot served as international headquarters for The Summit Lighthouse and Church Universal and Triumphant beginning in 1978. In 1986 the community of Camelot moved to the organization's new headquarters, the Royal Teton Ranch, in southwest Montana.

Elizabeth Clare Prophet:

Friends, neighbors, lightbearers, Keepers of the Flame, we welcome you to the circle of the guru-chela relationship. We welcome you to the circle of Serapis Bey and the Brotherhood of Light, and we welcome you to the community of the Holy Spirit called Camelot.

This day is the decision to make your ascension in this life. The ascended master Lanello says to mark an X at the goal and move straight toward it.

> *In the name of the light of God that never fails, I call to the mighty I AM Presence. In the name of Jesus Christ, Gautama Buddha, and the entire Brotherhood of Light, with gratitude for the outpouring of the love and concern and devotion of Paul the Venetian and the chohans of the rays, we call to Sanat Kumara, Lord Maitreya: seal now all energies released this night within the heart of the Christ Self of each one. Let them never be requalified by the human but taken to be used in the service of all life.*
>
> *Seal each one with the sign of the heart, the head, and the hand. The Brotherhood Eternal saluteth thee. So may the service of thy heart of light be sealed by the power of the Father, the Son, the Holy Spirit, and the Mother. Amen.*

CHAPTER FIVE

That Every Man Can Realize Christhood

In the name of the Word that was made flesh and dwelt among us, I AM THAT I AM, I bow before the universal light of God. I bow before the light within these souls who are becoming day by day more of thee, O LORD *God Almighty.*

As thou hast manifest thy miracle presence in the hearts of the saints, so God, our Father, we pray to thee in this hour, let personal and planetary crisis recede before the Great Central Sun of Being that I AM. Let that Central Sun as thy heart, a flaming fire within us, roll back the darkness of death and degeneration. Roll it back. Roll it back. Roll it back. Let light spring forth within these hearts as a garden of light, a fountain of living flame.

Let this flame which we bear, O God, secure life where I AM, where the I AM is manifest in thy heart, in these temples. And let that burning and shining light, which we have witnessed in John the Baptist and

Jesus Christ and the procession of saints from thy heart, now appear in full glory.

Because thou hast ordained it and called us to this purpose, we give thee our life and our temple, Spirit Most Holy, Father and Son, blessed Mother. Come into our temple and live that all life might live to praise thy name. Amen.

When we pursue any earthly endeavor or discipline, we go to someone who is an expert. I'm sure you've all had that experience in college or in life, something that you wanted to learn and you wanted to know the real living, tested, tried and true method or discipline. You've sought out the experts and you've found the answers.

When you want the ascension with all of your heart, not as an escape hatch from the unpleasantness of your karma, but because it is the supreme offering of the Self—that all life might live—you go to those who have made it. You go to the ascended masters because they are intimately acquainted with the process.

They understand the path. They know its blessings. They know what is absolutely necessary. They know the pitfalls of the human ego. They know the compartments of consciousness. They know all about psychology and the meager offering of that study which we have today in its discipline in our universities. They know all about the teachings of religion, of which Serapis Bey says, "Though there be errors in religion today, these errors are covered over by the very sincerity and heart flame of the people."

And so, even while these errors are covered over with the holiness and devotion of people who truly, in spite of the false doctrine that binds them, do contact the living Word, we nevertheless find that what we have given to us in our religion or in our studies of psychology or life or philosophy entirely misses the path of the ascension.

I searched high and low all over the world with every teacher I could find, asking if anyone knew of the path of the ascension. No one knew. The most dedicated Christians had very nebulous ideas about the ascension. Some were very certain that only one individual had the right to ascend, and that was Jesus Christ.

In fact, Catholic doctrine is that Mother Mary did not ascend; her miraculous transition is called the assumption. Her assumption into heaven is considered to be not like the ascension—for if it were, it would make her equal to Jesus Christ and therefore somehow detract from the majesty of the Saviour.

Well, if any of you have ever taught anyone anything, you have known the joy of the moment when your pupil was able to execute to perfection that which you taught. Whether you taught a little child how to bake a cake or you enabled someone else to become proficient in something that you could do, you felt that a part of yourself was fulfilled because you could transfer that which you were. It is so with the ascended masters. Each time a soul ascends, the ascended master Jesus Christ is glorified, is magnified. His very person is multiplied. In fact, he increases himself by the law of transcendence.

To Walk in the Footsteps of Jesus Christ

Some who are involved in a sentimental religion do not like to think about the fact that the ascended master Jesus Christ is today a person of infinite magnitude, multiplied many times over, compared to what he was in the hour of his ascension. Do people think that for two thousand years an ascended master has done nothing?

We understand that the ascension is truly the moment when the soul is born to eternal life—unlimited potential and possibility—because it is the moment of integration of the soul with the Father, the Son, the Holy Spirit, and the Mother. Jesus Christ demonstrated to us that integration while he was on earth.

He is considered by the Great White Brotherhood to be the greatest example of the path of the ascension to have been recorded in all of recorded history.

The position held by Jesus Christ within the Great White Brotherhood is held by none other, and there is not a cosmic being or Elohim or archangel that does not bow before the name of Jesus when it is spoken. But just because this is true, that does not mean that praise and honor should not be given to Saint Germain or to El Morya or to others who have walked the path. And so the ascended masters, key among them Jesus Christ, do not apologize for the teaching that every man can realize Christhood.

Jesus proclaimed in the final hours of his mission that those who believed on him did not believe on him, but the one who had sent him, and those who heard his Word did not hear his Word, but the Father which spoke through him.[1] When he said that, it is written that "Jesus cried and said . . . " The word "cried" stands out to me because I feel in it the intensity of his heart, knowing how people are so prone to idolatry.

People Have Believed the Lie

The thing Jesus feared most is that people would worship him and not emulate him, would so remove him, so exalt him, so make a God of him, that they would automatically conclude that their sin or supposed sin or their sense of sin would make them something apart, something not capable of doing what he did.

Therefore everything that Jesus did becomes totally natural because he is a God. "Why of course Jesus could do it, because he is God. But we poor mortals, we poor sinners, we are not in that category. We are subject to the flesh; we are subject to original sin. We're subject to all of these conditions of consciousness."

That is the overlay of condemnation that somehow says, "Why I'm not as good as Jesus, and therefore I cannot walk in his footsteps." That is idolatry; it is the worship of the flesh and blood master.

Many of you may know what I am saying, you may be wholly convinced of what I am saying, but the majority of the world is not. And herein lies our concern—that people today have believed in the lie that he came to be the exception instead of the rule, and because of that, the path of the ascension and the path of sainthood is not the central path of Christianity or Judaism or the Muslim faith.

The Mother Flame

Even in Hinduism, the concept of many, many more existences and lifetimes and balancing of karma seems to be a long dusty road approaching infinity into the future. There is no longer any urgency; there is no longer any need to challenge what is facing us. There is no longer the sense that hour by hour and day by day things are happening of supreme importance.

It's the sense that you cannot change maya or the astral condition, and therefore you can retreat into the mountain and meditate. And someday in the next hundred thousand years you may attain soul liberation. And in the meantime, you see all sorts of perversion of the original path of Hinduism in the misuse of the sacred fire, immorality, even the use of drugs, the squandering of the life force in all sorts of sexual experimentations.

I have people coming to me from the Eastern gurus speaking of the sexual experimentations that are taught as part of the path. Well, the sexual energy is the force of light and of the Mother flame. It is locked in the base-of-the-spine chakra. It is unlocked and spent in the sexual experience. Therefore, when people are taught that for the biological or psychological survival of the individual, the sexual energy must be continually spent, they follow a path that is really not compatible with the ascension, because it is a crystal cup of light—it is an elixir—either you drink that light and live forevermore, or you squander it daily. It is a natural resource; it is a choice.

The Mother Light Must Be Used Wisely

Americans are waking up to the fact that resources can come to a shortage, that the earth has so much oil, the earth has so much energy. In fact there is an abundance of energy, but it is being hoarded or not properly extracted for our use. It is being manipulated for the sake of manipulating the people, and all of the sudden there is no gas in the gas tank.

Well, that is a sudden realization to a people who have never known want for water or energy or light. We suddenly come to the realization that the energy that God gives to us materially and spiritually must be wisely used.

The path of the ascension is not a path of denial; it is not a path of suppression; it is not a path of "no, no, no, and if you do, you might go to hell." It is a path of great wisdom and great joy. It is the path of understanding, of the raising up of the Mother light in joy abundantly, joyously. And as the light rises within the temple, it reunites in each of the seven chakras of being with the Alpha and the Omega potential.

The descent of light from your I AM Presence is the light of the Father. It descends. That which descends must ascend. But the Father light does not ascend unless and until it is united with the Mother light.

The Mother light sealed in the base of the spine is the energy that is capable of creating a cosmos, of bringing forth life. It is also the energy that is capable of carrying the soul to the holy place, the Holy of holies in the secret chamber of the heart, and ultimately in the crown chakra.

The use of the life force is strictly a matter of human habit. We have long, long centuries of the human habit pattern of the descent of energy. When the energy descends from the I AM Presence, unless it is released from the heart in love and service and each day given back to life in order that life may give again, unless that process of the givingness of self is going on, the energy builds up. It builds up in the chakras, and unless there is a flow and an interaction with God and with every part of God in the earth, there is going to be a stoppage of energy.

That energy that collects in the lower chakras and does not flow collects there many times because of heavy diets. Diet itself will stop the flow of energy in the lower chakras. It is stopped there because of human habit patterns, of negativity, discord. Inharmony of every kind, especially in the feelings, locks the energies in the lower chakras. When people do not know how to meditate, simply to close their eyes, go into the heart, salute the living Christ, rise with that Christ into the upper chakras, they have no surcease from the endless round of the energy in the lower chakras that is in a constant state of interplay.

When you look at peoples' lives and how they are lived, it is no wonder that they have psychological problems, sexual problems, family problems, overeating problems, physical health problems. All of these have to do with not understanding how to use this ascension flame, not knowing how to raise it up and thus begin the flow of all energy back to God.

Energy that rises and ascends, when it passes through the heart chakra, when you use the violet flame, is transmuted. Energy that is purified becomes energy stored in the chakras and in the aura and finally in the causal body. Energy misqualified collects and creates the build up of energy, which has its outbursts in crime, in anger, in frustration and ultimately in sexual uses that become more than the natural or normal uses of sex—either perversions or obsession with sexual fantasy.

The Mother Flame Is Rising

We have today so much sexual symbolism in our advertising, in pornography, in regular movies that are playing. We have a tremendous upsurge of misuses of sexual energy. And we see that all of this is the rising of the Mother flame from Lemuria. And when that rising of the Mother flame takes place, it is the white light in every single person upon the planetary body that is activated. And when it is activated, it begins to outpicture the old stream beds and the old patterns. We have a long history upon this planetary body of civilizations and of dark ages. Therefore, in your own aura and etheric body there are the records of the descent of energy.

And so we see that the attempt to resolve the build up of energy in the lower chakras comes out in rock music, in disco, in discordant rhythms. There is such an intense build up of misqualified energy that has descended, along with the beginning of the raising up of that Mother light, that people's bodies begin to gyrate to a beat that lowers their energy lower and lower. It is a means of attempting to throw off that which is not being resolved through meditation, through integration, through the identity, realizing the point of the I AM Presence.

There are many activities that people engage in that are a misuse of this energy. For example, the use of the tongue in human gossip is a virulent force of the misuse of sexual energy. It is interesting to note that many people who gossip enjoy gossiping about other people's sexual lives, they themselves thinking that they are free from these unnecessary habits. But in fact their sexual expressions are through an unbridled tongue, and the gossip becomes just as offensive and discordant to the environment as the pollution from other chakras. So those who are self-righteous and proud and will tell you all of their virtues may have just as much bottled-up energy and just as much absence of the resolution of that light.

Nevertheless, I cannot tell you an untruth. I must tell you that your ascension is directly linked to the conservation of energy within your chakras, to the transmutation of energy misqualified, and to taking dominion of all of the centers, beginning with the heart, which is the real central sun of your being. The heart becomes a magnet, and it will magnetize the light of the Mother flame *gently,* rhythmically up into the higher centers.

The transcendence of the uses of energy is thereby natural, and it is not something that is forced. It is not forced upon you by the Law or by the ascended masters, but it comes to you naturally—not because of suppression, but because of replacement. You begin to replace the habits of the misuse of energy with the giving of decrees. The simple affirmation of the resurrection flame begins a spiral so intense as to find this energy rising and scintillating through your form. The rising spiral of the resurrection flame that is anchored in the heart of the Great Pyramid is itself the means for this overcoming. In and of itself, the flame and the dynamic decree takes the place of the descending energy.

A Path of Striving and a Higher Way

I have not set up rules and regulations, nor have the ascended masters. They have set forth a teaching and they have presented love—love in its highest essence. They have presented a teaching that gives you a motivation whereby in purity and comfort and compassion you can find yourself day by day enjoying the light, enjoying the unity and the wholeness of that light.

So, this path is a gradual path, and it takes a number of years for you to wean yourself from simple habits—habits of diet, perhaps habits of smoking, all sorts of things that you know in yourself are not really your ultimate desire. So you take them one by one. You work diligently, you pray fervently, you give the appropriate decrees and calls for the removal of entities that reinforce the misuse of energy. But the one thing you do not do is condemn yourself. Self-condemnation is simply the tool of the Antichrist and your own carnal mind.

Not to condemn yourself does not mean that you let yourself off without the necessary understanding that sin is a reality until it is forsaken and that repentance is a very important part of the path—to repent from those ways that are not lawful and not in keeping with the teachings of God. So sincerely, in your heart, ask for intercession, ask for the help of the angels and Jesus Christ and Saint Germain and Archangel Michael.

Not to condemn yourself for having a foul mouth or a foul temper doesn't mean that you simply allow it to continue to happen. You strive and you wrestle with those demons, but do not get into a spiral of self-condemnation that says, "Well, I'm a miserable sinner. I haven't balanced enough karma to come to grips with this. I'm not Jesus Christ, and therefore life will just have to take me the way I am. This is the way I am; take me or leave me."

I've heard people make this ultimatum to God, to the ascended masters, and to me. And of course, that is not the way of the path. The path is a path of acceptable striving, a striving that you can contain and not go off the deep end.

The ascended masters are not fanatics. They don't like fanatical fasting or fanatical decreeing or fanatical anything. They want you to be examples of a higher way, of an abundant life that you can live in and among your neighbors and your profession, on your job, and show that life lived for the goal of reunion with God can be viable, that people pursuing this path are indeed normal people, helpful people, understanding people, that have families and raise children and perhaps have problems with those children just as everyone else has problems with children, that they can become active and get involved in community service, that they are not aloof, and by all means they are not in a state of condemnation of other people who perhaps are living very good and beautiful lives but do not happen to be on the path of the ascension.

The Letter of the Law and the Spirit

Self-righteousness and fanaticism can be the very tools of Antichrist to discredit the entire path of the Brotherhood. I would like you to know that I see people who have taken up the teachings of the ascended masters who are far more fanatical and zealous than I am. It's a strange occurrence. It is as if they felt that somehow in the letter of the law—as Paul warned against going back to the rituals of Judaism, fulfilling the letter of the law without the Spirit[2]—they could somehow buy their way into the kingdom of heaven.

Once I was in a restaurant and I was next to a table where there were two Christians seated. They were discussing a theological question, and they were saying that if they sinned and then they asked for forgiveness, God would have to take them into heaven. It is as though they were looking at the law as legalists, as scribes, and saying, "Well, the law says this, this and this. And if I do this, this, this and this, then God will have to take me into heaven."

I could see that they were operating under the rules of Christianity by fear and not by love. They had not really overcome those things that they refrained from. It was good that they refrained from them, but it was not good that they were not overcoming their fear.

I have been shown the record of various priests and nuns in Christianity or Buddhism who have served in their monasteries in various lifetimes, and they have fulfilled the whole letter of the law. And when they have come to the conclusion of that incarnation and they have gone to the Karmic Board, they have not been given the initiations of the crucifixion or the resurrection or the ascension, because they didn't have the spirit of love. Love was the gaping hole in their entire experience. They sought to buy their way into heaven by perfect performance, but within them was seething resentment and a sense of injustice, a sense of martyrdom.

Understanding the Motive of the Heart

This is why the ascended masters Jesus and Kuthumi come with the path of the World Teachers. They come to teach us something about the psychology of the self. Why does the self want association with the ascended masters? Has it been rejected by the world and therefore it needs to have some kind of an imaginary association with imaginary beings of light who will now flatter that individual and flatter his psyche?

Or is it because of the basic love for every part of life, and the realization that these saints have given their lives, and because they have given them, we live, and that these ascended masters are not aloof? The masters are in the ghettos. They're in the places where people have the greatest want and the greatest need. And there they look for an instrument to minister to life.

The ascended masters are the bodhisattvas tarrying with this earth until every one of us discovers the key to the ascension, psychology, and the understanding of the motive of the heart. The heart has motives, but the subconscious desire body also has motives. Freud well outlined the desires of the id and the energies of the libido and how these desires really were the foundation of what is outpictured on the surface. This may be true, but once you know it, it does not have to continue to be true.

The Four Lower Bodies

The Four Horsemen of the Apocalypse, about which Sanat Kumara is lecturing in his current releases through the *Pearls of*

*Wisdom,** are symbolical of your four lower bodies. They are the vehicles of your consciousness. You—your soul with your Christ Self—are intended to be the driver, the single rider on all four horses. Unfortunately, the ego fragments itself into four persons and comes riding on the four horses and completely dominates the scene, and the soul has no say about what will happen or its future.

The unsealing of the seven-sealed book by Sanat Kumara opens the way for us to realize that until the Christ person within us is crowned King of kings and Lord of lords and sits upon the throne, these four horsemen have a heyday. The ego itself, that carnal mind, that impure desire and the impure motive of the heart, is given complete freedom to run rampant, to bring hell and death and famine and pestilence and all manner of disturbance within this temple.

So the desire body is a horse that we ride. The soul takes dominion and becomes aware of impure desire, and the soul meditates upon God and discovers what is God's desire in the universe. God's desiring to be himself in all of us is the desire for life to be lived abundantly, joyously, lovingly. When we meditate upon the desire of God, we realize that there is no conflict between our soul and the Spirit of God, that impure desire leads to death and self-annihilation. We don't really want it. It is the not-self, the unreal self.

And so we begin the path of invoking the violet flame into the impure desire to transmute its momentum—the cause, effect, record and memory of all previous lifetimes. And we invoke the desire of God to come into this temple and transform us.

And do you know what you find—what I have found? The desire of God is so all-consuming that moment by moment and breath by breath, you have no other desire than to be in God, to do his will, to outpicture his desire. There is no other desire

*These teachings by Sanat Kumara are published in the 1979 *Pearls of Wisdom* and in the book *The Opening of the Seventh Seal: Sanat Kumara on the Path of the Ruby Ray.*

left within you but to know him. There is nothing that God has ever taken from me or deprived me of in order to give me the victory of my ascension.

I am no martyr. I am not a deprived person. I enjoy the fullness of life. The life that I enjoy is the fullness of God's love, and therefore what would seem to some as temptation is not temptation, because it is of no interest, because God has filled me with his life; he has filled me with his Holy Spirit. All of my needs, all that I could possibly ever want is fulfilled by that Holy Spirit.

And so the message that I bring you is that the path of the ascension is not a path of suffering. It is only a path of suffering to those who are the prisoners of the carnal mind, who are so convinced that they need all of those activities of the carnal mind that the very thought of giving up those activities is death itself.

You've all heard the stories of people dying of lung cancer who are smoking away even when they've had operations. They would rather die than stop smoking. I hear it very often about relatives of people on the path who are making their transition, for whom I pray.

But is that their true desire? No, it is not. That is the possessing demon. That temple of that individual who is bound by the nicotine and cigarette habit is invaded by the nicotine entity, virulent and vicious to the very death of the individual. It has a worm manifestation; it has a demon manifestation. It enters the temple; it takes it over; it creates the insatiable desire for cigarettes until a person is a habitual chain smoker. It destroys the body; it eats the body.

And what does it get? All of the light stored in the cells of the temple. Therefore it perpetuates its existence and goes forth to come upon other houses, other temples. When a person says, "I would rather die than not have a cigarette," he is not expressing his free will. He is enslaved by possessing demons.

The Message of Sanat Kumara

The message that I bring to you this morning comes from Sanat Kumara. You will read it in the coming *Pearls of Wisdom*. He brings to you the message of the great commission: to go forth into all the world and preach the gospel to every creature.[3] He brings us the understanding that to preach is to have the *p*ower to *reach* the soul that is in a state of demon possession.

You begin with yourself. We begin with one another. And when God is raised up within us, and when the Holy Spirit is in us, then when we speak, the power of the Word goes forth. It goes forth from the heart of your I AM Presence to your Christ Self. And what does it contact in that poor soul that is enslaved to a possessing demon?

It first contacts that soul's real identity, who is the person of the Christ. This is why Christian leaders today have no power to exorcise the demons in Church and State, even while all of America is rampant with these demons that possess our children —whether alcohol or nicotine or sugar. Sugar as an entity is just as addictive and destructive as drugs and rock music and the death beat itself. We have a nation that is in a state of demon possession, and where are the religious leaders who can go forth and exorcise them in his name?

"O ye of little faith."[4] If they have the ultimate Word, let them prove the Word by their works. The ascended masters' chelas are proving their word by their works, and Jesus Christ has given to them the knowledge of the Elohim Astrea. The call to Mighty Astrea—one of the seven Elohim, the seven spirits of God described in the Bible[5]—brings down upon us the action of the light of a circle-and-sword of blue flame for the binding of demons.

I have seen the calls of the students singly and in unison bind entire hordes of rampaging demons of murder, of destruction, of war, of riot. I have seen all kinds of conditions in our cities and in our nation stopped by the dynamic decrees. The dynamic decrees work, and you must begin with yourself, because unless you are free from any form of mental suggestion that comes from discarnates, entities or demons, you do not have the full faculties of your free will.

The Power to Preach

Sanat Kumara says that in order to have the power to preach, the Holy Spirit must come into you, and if you desire that Spirit, you must begin the exercise of the Word; you must begin to witness. This is why Jesus taught his disciples to witness unto him and his person.

When you speak of Jesus Christ or El Morya or Saint Germain, their very name spoken through you draws their presence into you. When you witness to their reality and the reality of Almighty God in your life, you are confirming that presence where you stand. And so daily the Word is confirmed—the person of the Word and the power of the Word.

So, in order to get the power to preach, you have to begin to preach. That's the message of the World Teachers. If you want to receive the Holy Spirit into your temple to transform lesser desire into greater desire and to know the joy that is my daily cup that I speak to you of, you have to start the ball rolling. You have to thread the needle. You have to pull that thread of consciousness through the eye of God. You've got to begin; it just doesn't happen.

Many years ago, when I was making my decision to be or not be a chela of El Morya, to leave everything and to follow the path of my ascension, one very interesting religious teacher said to me, "Why, the ascension is something that just happens at the end of your life, if you lead a good life."

And I thought, "Life should be so simple." And I looked at him and I knew that I had outgrown that teacher, and I knew that I must go on.

To walk alone is better than to walk with a false teacher who is limiting your expression. It's better to walk with your mighty I AM Presence. Walk the streets and pace the floor and talk to God and say, "God, cleanse me and purge me, raise me up. I want to do your work, but my life is not yet in a condition where I can serve you, because I myself am still bound."

When you have that point of realization, you know that you have joined with the discontented ones, those who are dissatisfied—and dissatisfaction itself is the only condition of consciousness calculated to make an avatar. If you are content with your slavery and refuse to see that you are enslaved, then you will be enslaved—as were the Israelites in Egypt.

Awakening Those Who Sleep

This is what Sanat Kumara teaches us: when you begin to preach the Word and that fire is hurled forth from you, you contact the living Christ in your hearers, and it is that person of the Christ, the Christ Self, the blessed mediator of that one, who reaches down and lets a light ray descend and quicken that soul.

Have you ever been asleep and not wanted to be awakened? You got home late, you've only slept a few hours, you want to sleep in. Somebody comes along and shakes you, and you get very annoyed. You find yourself feisty and nasty and saying, "Don't wake me up!"

Well, that's the way it is with the soul. It is comfortably asleep. It knows it is asleep, and yet it wants to be asleep. It wants to sleep on and on like someone who is sleeping off drugs or alcohol. They want to sleep and sleep, and when they awaken they start the round again so they'll go back to sleep. They don't want to face life.

Sanat Kumara says that when you begin to preach, you arouse anger on two fronts: the anger of those demons that are possessing and inhabiting the temple of the one you desire to rescue, and also the resistance of the soul to being awakened. "Go away, leave me alone. Don't tell me all of this truth. I can't stand to hear it, because if I hear it I'll have to do something about it. Let me sleep on." Sleeping that sleep of death, this is where we find the self-induced hypnosis of our people.

Why are people glued to the TV set? It is because they really want to be hypnotized, because no one has shown them another reason for living, another way of living, a joyous way of living. And all the dos and don'ts of religion or society are just too painful.

Experiment with the Law

If you have the courage to listen to the truth, even a small amount of the truth, you can hear the door creaking open and the soul will come forth from its tomb and begin to live. And day by day, you have the opportunity for more and more self-mastery, and you realize that every point of self-dominion is such a joy. You say, "Praise the Lord. In the name of the ascended master Jesus Christ and Saint Germain, I have lived this day to prove that the Law works, that when I give a dynamic decree, light descends and my life changes! And things start happening for the better and I start finding out my divine plan."

To experiment with a law that is precise, a law that is mathematics, that is yours for the taking, and then to watch it work, is like the delight of a child who takes his first step, because you've done it yourself. You, a soul, have risen up. You have contacted your personal Christ Self, your I AM Presence, and you realize that in actuality there is a path back Home that doesn't come by superstition or witchcraft or psychic formulas, or all kinds of necromancy.

In this hemisphere, in North and South and Central America, millions of people today are practicing witchcraft or superstition mixed up with their Christian religion, conjuring up psychic entities, spiritualism, charting their lives on worldly astrology. Do you realize how many devious pathways there are, when the one supreme path of the mighty I AM Presence is there and can be walked step-by-step?

I would like you to know that I have been walking this path a long time, that I am no different from any one of you. I happen to remember my past lives. I do not fear to confront them. When I see an akashic record that tells me that I have sinned or done something that was not the better part of wisdom in the past, I thank God for the opportunity today to do ten or a hundred things to undo that and make it right. I can face the fact that I've made mistakes. I can face the fact that the self I was yesterday is not the self I want to be today or tomorrow.

I don't have to condemn myself. I can say, "Thank you, God, for giving me the opportunity to experiment in free will with consciousness and life and with my four lower bodies. I've made terrible mistakes. I am very sorry and I am here to atone for them. Let me go to work and do some things right and show that by your law people can rise up."

You know, there are those who always want to quote the words of Paul, who said, "We've all sinned and come short of the mark."[6] We've all sinned—well, that may be true. But isn't there ever a day when someone can stop sinning and say, "I'm going to live the life of righteousness"? When does it end? When does the condemnation end? Possessing demons will continue to tell you that sin goes on and on along with the suffering of sin.

But the individual who truly is saved and knows God is no longer a sinner, and he does not fear his sin, because he knows that it is swallowed up and transmuted by the Holy Spirit when he will stand, face and conquer. Have the courage to be a saint. Have the courage to say, "I am walking the path of sainthood, and God has placed his spark within me, and by his grace I'm capable of walking that path and it is my inheritance."

The Fruits of Following the Path

I tell you this because I have seen the fruits of following the path in my own life. I have been through the testings of Luxor. I have been with Serapis in the King's Chamber. I have passed through the trials of the long dark night. I have seen the labyrinth. I have been sent into hell to preach to the rebellious spirits. I have seen the devil face-to-face. And what have I learned?

I've learned that only God is power, only God is real. And the moment you say his name, all that is unlike him trembles and fears before your footstep. I have learned that there is no dragon or beast that can confront a single soul when that soul is wedded to God. I have seen conditions of power and the attempt to destroy my life or the lives of other people entirely swallowed up by the name of God by the person of Archangel Michael. I have seen the threats of the ultimate fear of death. I have looked at death face-to-face and I have seen the living proof of Jesus Christ that death is not real, that there is no death, that the coming and the going within this temple and other temples is provided by God and he has many mansions celestial and terrestrial.[7]

When you cease to fear death, you work backwards because all other fears are lesser. Mark used to tell me, "If you fear what will happen, contemplate the ultimate threat. The ultimate threat is always death. If that's not so bad, then nothing else will bother you." It really works.

Terrestrial and Celestial Bodies

I saw Mark Prophet go through the experience of what appeared to be physical death. I saw him, I took his hand. I realized I would not see him again in this octave in a physical form. Something inside of me died, and something inside of me was born. I saw the temple—but I also saw the soul. I saw the soul rise into the ascension, and I whispered to him, "You've won, you've made it. You're the victor."

And that is what he wanted to know that I learned from that experience. I didn't descend into the idolatry that because the flesh and blood were no longer functioning, that somehow he was not there. That would have been a worship of his physical person. But I had a very human prayer in my heart when I took his hand, and I said, "Dear God, I cannot believe that somewhere in this universe I will not take that hand again." That is something you say when you are required to place that loved one upon the funeral pyre in the cremation chamber.

We become so attached to the body, but the body is Mother, the body is renewed. And as Paul said, there are terrestrial bodies, and there are celestial bodies.[8] And that ascended master light body of Mark Prophet is here and now where I am. It is superimposed where I am, and we are one. And therefore that which dies in oneself is the one-on-one human relationship, and that which is born is the awareness of androgynous being, that you and your twin flame here and now occupy the same time and space and that you are one.

The human mind, from time to time, is tempted to believe in separation. That's simply the law of time and space. But I have a retreat in my heart where I go when I am tempted with that temptation. And in the secret chamber of the heart, I renew again my awareness of the total cosmos. It is not far from me. It is not far. But so long as we live in this octave, we will deal with those situations. And when you can deal with them fearlessly, you know you are on the path of the ascension.

You Can Make Your Ascension

And I want to tell you that every one of you can make it. I am not so old as years go in this embodiment. It didn't take me all of my lifetime to come to this realization. Very early in life, I had that awareness of God consciousness. That was from other incarnations and other lifetimes. But you have your momentum, too.

Did you ever consider that while you are bound by this or that human habit, you are not opening the great floodgates to the descent of your God consciousness, that locked in your causal body, right now, is attainment, that on other battlefields in other lifetimes you have won victories over yourself, and that right now you don't have the full momentum of that discipline in your outer four lower bodies, because you haven't made room for it? Kick out those unnecessary things.

You know, I came to San Francisco, and I came as the messenger of Serapis. I came in his consciousness and in his mantle. And one of the first students I met had two requests to make of me. These requests were quite mundane and quite concerned with mundane life. And I thought to myself, "Just think if he could have understood what really happened. If he could have really seen Serapis standing where I stood."

If you had the opportunity to speak with Serapis Bey, what favor would you ask him? Would you treat him as a genie and say, "O Serapis, give me human happiness, solve my financial problems, make all things comfortable for me?"

I hope you would say, "Serapis Bey, come into my temple and show me why I don't have more God consciousness. Reveal to me how I can transmute, by the sacred fire, what is standing in the way of mastery. Serapis Bey, initiate me in the very first steps of Luxor."

I hope that would be on your mind. But sadly, of course, Serapis comes looking like any one of us, and any one of us happens to be me. And so little old me gets asked these mundane questions, "Can I do this?" or "Can I do that?"

The Initiations of the Path

You know, there came a time in my life when I was determined that nothing would stand in my way, and I demanded those initiations and I received them, and they were like the flood of arrows darkening the sky at Thermopylae. But the Christ is standing there, and God really never gives us more than we can take.

Sometimes we have to catch up. Sometimes we've allowed ourselves to sleep, we've indulged ourselves for a long time. It's like collecting your dirty laundry. It piles up, and all of a sudden one day you have an extraordinary burden, and then you demand to be free and it all comes out, and then someone asks, "Why am I having so many problems? I don't understand why, when I just came back from the retreat of the World Teachers, that suddenly I have such burdens."

Well, you came to the retreat of the World Teachers to learn how to challenge those burdens!* Did you think you would go away from the retreat and life would be a bed of roses? You have to have something to sharpen your sword on. How will you know what the muscle of the heart can do if you don't have a challenge of that burning in your heart? A burning in the heart is something that is very natural to the saints. Some people panic even if they're twenty-two and they say, "Oh, I have this terrible heart condition!"

The Fire in the Heart

No, your heart is becoming a fiery furnace of the ruby ray. The intensity of the white light is burning, and it's burning as a fiery vortex for transmutation, and God is using you to clean up the earth. He needs his fiery furnaces all over the place.

Remember when they stopped letting you burn your garbage and your leaves? They won't even let the fiery salamanders come and clean up the garbage of the planet, because it might pollute the air. They didn't stop the trucks and the buses and the planes. They didn't stop the chemical factories from polluting the air. But you can't burn your leaves in your backyard anymore.

* The *Seminar of the World Teachers* was held July 9–20, 1979, at Camelot.

We need to burn physically and we need to burn spiritually. And it's a burning and a shining light that came with John the Baptist[9] and Jesus Christ who said, "I AM come to send fire on the earth."[10] And that fire begins as the fire in your heart. And when you first come into the dictations of the ascended masters, sometimes you get very hot, because of the alchemy of transmutation. And after a while you feel very cool and you find that the sensation of fire is coolness.

If you went to the sun of our system today, would you be hot or cold? It depends on your vibration. Whether you can pass through the sun and feel heat or feel coolness depends on the level of your consciousness, depends on how much misqualified energy is within you.

The burning in the heart is God loving life through you. God loves life so much, and especially God loves those whom you think are your enemies. And when those enemies are gossiping or maligning or persecuting, as Jesus promised they would to those on the path,[11] what happens to your heart? It gets on fire. And the burning process is the flame. And the flame is consuming that anger and that hatred, because if it didn't, the anger itself might very well remove you from the screen of life.

God protects you. He lights the light in your heart. And if you experience a little pain, it's because you haven't put enough into the fire. You need some more kindling wood. You need some more to burn to make it hotter. In other words, you need to give some more violet-flame decrees. Increase the fire, the burning will increase, the consuming will increase, and you'll discover that your fiery vortex has grown. You're becoming a Great Central Sun, and you're moving on that path that Sanat Kumara is talking about in *The Opening of the Seventh Seal.*

The Chart of Your Divine Self

There are three figures represented in the Chart of Your Divine Self. We refer to them as the upper figure, the middle figure and the lower figure. These three correspond to the Christian Trinity: The upper corresponds to the Father, who is one with the Mother, the middle to the Son, and the lower to the temple of the Holy Spirit.

We address our Father-Mother God as the I AM Presence. This is the I AM THAT I AM, whom God revealed to Moses and individualized for every son and daughter of God. Your I AM Presence is surrounded by seven concentric spheres of rainbow light. These make up your causal body, the biding place of your I AM Presence. In Buddhism it is called the *Dharmakaya*—the body of the Lawgiver (the I AM Presence) and the Law (the causal body).

The spheres of your causal body are successive planes of God's consciousness that make up your heaven-world. They are the "many mansions" of your Father's house, where you lay up your "treasures in heaven." Your treasures are your words and works worthy of your Creator, constructive thoughts and feelings, your victories for the right, and the virtues you have embodied to the glory of God. When you judiciously exercise your free will to daily use the energies of God in love and in harmony, these energies automatically ascend to your causal body. They accrue to your soul as "talents," which you may then multiply as you put them to good use lifetime after lifetime.

The middle figure in the Chart represents the "only begotten Son" of the Father-Mother God, the universal Christ. He is your personal Mediator and your soul's Advocate before God. He is your Higher Self, whom you appropriately address as your beloved Holy Christ Self. John spoke of this individualized presence of the Son of God as "the true light, which lighteth every man that cometh into the world." He is your Inner Teacher, your Divine Spouse, your dearest Friend and is most often recognized as the Guardian Angel. He overshadows you every hour of the day and night. Draw nigh to him and he will draw nigh to you.

The lower figure in the Chart is a representation of yourself as a disciple on the path of reunion with God. It is your soul evolving through the planes of matter using the vehicles of the four lower bodies to balance karma and fulfill her divine plan. The four lower bodies are the etheric, or memory, body; the mental body; the desire, or emotional, body; and the physical body.

The lower figure is surrounded by a tube of light, which is projected from the heart of the I AM Presence in answer to your call. It is a cylinder of white light that sustains a forcefield of protection 24 hours a day, so long as you maintain your harmony in thought, feeling, word, and deed.

Sealed in the secret chamber of your heart is the threefold flame of life. It is your divine spark, the gift of life, consciousness and free will from your beloved I AM Presence. Through the Love, Wisdom, and Power of the Godhead anchored in your threefold flame, your soul can fulfill her reason for being on earth. Also called the Christ flame and the liberty flame, or fleur-de-lis, the threefold flame is the spark of the soul's divinity, her potential for Christhood.

The silver (or crystal) cord is the stream of life, or "lifestream," which descends from the heart of the I AM Presence through the Holy Christ Self to nourish and sustain (through the seven chakras and the secret chamber of the heart) the soul and her four lower bodies. It is over this "umbilical" cord that the light of the Presence flows, entering the being of man at the crown chakra and giving impetus for the pulsation of the threefold flame in the secret chamber of the heart.

The lower figure represents the son of man or child of the light evolving beneath his own "Tree of Life." The lower figure corresponds to the Holy Spirit, for the soul and the four lower bodies are intended to be the temple of the Holy Spirit. The violet flame, the spiritual fire of the Holy Spirit, envelops the soul as it purifies. This is how you should visualize yourself standing in the violet flame. You can invoke the violet flame daily in the name of your I AM Presence and Holy Christ Self to purify your four lower bodies and consume negative thoughts, negative feelings and negative

karma in preparation for the ritual of the alchemical marriage—your soul's union with the Beloved, your Holy Christ Self.

Shown just above the head of the Christ is the dove of the Holy Spirit descending in the benediction of the Father-Mother God. When your soul has achieved the alchemical marriage, she is ready for the baptism of the Holy Spirit. And she may hear the Father-Mother God pronounce the approbation: "This is my beloved Son in whom I AM well pleased."

When your soul concludes a lifetime on earth, the I AM Presence withdraws the silver cord, whereupon your threefold flame returns to the heart of your Holy Christ Self. Your soul, clothed in her etheric garment, gravitates to the highest level of consciousness to which she has attained in all of her past incarnations. Between embodiments she is schooled in the etheric retreats until her final incarnation when the Great Law decrees she shall return to the Great God Source to go out no more.

Your soul is the nonpermanent aspect of your being, which you make permanent through the ascension process. By this process your soul balances her karma, bonds to your Holy Christ Self, fulfills her divine plan and returns at last to the living Presence of the I AM THAT I AM. Thus the cycles of her going out into the Matter cosmos are completed. In attaining union with God she has become the Incorruptible One, a permanent atom in the body of God. The Chart of Your Divine Self is therefore a diagram of yourself—past, present, and future.

CHAPTER SIX

The LORD's Ritual of Exorcism

The word in the last chapter of the book of Mark is, "Go ye into all the world," which is in every plane of consciousness, "and preach the gospel to every creature."[1] Then it begins with five signs that will follow them who will accept that calling, and the first sign is the casting out of devils.

Sanat Kumara has taken three entire chapters to address himself to the subject of casting out devils. And he says that you can go nowhere until you determine to enter the ritual of exorcism, the ritual of casting out devils. The world is rampant with devils and discarnates and unseen forces, and all the while we are taught a philosophy that they do not exist. And how are we taught to control these forces of possession that create psychological problems? With chemical drugs.

It's very interesting that the drug Thorazine, which is often used where people have a severe psychological problem, does in fact set up a chemical barrier to the penetration of discarnates into the temple. And so for want of self-mastery, it becomes a stopgap measure.

Well, we all know that drugs for physical or psychological conditions are stopgap measures. I don't advise people to get off their prescriptions the moment they discover the teachings of the ascended masters. I only advise you that medication is certainly not the ultimate solution. It is temporary until you can summon the light and gain self-mastery, and that takes a little while. God doesn't take a while. God is instantaneous. But we have cycles and signs and times and spaces in our evolution, and the four lower bodies need healing.

If you need proof of that, you can read the account of Saint Germain where he as an ascended master went to heal one who was in a state of severe illness, and it was not a mere instantaneous touching of this person that brought about the healing.[2] It was a prolonged working with that individual, the action of the sacred fire in the casting out of devils.

Sanat Kumara explains that when souls in karmic experiences and in past embodiments have had confrontations that are extremely painful and they have not been able to meet those confrontations, the souls have receded into the subconscious.

It's very easy for a soul, given the mechanization of our civilization, to do this. Why? Because our education, our TV and our media is primarily concerned with the training of the outer mind, or the mental body, which becomes the carnal mind or the intellect. There is not much stimulus for soul development. The soul can go into its sleep, its self-hypnosis, or even in a state that's like a coma, and the outer person can function and appear to be totally normal.

When I look at the auras of people in our government today, I see that they are considered to be powerful, that they have vast disciplines, they are intelligent, they are capable of running departments, et cetera. But I see that they are running totally on their mental bodies, not by contact with a flame, not by contact with a God source, and that the soul is not even a participant in what they are doing, I realize that the carnal mind that can reach such levels of ability is also always vulnerable to be used at the moment when the fallen ones desire to use that mind to wreak havoc and to make decisions to destroy an economy, a nation or a people.

We have a lot of people who hold the destiny of this state and this nation in their hands today who have no contact with the living Word. In the absence of that contact, by the lives that they lead and human habit patterns that you are well aware of, they are invariably surrounded and filled with all sorts of discarnates and demons.

Therefore, when Isaiah wrote, "The government shall be upon *his* shoulder,"[3] he was prophesying the triumph of the Christ in the individual person, the raising up of that Christ, and the Christ governing the individual and then governing the community. We do not see that in America today. And that is why we are losing this nation and losing our opportunity to be an example in the world of the true teachings of the living Christ.

We are losing it fast, and if we don't individually give accounting, we are going to see that the ascended masters and the Great White Brotherhood will have to figure out how to start all over again. It has taken over two hundred years to bring to this moment a people, a nation, a destiny and a calling of freedom. The calling of freedom is the calling of the Holy Spirit, and the calling is for wholeness. America will not be whole, you will not be whole until the Holy Ghost comes into your temple. The Holy Ghost will not come into your temple until, in the name of the Son of God, you cast out the invading entities.

Entities and the Individual

Sanat Kumara says that many of these entities are very comfortable. They're very similar to the personality of the person they are with. They imitate, in gray tones, the soul's own identity.

And if the soul has receded to the subconscious, then these entities are simply a part and parcel of the functioning intellectual mind, so that the identity, or in this case actually the id itself, the pseudo-self or the mental body, considers itself to be the real self. That is the equation you face when you preach the Word. And this is why the Word is preached and not merely taught.

I really learned an appreciation for preaching the Word when I received these dictations from Sanat Kumara. Preaching the Word means the transfer of the Holy Ghost, the power of the Holy Ghost to reach down into the subconscious, awaken that soul, wrestle with it while it gets feisty and says, "Don't wake me up!" draw it forth, bring it to the inner temple of the heart, place the hand of that soul in the hand of its Christ Self, guard that alchemical marriage, and protect it until the soul is strong enough to maintain its own contact with its own inner Christ Self.

The ascended masters are the true shepherds of the people who come to guard that process and bind the hordes of entities that prevent the individual from contacting his own free will. People are not in possession of their free will when they murder, when they lie, when they cheat, when they steal, when they indulge themselves and gorge themselves and rebel against God or Church or religion in some form. That is not the free will of the soul; that's the free will of a miseducated carnal mind functioning with all kinds of discarnates.

A discarnate may be someone who has been in embodiment and who is now functioning on the astral plane, who has passed through death and doesn't have enough light to go into the higher octaves. The world and the cities are filled with discarnates. Those who die and cannot accelerate remain just about where they were when they died.

When you see traffic accidents on the highway, a day later you can see people who died trying to find their bodies. They don't really go anywhere special. People think they go off into heaven. Well, the few make it who have light and devotion. But those who are in the mass consciousness stay in a very low level, and they gather around people with whom they affinitize. So when you have a bad habit, that bad habit becomes a magnet for discarnate entities who had the same habit when they were in embodiment.

The Sugar Entity

This is why it becomes such a tremendous struggle to wage a war, let's say, against the sugar entity. This craving for sugar is increased by the presence of discarnates and demons. It becomes an enslaving habit. And we have an entire generation of children enslaved to that sugar entity.

I have seen that entity. It is a *deadly* entity. It needs to be replaced. You can't just take away sugar from people's diets. You have to begin to give them things like honey or maple syrup or fresh fruits, translate and reeducate the taste buds, and let them begin to realize that all of the vegetables and even the sprouted grains have their own natural sweetness, that the body really doesn't need all of that sugar.

Why is sugar so deadly? Because it imbalances the bloodstream and the body temple, and it prevents the soul from direct contact with the mighty I AM Presence—just like alcohol, just like nicotine, just like drugs. That is why it is such a subtle force. And when these habits are present and you feel they are overwhelming, you're not just dealing with yourself, you're dealing with hordes of entities that want to keep you enslaved because they are depriving you of life, keeping you from that God-mastery, because when you get God you're going to have the all-power of heaven and earth in your temple, and you're going to count for world salvation, you're going to make a difference to this planetary body. And the hordes of the night are going to tremble when many sons and daughters rise up with this flame.

So as a point of victory, it is necessary to put them down. You might say, "Well, it doesn't really matter that I have this habit, it's really not harmful," or "I only do it once in a while." It's the factor of whether you really *can* stop smoking if you want to. After you've smoked, it's always easy to say, "Well, I don't really have to smoke," because you have satisfied the entity.

The casting out of demons cannot be done unless you have personal contact with the legions of angels and the Elohim. Remember, it is your office to speak the Word. But it is the office of the hosts of the LORD to engage in Armageddon. You do not have to personally annihilate those demons. All you have to do is say:

> In the name of Almighty God, I call to beloved Archangel Michael! Beloved Archangel Michael, stand in this room! Come into my house! Bind this discord! Bind this division in our family! Bind this drug habit! Bind the marijuana entity! *Burn* through and set the captives free!

The Formula for Exorcism

Sanat Kumara gives a very precise formula for exorcism, and he takes it from the passage of Jesus that is in the eighteenth chapter of the Book of Matthew. It is written that Jesus gives to the apostles the power to bind, and he says, "Whatsoever you shall bind on earth, it will be bound in heaven."[4] Then he says, "For where two or three are gathered together in my name, there am I in the midst of them."[5] "If two of you shall agree on earth as touching any thing that they shall ask, it shall be done."[6] Those three points of scripture are three steps in the Ritual of Exorcism.

First comes the call for the binding. Sanat Kumara says we should give Jesus' I AM Lord's Prayer three times, give the call to the Hail Mary three times, and then give the Judgment Call. Before the Judgment Call is given, you give to the ascended masters in your own words either the name of the demon or discarnate, or you describe its condition and the state of its consciousness. If you perceive in yourself a habit of human selfishness and self-indulgence, you so describe it and you demand it be cast out. And then give the Judgment Call for the judging of both the person and the principle of that manifestation.

Remember, I spoke to you of Alpha and Omega. All manifestations of God have a person. They also have an energy or a power. The essence of God is the impersonal spirit of Alpha. The person of God is in the personal manifestation of Omega. So whenever you have an imitation of the Godhead or a perversion of the Godhead, you have an imitation of those two forces. So you will have a demon that has become the person of a drug entity. You can see it; it has eyes; it is very ugly; it is terrifying to look at. In addition to the demon, it has a forcefield, just like you have an aura. And that forcefield is an accumulation of energy.

And what is that energy? It's an accumulation of a cesspool, a momentum of energy that has been generated by that demon, getting you to misqualify energy. The demon gets you to smoke a cigarette. When you smoke a cigarette, you are misqualifying energy. And here it sits, this big black cloud of misqualified energy. The demon takes it, adds it to his forcefield. He gets power.

Discarnate Entities and Mass Entities

There are two kinds of entities. There is the discarnate that is the personal entity. And then there is the floating grid or forcefield that is called a mass entity.

For example, war is the means of the building up of vast reservoirs of war energy, of hatred and of bloodshed. These mass forcefields collect in the atmosphere of the astral plane over the planet. And when the fallen ones desire to create murder or war or mayhem, they actually move those forcefields over the physical place where they desire to stir up the people into a war.

So people go to war and they are agitated and aggravated by this tremendous force of war and by the war entity. You have a mass war entity that looks like a great beast or a great dragon, and then you have millions of individual demons of war. Now war is something that must be cast out of the earth. It hasn't been overcome in thousands of years. But the Prince of Peace has come, and he has said, "I came not to send peace, but a sword."[7] And the sword is a sword of living truth, and it divides asunder the Real from the unreal.

What you do not know is that the sword that he came to send, he has placed in your right hand. And your teachers have not taught you how to wield that sword. And therefore, they are found wanting. They may be well-meaning, but they are found wanting because they have not given you what you need to fight the battle on the threshold of consciousness—the threshold where the conscious mind must deal with subconscious and unknown forces; the threshold where the conscious mind must reach up into the superconscious mind, the mighty I AM Presence, become one with it, and therefore have the power to slay that demon and his entire forcefield.

You cannot do it alone. I am continually amazed at the pride of politicians who daily announce themselves for candidacy for president or any other office. Right and left they come. "Choose me. I can do it. I can save America. I can save the economy." What folly! The only son of God who is going to make a difference in this country is the son of God who says, "I of mine own self can do nothing. It is the Father in me who doeth the work."[8]

You Must Call on the Name of the LORD

These are fools who rush in where angels fear to tread. You do not rush into the midst of a seething vortex, of a nicotine entity or a cancer entity or a dope entity and think that you alone are going to somehow save a soul. This is folly. You must call upon the name of the LORD, and with that, give the names of his saints, his hosts, his archangels, his ascended masters. Those names have been given to us as messengers for the Great White Brotherhood, because we need the names. Jesus had to know the names of the demons to cast them out.[9] So you need to know the names of the archangels and the ascended masters to invoke their presence.

When you invoke Saint Germain, no other name will do. And don't believe those psychic impostors who tell you that he or Jesus Christ have changed their names—because they haven't. Those other names are the names of psychic impostors who want to be invoked in place of the real and living ascended masters. The name of Jesus Christ is the name whereby you are saved, and there is no other name.[10] And you have to know that that is a true word when it is understood. Isaiah says that God calls his saints by name,[11] and these are the angels.

There is a very blessed brother on the path whose name is Ernest Angley. He's in Akron, Ohio. And he calls his ministry the "ministry of angels." He's a very sweet child of the light imbued with the Holy Spirit. He has seen the Lord Jesus Christ face-to-face and his Holy Spirit and his angels. He calls them angels; they are ascended masters.

Ascended masters is a new word in the lexicon; it's not in the Bible. But it more accurately describes the sons and daughters of God who descend from heaven, embody, and go through the process of overcoming and ascend. When they ascend, they are beings of light and they look like angels.

Angels are a different order of evolution. They were created by God to serve his sons and daughters. And before the great fall of Lucifer, none of them had embodied in these Matter spheres. Since that time, they have embodied and volunteered to save the souls who were lost by the rebellion of Lucifer. So the angelic hosts, when they are appearing in their light bodies, look very much like ascended masters.

Although Ernest Angley might repudiate—perhaps, perhaps not—this teaching, yet, by the Holy Spirit, he is one with those very "angels." Well, you need those angels, you need those ascended masters. And when you say, "In the name of Saint Germain, *be thou removed!*" and you speak to that mountain of adversity, it is removed.[12]

The First Step

This is what Sanat Kumara teaches in these three steps of the Law:

First, begin with the Lord's Prayer that seals you in the Father and the Son. Give the Hail Mary, for it is Mother Mary herself who carries the authority for intercession and for judgment. When judgment descends, it descends through the Son of God and through the right arm of the World Mother, Mother Mary.

Then there is the naming of the demon or demons, the naming of their condition and consciousness. If you don't know the name, Sanat Kumara says, call to the twin flames of the Two Witnesses.[13] Call to our twin flames, to Lanello and to me, as we have been given the office of naming the demons.

When you call to our mighty I AM Presence, to our twin flames, we stand with you at inner levels and we will pronounce the name of the fallen one that must be bound for the healing of your loved one, the healing of your child or yourself. So the name is pronounced, you describe it, you ask us to pronounce the name, and we do.

Then you give the Judgment Call. You can give it once, three times, twelve times, whatever the momentum that you desire to give it.

Now that is the ritual of the binding. You pronounce the Word, but it is God—God in his emissaries and the archangels and the Elohim—who doeth the work. And you never, never, never forget, "I of my own self can do nothing. It is the Father in me who doeth the work."[14] And the Father includes all of his hosts of light and legions. He has created them in the service of the light.

The Second Step

"Wherever two shall come together on earth and agree as touching any thing, it shall be done unto them."[15] This is the action of illumination. You come together. You seek out chelas who have perhaps a greater understanding of the Law, or you seek our ministers. You seek the ascended masters and you take counsel with the sons of God.

You arrive at the best understanding of a course of action. And then you pray to God the Father, in the name of the living Christ, that it shall be done. And when you pray, you ask that this call be adjudicated according to the will of God, and that if it is not the will of God, it be accelerated and that your own consciousness be transformed in the understanding of the will of God.

Where two agree together that a certain thing should occur, it will be done—that is the promise. It must be done fervently, and it must be done as a part of this ritual. You've given the Judgment Call; now you are in deep prayer, and you pray to God on your knees with all of your heart that your son or your daughter should be healed of this particular condition that you are praying about.

That second step is the step of the office of the Son of God. The first step, the action of the calling of the judgment, is the step of the Father, the person of the Lawgiver and of power and authority. The second is the illumined action of the sons of God counseling together as to what is the best course and manifestation that is needed.

The Third Step

The third step of your exorcism is the action of the Holy Spirit. And this is where it is written, "For where two or three are gathered together in my name, there am I in the midst of them."[16]

The gathering together of two or more—in the name of God—is for the affirmation of that name, I AM THAT I AM. And whatever follows that affirmation is multiplied by the person of Jesus Christ who has promised, "There am I in the midst." And when you come together in the name of Jesus Christ, Saint Germain, El Morya, Serapis Bey, and finally you say "the entire Spirit of the Great White Brotherhood, the World Mother, elemental life—fire, air, water and earth," then you have the entire company of the hosts of the LORD multiplying the Word.

The third step, coming together in the name of God, is coming together for the grand ritual of the recitation of the Word. And Sanat Kumara gives to us the tremendous teaching that the recitation of the Word of Jesus Christ or the avatars is the greatest praise that we can give them. When we recite their word, we become one, congruent with their person. The person of Jesus Christ *is* the Word; your Christ Self *is* the Word. And when you ascend into the Presence of God, you have *become* the Word.

The Word, then, is not just the speech of God that goes through you. When you speak in the name of God, and when you speak the words of Jesus Christ, the I AM affirmations, "I AM the way, the truth and the life,"[17] it is not merely his words, but the *person* of the Word that manifests through you. And he said, "My word shall not return unto me void."[18]

Sanat Kumara shows the rhythm of the stars, the rotation of the planets, the turning of worlds, the cells, the movement of the electrons. And he shows how this is a ritual of life in which the Holy Spirit through the seventh ray constantly repeats the affirmation of the Word. He says there is a Word that is heard, the Word that has sound, and there is the soundless Word. But in actuality there is a sound to all movement of life that is the Holy Spirit. And that sound is the sound that goeth forth like the dynamic decree.

You can hear the sound of electrons. Keppler had the hypothesis that the planets turning around the sun created the music of the spheres. He wasn't far from right. There is a sound and there is a harmony. And when the Word flows through your lips—giving the mantras, the dynamic decrees and the prayers and repeating them—you are placing yourself one with a cosmic tone.

The cosmic tone begins to sound through you. You build a momentum when you do this every twenty-four hours without fail, and you find that when you repeat the names of the masters, not only their Word, but their person lives in you. Jesus Christ can actually live in your temple, Serapis Bey can live in your temple.

The Presence of the Holy Spirit

Sometimes I used to listen to Mark Prophet's footsteps coming down the hall, and I could tell by the footstep what master was walking with him. I would know the footsteps of the masters and the footsteps of Mark would be the same. I would see the masters in their dictations. I would see Mark's face dripping with the light of their presence, each one distinct and unique, and I realized that the Holy Spirit *is* the person of the ascended masters. They have become one with that Spirit, and this is something that gives us the understanding of how it is the Holy Spirit that is speaking to us when the ascended masters are speaking.

It is the portion of the person of Paul the Venetian that became the Holy Ghost that communicates the teaching, because it's the office of the Holy Spirit to be the teacher and the comforter and to bring all things to our remembrance whatsoever Jesus has taught us.[19] Everyone who ascends back to God becomes the fullness of the Holy Ghost.

Is it so hard to understand that the Holy Ghost may manifest as a living person once or a million times? If you suddenly become the cover girl of *Ladies' Home Journal,* or your face appears on *Time* magazine, how many images appear throughout the world? A million copies? Does that make you a million persons? Are you so superstitious as to think, as they do in the jungles, that you mustn't allow your picture to be there, because if it is there, you yourself are multiplied and you yourself are wherever the picture is and you become vulnerable to your enemies?

Well, are you so superstitious as to think that the Holy Spirit cannot manifest once or twice or a million times and not still remain one? If you are still one person and can have a thousand pictures of yourself, why can't the Holy Spirit be one person and have a thousand manifestations or a million in all octaves and planes of being and be in the ascended masters and be in their disciples? Is anything too hard for the Lord? Has he kept himself as three persons only, concrete?

Let us raise up three statues and say, "Here they are and nevermore can they be anywhere else in the whole universe. Come and worship here at these three statues." Isn't that what the disciples wanted to do when Jesus was transfigured?[20] How long will we live among this idolatrous generation? I will tell you how long—just so long as we fail to exorcise those devils that are perpetuating this ignorance of the living Word. It is sheer ignorance, and it is exposed by the truth that you bring.

But that is not enough. The teaching is not enough. It must be preached, and the Word passing through you will be accompanied with the sign following, that those demons flee. They will flee before they're exorcised. I've seen it happen. But you don't want to let them go. No, you're not going to let them go, because they're going to flee and go somewhere else, to torment some other poor soul who lacks the power of the Holy Spirit.

The End of Evil

The power of the hosts of the LORD in the ritual of exorcism is not merely to rearrange the dust of this planet. The power of these hosts of the LORD is to bind them on earth, bind them in heaven, take them to the Lake of Fire,[21] which is an intense sea of living liquid light, the universal solvent that dissolves them and their creations.

The Lake of Fire is nothing to be feared; it's where all miscreation goes when you invoke it in the name of God. And when a demon is bound in the name of Almighty God, in the name of the Son, that demon is no more upon the earth. There may be others, and people by their evil may create others. Demons are created by anger tantrums, they are actually formed by misuses of energy, but they can be just as well uncreated when you rise to the wisdom of your actions.

The cleaning up of the earth is not some process that has no end, like the story of the little mother squirrel whose offspring were swallowed up by the ocean deciding to get even with the ocean and take her tail and remove the ocean from its bed. No, the cleaning up of the astral plane has an end.

It is prophesied, it is sealed, it is in scriptures, and the day appears when the Ancient of Days and the hosts of the LORD swallow up the last vestiges of these rebels against the light. That day is at hand, and we all know it. We know it is at hand, and that's why we come together. We know that there is a power of Almighty God that is right here—it is so here that we could reach out and touch it. It's the imprisoned lightning, and it comes forth by the Word of God in you.

Cycles for the Fulfillment of the Law

The first of the three steps is the giving of the Lord's Prayer, the Hail Mary, the Judgment Call.

The second is agreeing together on earth, in prayer—heartfelt, deep prayer for that which is the desired result.

And the third step is the coming together and giving the glorious ritual of the seventh ray, the repetition of the Word in dynamic decrees.

Sanat Kumara said that this ritual should be repeated, for whatever purpose you are working on, once or more *every day until the desired results are fulfilled.*

The Elohim took seven days for the creation.[22] Those were seven days or seven ages, whatever your perspective is. The point is, it took cycles—whether millions of years or the twinkling of an eye. Some people would rather think of millions of years, but millions of years can also be seen on the head of a pin. It's a point of relativity.

There is a process involved. If the first time you open your mouth and begin to work on this condition, it doesn't happen, by no means is that an indication that the science of the use of the Trinity in the Ritual of Exorcism does not work. It does work. I've watched it work for years.

I've watched it work on the inner planes. I've watched souls freed from all kinds of impositions. I've seen people walk through the halls of Summit University, enter in bondage and walk out free, sons and daughters of God. And I've said in my heart, wherever they go, they will be free if they maintain the light they have gained. This is my great reward and my only desire, to see you free.

The Mysteries of the Ruby Ray

Sanat Kumara has introduced to us in *The Opening of the Seventh Seal* the original teachings of the ruby ray that were intended for the children of Israel. You may recall that when Moses first went on the mountain, he came down and saw that they had builded a golden calf, and their sin was that they would have their ritual without Moses, without the guru.[23] They decided he wasn't a God-man, but he was ordinary like themselves. Why should they follow him, take orders from him?

They would have their ceremony, which was based on a very ancient symbol of God out of Hinduism. The concept of the calf is in Ezekiel and in Revelation: the four cosmic forces are illustrated as a lion, a calf, a man and a flying eagle.[24] The calf is symbolical of that upon which the LORD God rides. It's the symbol of the altar. But their symbol of the calf descended to the consciousness of the Canaanite fertility rites and sensuality and rebellion.

So Moses came down and broke those tablets, and what was written on those tablets was never written again. When Moses went up the mountain the second time, he received ten words, ten commands. Those commandments were given for the bridling of the outer self. They are dos and don'ts of human living. They are not the great mysteries of the path of initiation. Those mysteries that were originally written on those first tablets have never been given since, because the children of Israel proved themselves not ready for the path.

Sanat Kumara says that not until the age of Aquarius and the assembling of the lightbearers on this golden shore, the West Coast of the United States, would it have been possible to bring forth once again those mysteries. They are the mysteries of the path of the ruby ray, and this is what he is presenting in his *Opening of the Seventh Seal.*

I can only tell you, to sit in the presence of Sanat Kumara and write these down is the most humbling and beautiful experience I've ever had. The light and the glory and the beauty of his person, the intense love of his being for you, this offering is so great, that none of you should be without them, and these teachings are your daily bread. As you read and reread them, you discover that all mysteries are spherical and all mysteries are accompanied by music. You begin to hear the inner music of the mysteries; they are spherical.

As you read, you reread, and you go back and you read again, you will find that all these pieces are like stones in the pyramid, and you see things that come together, and you begin to see the dimensions. The writing is linear, one thought comes after the other, and yet the thoughts are all spherical. And as I am seated receiving those messages and feeling a sphere of consciousness that is going to have to finally come one grain at a time through the nexus of my being, it seems like the supreme challenge, and yet I know that it is God who is equal to the challenge.

In this mystery of the ruby ray, Sanat Kumara explains that there is an order of hierarchy of the ruby ray. And so when you make the call for exorcism, it is important that you address the individuals who are holding the offices for the ruby ray, beginning with Sanat Kumara, Gautama Buddha, Lord Maitreya, Jesus Christ. And then we come to the earth, we come to the two messengers and all of the saints, and finally the great multitude who will follow the saints.

We are in the era and the dispensation today of the Two Witnesses setting forth the prophesyings that are foretold in the eleventh chapter of the Book of Revelation. When that witnessing and that prophesying is set and taken up by the saints—the saints being the advanced initiates and the chelas—there comes a moment when the saints transfer the teachings and the mysteries to the vast multitude who are the sheep on the hillsides of the world waiting, waiting for that daily bread.

The World Teachers this summer have given a two-week seminar for those who are seeking the initiation of receiving the mantle of World Teacher. They will be at Summit University this fall with Lord Maitreya and with the Goddess of Liberty. And so that seminar will be given again. It is a seminar that is a transfer of light, it is an initiation.

The action of the ruby ray is, then, the teaching that the World Teachers' representatives must teach, and that teaching can only be learned by meditating and studying and becoming active in the preaching of the Word, the transmittal of the message. And that is what we are doing in our Mission Amethyst Jewel,[25] in our lecture tours, in our teams of students going forth two by two through the United States and through the nations.

The Hierarchy of the Ruby Ray

The ruby ray must be invoked in the order of those who hold it, because it is held and it is stepped down. And it is a geometry of the Great Pyramid itself. So it begins with Sanat Kumara, Gautama Buddha, Lord Maitreya and Jesus.

The ascended masters have explained that those four beings represent all other beings. In other words, when you say Jesus Christ, you are actually speaking to all the ascended masters, all who are with him in the same vibration, all the ascended masters of the Great White Brotherhood.

When you are directing your attention to Lord Maitreya, you are speaking to all of the bodhisattvas and those on the path of becoming the Buddha and following the flame of the White Goddess.

When you are speaking to Gautama Buddha, you are addressing all those who are on his band or frequency of consciousness: Lords of the World, Solar Logoi, twin flames, beings of the elements.

And finally, with Sanat Kumara, you get cosmic beings as well as Elohim, and you get the eternal Gurus.

So it is not that there are only four ascended masters who

embody the ruby ray: there are four masters who are the keys to unlocking the ruby ray in your heart. And so they are always named in the invocation, and then the Two Witnesses who bring forth the message and the saints who receive it. The saints who receive it, their hearts are already a part of the release of the ruby ray, and therefore, we call in the name of their Christ Self and the light within their hearts. So that is the descent, and when I make the invocation now for this exorcism, I will do it in that order.

The Ritual of Exorcism

The first thing that I do when I come before the altar for this ritual, is that I kneel in prayer and I ask Almighty God, "What shall I pray for? What is your desire? What is it that you desire to have me pray for in this moment of our oneness? O God, I am so grateful for your Presence, that thou hearest every call, that thou dost answer my every call. I ask you tell me then, what is the great need of souls upon earth in this hour, and how shall I dedicate this invocation."

> *In the name of the I AM THAT I AM, I call forth the light of the living Word. I call forth the light of God that never fails. I call for the descent of Elohim, the seven beloved archangels and the chohans of the rays. I call to God the Father, God the Son, God the Holy Spirit. In the name of Sanat Kumara, Lord Gautama Buddha, Lord Maitreya, Lord Jesus Christ, the twin flames of the Two Witnesses and the hearts of the saints, I summon now the full power of the ruby ray. I call for the light and the action of that ray. I call for the legions of the* LORD*, beloved Mighty Victory, the legions of the seven archangels.*
>
> *Go forth now in the name of the Word, in the name of the I AM THAT I AM. Go forth now. I demand the exorcism within this planetary body. I demand the*

casting out of those devils that are the impostors of the Holy Spirit, those devils that perpetuate their false doctrine and dogma, and those working in Church and State to prevent the true light, the light of every son and daughter of God from coming into full manifestation in every nation upon earth. I demand the binding of those devils. I demand the binding of the wolves in sheep's clothing. I demand the binding of the fallen ones who have invaded the temple of the people and the temple of our God.

I call thee forth, O Elohim. I call thee forth, O living Word. Bind now all that opposes the light of the archangels and the ascended masters coming into the hearts of the children of God upon earth. Bind that which would prevent the Word from descending in the true spirit of prophecy from Almighty God, into the hearts of the messengers, into the hearts of the saints and into the hearts of the great multitude. Blaze forth your light! Blaze forth your light! Blaze forth your light!

In thy name, O God, in the name of the Father, the Mother, the Son, and the Holy Spirit, we pray the Lord's Prayer for the confirmation of our word.

STEP ONE

I AM Lord's Prayer

Our Father who art in heaven,
Hallowed be thy name, I AM.
I AM thy kingdom come
I AM thy will being done
I AM on earth even as I AM in heaven
I AM giving this day daily bread to all
I AM forgiving all life this day even as
I AM also all life forgiving me
I AM leading all men away from temptation

I AM delivering all men from every evil condition
I AM the kingdom
I AM the power and
I AM the glory of God in eternal, immortal manifestation—
All this I AM (3x)

The first step continues with the giving of the Hail Mary three times. This is the salutation to the Mother light within you, to the white light. It is the all-power of God in Matter.

In Matter, God has created the Mother flame as the polarity of the Trinity. It is absolutely necessary that you resolve your relationship to Mother—Mother within you as the light, Mother as the person who bore you in this life, Mother who comes in the person of the Guru. The teacher, whoever that teacher is, is always the figure of Mother.

Many people have very great problems with the person of the woman or with the Mother. These problems are psychological, they go through many incarnations. They must be resolved. The resolution is through the recitation of the Hail Mary, for Mother Mary comes into your temple and resolves all misuses of the Mother light, the white light of purity. We give our devotion to her because she represents the universal Mother. She is not the only Mother, but she is the great avatar of the Piscean age who is Mother. If we do not see the Mother in her, we will not see it in ourselves.

So we say her name, but we understand it is not confined in her. *Mary* means "Mother ray"—universally manifest, individually manifest in her, and particularly manifest in you where you are. When you give devotion to the white light, the white light gives devotion to you. When you send your heart flame to it, it will not fail to give you an answer. And the answer is the loving of your soul, the wrapping of your soul in the swaddling garment, the caring for the newborn child.

In this particular Ritual of Exorcism, it is Mother Mary who occupies the office of the judgment with the Son Jesus. She is the one before whom Sanat Kumara says the very demons tremble. And if you desire intercession for a loved one, you must give this Hail Mary not merely three times as in this ritual. We have our daily rosaries, which you must not omit, because each time you give them, the ascension flame rises in you. So let us give the Hail Mary together.

Hail Mary

Hail, Mary, full of grace.
The Lord is with thee.
Blessed art thou among women
And blessed is the fruit of thy womb, Jesus.

Holy Mary, Mother of God,
Pray for us, sons and daughters of God,
Now and at the hour of our victory
Over sin, disease, and death. (3x)

The Lord's Prayer and the Hail Mary are an immense protection. You need protection and that oneness with these flames as you begin the call of judgment, "They Shall Not Pass."

Jesus gave us this call in a dictation and he told us how to give it. He told us to stand and raise the right hand, using the mudra of fearlessness, the right hand forward. And through the chakra of your right hand flows the power of God to turn back the forces of darkness. It doesn't matter if it's one demon or a horde of millions, the power of God is able. He said we should place the left hand on the heart, making contact with the heart chakra, and therefore the flow is from the heart through the head, the spoken Word, through the hand, the Trinity in action in you.

If you are giving this decree day by day and not as a part of the Ritual of Exorcism, you would make your invocation right with the Judgment Call. I'm going to make the invocation again as we are separating this ritual with periods of instruction, and I want to reinforce my call.

In the name of Almighty God, I call to the hosts of the LORD. *Beloved Archangel Michael, beloved Sanat Kumara, I call forth the entire legions of the Great White Brotherhood. I demand the binding in the earth and in the heavens of all those forces and forcefields, persons embodied or disembodied, moving against the children of the light and the transfer of the Word of God and the true teachings of the Lord Christ in this age.*

I demand the binding of all demons and discarnates, binding the children of God and preventing their free-will choice, of choosing to be God, choosing to be in the light, choosing the path of the ascension in this life. Bind them in the earth. Bind them in the heaven. Bind them by the authority of the Word.

In the name of the Father, the Son, the Holy Spirit, and the Mother, in the name of Sanat Kumara, Gautama Buddha, Lord Maitreya, Jesus Christ, the Two Witnesses and the saints, I decree:

The Judgment Call
"They Shall Not Pass!"
by Jesus Christ

In the Name of the I AM THAT I AM,
I invoke the Electronic Presence of Jesus Christ:
They shall not pass!
They shall not pass!
They shall not pass!
By the authority of the cosmic cross of white fire
 it shall be:
That all that is directed against the Christ
 within me, within the holy innocents,
 within our beloved messengers,
 within every son and daughter of God

Is now turned back
by the authority of Alpha and Omega,
by the authority of my Lord and Saviour Jesus Christ,
by the authority of Saint Germain!

I AM THAT I AM within the center of this temple
and I declare in the fullness of
the entire Spirit of the Great White Brotherhood:
That those who, then, practice the black arts
against the children of the Light
Are now bound by the hosts of the LORD,
Do now receive the judgment of the Lord Christ
within me, within Jesus,
and within every Ascended Master,
Do now receive, then, the full return—
multiplied by the energy of the Cosmic Christ—
of their nefarious deeds which they have practiced
since the very incarnation of the Word!

Lo, I AM a Son of God!
Lo, I AM a Flame of God!
Lo, I stand upon the Rock of the living Word
And I declare with Jesus, the living Son of God:
They shall not pass!
They shall not pass!
They shall not pass!
Elohim. Elohim. Elohim. [Chant the last line.] (3x)*

We've completed the first step. There are two more steps.

STEP TWO

The second step is that two of us or more have come together to agree on earth as touching this particular call of exorcism. We have counseled with the sons of God, we have prayed to

*The most effective posture for giving this decree is to stand and raise your right hand to shoulder height using the *abhaya mudra* (gesture of fearlessness). The palm is turned outward and the fingers pointed upward. Place your left hand at the center of your chest, where your heart chakra is located, with the thumb and first two fingers pointing inward.

know the will of our ritual, so now we're going to join hands.* Wherever you are, simply join hands with the people near you. We're going to feel this oneness. We're going to agree together in very deepest, most concentrated prayer. Go into your heart now and pray with me as I pray.

Our Father-Mother God, Alpha and Omega, we are assembled together on earth in the name of Jesus Christ and every son of God whom he has initiated in the path of true sonship. We have come together in the name of Gautama Buddha, Lord Maitreya, Sanat Kumara, the saints and the Two Witnesses serving the ruby ray.

In the name of the I AM THAT I AM, we agree together on earth in this hour that there shall be the binding of the seed of the wicked who have prevented the souls of light from contacting Almighty God and the living Word within them. We agree together on earth that those shall be bound who have perpetuated the false doctrine and dogma. We agree together for the binding of the demons and the discarnates that have invaded the temple of God, the impostors of the Holy Spirit, the impostors of the Father, of the Son, and of the Mother.

Go forth, O LORD God Almighty, by thy invincible Word, by the Word of God, by the Faithful and True, and by the legions of light. Now bind that force and forcefield on the astral and physical planes. We demand the staying action of the LORD God this day of all seed of the wicked in Church and State who are determined to take from the children of God their rightful inheritance of the abundant life in Spirit and Matter.

This is our prayer. We have come together in thy name, O God, and in thy name we trust the fulfillment

*The messenger asked members of the congregation to join hands to emphasize the oneness that is the basis for Step Two of the ritual. However, joining hands is not a necessary part of the ritual and is not usually done by those participating in it.

of our call according to thy will and in the name of the entire Spirit of the Great White Brotherhood and the World Mother. Amen.

This is a prayer for the second step.

STEP THREE

The third step is two or three gathering together "in my name" for the repetition of the Word in dynamic decrees.

This afternoon, after we have taken our break for lunch and a little bit of fresh air, we will come back and we will give the sounding of the Word for the anchoring in Matter of what we have called for.

Dynamic decrees give your energy to the hosts of the LORD to implement God's will in Matter. It is the law of octaves that not a single angel may come into your life and help you unless you ask, unless in some form of your being you pray and it is your desire to enter into conscious cooperation with God. The ascended masters will not touch your life unless you ask them. This asking becomes the command of Isaiah, the "command ye me,"[26] the dynamic decree.

So we will give calls to Astrea for the binding of this force of Antichrist in the world. We will give calls to Archangel Michael. We will give the violet flame. And each of these will be explained to you as to why we are giving them. And all of them clear the way for your temple to be the instrument of light.

When the disciples could not cast out a possessing demon, Jesus rebuked them for their little faith and invoked the power of Elohim.[27] He has told us that. Astrea has told us that. Astrea is the Elohim of the fourth ray, the very same ray on which Serapis Bey is serving. The fourth ray is the ray of purity, the power of the Mother, the power of the sword of Kali, the power to bind all the demons that assail the children of the Mother and prevent them from expressing their true freedom. So that will be the third phase, the Holy Spirit phase, of the ritual.

The Finishing of the Mysteries of God

How do we understand that it is true and right? It is prophesied in the tenth chapter of the Book of Revelation that the seventh angel will come to finish the mysteries of God as he has declared them to his servants, the prophets. That seventh angel is the ascended master Saint Germain, the lord of the seventh ray and the seventh age. He is finishing the mysteries.

The mysteries that were lived by Jesus Christ were spoken in the Upper Room to his disciples. But they were not written down. The finishing of those mysteries comes two thousand years later as he prophesied.

How do you know that the Word is true? You know it by the Holy Spirit within you. The Holy Spirit will testify in you of me and of Almighty God—and there is no other way that you can know the truth. So to get the Holy Spirit, you need to cleanse the temple and judge righteous judgment.[28]

We have explored the first phase of the path of the ascension. The path is straight and narrow, but it is spherical. There are many processes and initiations that go on simultaneously. We have taken up this one today because it is so key as we look at the needs of our friends, family, and our neighbors.

O beloved mighty I AM Presence, bless and seal each heart. Seal these hearts with thy living Word and Presence. Let it be so in thy name I AM. Amen.

Dynamic Decrees

For Step Three of the Ritual of Exorcism

Violet Fire and Tube of Light Decree

by the Ascended Master Saint Germain

O my constant, loving I AM Presence, thou Light of God above me whose radiance forms a circle of fire before me to light my way:

I AM faithfully calling to thee to place a great pillar of Light from my own mighty I AM God Presence all around me right now today! Keep it intact through every passing moment, manifesting as a shimmering shower of God's beautiful Light through which nothing human can ever pass. Into this beautiful electric circle of divinely charged energy direct a swift upsurge of the violet fire of freedom's forgiving, transmuting flame!

Cause the ever expanding energy of this flame projected downward into the forcefield of my human energies to completely change every negative condition into the positive polarity of my own Great God Self! Let the magic of its mercy so purify my world with light that all whom I contact shall always be blessed with the fragrance of violets from God's own heart in memory of the blessed dawning day when all discord—cause, effect, record, and memory—is forever changed into the victory of light and the peace of the ascended Jesus Christ.

I AM now constantly accepting the full power and manifestation of this fiat of light and calling it into instantaneous action by my own God-given free will and the power to accelerate without limit this sacred release of assistance from God's own heart until all men are ascended and God-free in the light that never, never, never fails!

Lord Michael

In the name of the beloved mighty victorious Presence of God, I AM in me, my very own beloved Holy Christ Self, Holy Christ Selves of all mankind, beloved Archangel Michael, beloved Lanello, the entire Spirit of the Great White Brotherhood and the World Mother, elemental life—fire, air, water, and earth! I decree:

1. Lord Michael, Lord Michael,
   I call unto thee—
   Wield thy sword of blue flame
   And now cut me free!

Refrain: Blaze God-power, protection
   Now into my world,
   Thy banner of faith
   Above me unfurl!
   Transcendent blue lightning
   Now flash through my soul,
   I AM by God's mercy
   Made radiant and whole!

2. Lord Michael, Lord Michael,
   I love thee, I do—
   With all thy great faith
   My being imbue!

3. Lord Michael, Lord Michael
   And legions of blue—
   Come seal me, now keep me
   Faithful and true!

Coda: I AM with thy blue flame
   Now full-charged and blest,
   I AM now in Michael's
   Blue-flame armor dressed! (3x)

And in full Faith I consciously accept this manifest, manifest, manifest! (3x) right here and now with full Power, eternally sustained, all-powerfully active, ever expanding, and world enfolding until all are wholly ascended in the Light and free!

Beloved I AM! Beloved I AM! Beloved I AM!

Decree to Beloved Mighty Astrea—
"The Starry Mother"

In the name of the beloved mighty victorious Presence of God I AM in me, mighty I AM Presence and Holy Christ Selves of Keepers of the Flame, lightbearers of the world and all who are to ascend in this life, by and through the magnetic power of the sacred fire vested in the threefold flame burning within my heart, I call to beloved Mighty Astrea and Purity, Archangel Gabriel and Hope, beloved Serapis Bey and the seraphim and cherubim of God, beloved Lanello, the entire Spirit of the Great White Brotherhood and the World Mother, elemental life—fire, air, water, and earth! to lock your cosmic circles and swords of blue flame in, through, and around: my four lower bodies, my electronic belt, my heart chakra and all of my chakras, my entire consciousness, being, and world.

[Insert your own prayer here for the specific situation you are working on.]

Cut me loose and set me free (3x) from all that is less than God's perfection and my own divine plan fulfilled.

1. O beloved Astrea, may God Purity
Manifest here for all to see,
God's divine will shining through
Circle and sword of brightest blue.

First chorus:* Come now answer this my call,
Lock thy circle round us all.
Circle and sword of brightest blue,
Blaze now, raise now, shine right through!

2. Cutting life free from patterns unwise,
Burdens fall off while souls arise
Into thine arms of infinite love,
Merciful shining from heaven above.

*Give the decree once, using the first chorus after each verse. Give it a second time, using the second chorus after each verse. Give it a third time, using the third chorus after each verse. These three sets of three verses followed by each of the three choruses comprise one giving of the decree, or one Astrea pattern.

3. Circle and sword of Astrea now shine,
Blazing blue-white my being refine,
Stripping away all doubt and fear,
Faith and goodwill patterns appear.

Second chorus: Come now answer this my call,
Lock thy circle round us all.
Circle and sword of brightest blue,
Raise our youth now, blaze right through!

Third chorus: Come now answer this my call,
Lock thy circle round us all.
Circle and sword of brightest blue,
Raise mankind now, shine right through!

And in full Faith I consciously accept this manifest, manifest, manifest! (3x) right here and now with full Power, eternally sustained, all-powerfully active, ever expanding, and world enfolding until all are wholly ascended in the Light and free!

Beloved I AM! Beloved I AM! Beloved I AM!

I AM the Violet Flame

In the name of the beloved mighty victorious Presence of God, I AM in me, and my very own beloved Holy Christ Self, I call to beloved Alpha and Omega in the heart of God in our Great Central Sun, beloved Saint Germain, beloved Portia, beloved Archangel Zadkiel, beloved Holy Amethyst, beloved mighty Arcturus and Victoria, beloved Kuan Yin, Goddess of Mercy, beloved Oromasis and Diana, beloved Mother Mary, beloved Jesus, beloved great Karmic Board, beloved Lanello, the entire Spirit of the Great White Brotherhood and the World Mother, elemental life—fire, air, water, and earth!

To expand the violet flame within my heart, purify my four lower bodies, transmute all misqualified energy I have ever imposed upon life, and blaze mercy's healing ray throughout the earth, the elementals, and all mankind and answer this my call infinitely, presently, and forever:

I AM the violet flame
In action in me now
I AM the violet flame
To light alone I bow
I AM the violet flame
In mighty Cosmic Power
I AM the light of God
Shining every hour
I AM the violet flame
Blazing like a sun
I AM God's sacred power
Freeing every one

And in full Faith I consciously accept this manifest, manifest, manifest! (3x) right here and now with full Power, eternally sustained, all-powerfully active, ever expanding, and world enfolding until all are wholly ascended in the Light and free!

Beloved I AM! Beloved I AM! Beloved I AM!

CHAPTER SEVEN

The Story of the Crystal Cup

I would like to speak to you of the crystal cup, and I would like to give you the experience of Godfré and David Lloyd and the crystal cup. It is a very important initiation that occurred in that encounter. It comes from the book by Godfré Ray King, *Unveiled Mysteries*. Godfré writes:

> On the morning of the seventh day, I left my lodge at four o'clock and reached our meeting place at ten-thirty. I sat down on a log to wait with a feeling of wonderful exhilaration, which I knew to be the result of my meditation. I was so deep within the contemplation my God Self, I did not hear anyone approaching until a voice spoke to me.
>
> I looked up and saw an old man with white hair and beard, whom I thought at first sight was an old prospector, although his clothing was too clean for that occupation. As he came up to me and held out his hand, that too confirmed my feeling—he was not a laboring man. We exchanged greetings, chatted for a few moments on generalities, then he turned to me, and said:

"My friend, I would like to tell you a story. It won't take long. I haven't told it to anyone for a long time. I would like to try once more."

By that time, I began to have a feeling of intense interest. It occurred to me he might be thirsty, and as I reached for a cup to get him a drink, from the spring by which we stood, a crystal cup formed within my hand, like the one Saint Germain had held out to me several times. The old man looked up and with eyes shining and excited, almost shouted:

"It is he! It is he!"

I did not know what to do, so I insisted he drink. As I looked within the cup, I saw it was filled with the same clear, sparkling liquid the Master had given me. The old man grasped it eagerly, and, with an intense expression of the deepest gratitude I have ever seen, drank the contents. He immediately became very calm and quiet, but with it all a deep, intense sincerity. I asked him again to tell me the story, and he began by saying:

"My father was a British officer stationed in the Punjab of India where we made our home. When I was sixteen, he financed a friend who went to South Africa to try his luck in the diamond mines, but my father never heard from him afterward.

"The year I was twenty, a tall, handsome stranger, a man of great wisdom, visited my father at our home. He had come to bring a message from father's friend.

"'I bring you news,' he explained, 'from the friend whom you financed four years ago. He met with great success on that venture, in fact became very wealthy. He has recently passed on at the mines and left no relatives. His entire fortune has been left to you and in case of your passing, it is to go to your son. If you desire,

I will take charge of the matter and have it transferred at once.'

"'I cannot leave India at the present time,' my father replied, 'for I am on government duty here. I appreciate greatly your offer to take care of the matter for me.' I was standing near-by during their conversation, and when they had completed arrangements, the stranger turned to me.

"'My son,' he said, 'when you find the man who will offer you a crystal cup of sparkling liquid, you will have met the one who can assist you in raising the body. I cannot tell you more than this, except that you will find him on a great mountain in North America. This may seem vague to you now, but it is all I can say.'

"The stranger left, and a month later my father, who had ridden out to adjust certain government matters with the natives, was shot and passed on before he could be brought home. I was an only son, and after another month, mother and I prepared for our return to England. Just before we left, the same stranger came again and said he was ready to transfer father's fortune to me. I explained father had been shot.

"'Yes,' the stranger replied, 'when I left two months ago, I knew your father would pass on before my return. I have arranged for the fortune to be transferred to you, or rather to the Bank of England for you. Here is money you may wish to use on the journey home, also the papers of transfer, and the credentials you will need at the bank. Present them, and you will receive custody of your wealth. Much of it is in diamonds of the first quality.' I thanked him and offered to pay for his services, but he replied:

"'Your kind intent is greatly appreciated but that is

already adjusted. I will be happy to accompany you to the steamer at Bombay.'

"The trip revealed to me his great wisdom, and beside him I felt like an infant. I know now he enveloped me in a Radiation which has stayed with me throughout the years. He arranged for transportation, accompanied us to the boat, and his last words to me were:

"'Remember—the "Crystal Cup." Seek and you shall find.'

"After a most wonderful voyage, we arrived at Southampton, went on to London, and presented my credentials to the Bank of England. The official to whom I presented them remarked:

"'Yes, we were expecting you today. Here are your bank and check books.'

"I looked at them to see how much my fortune amounted to and was amazed to learn a hundred thousand pounds had been placed to my credit. Five years later, my mother passed on. I transferred one half of my wealth to a bank in New York and began the search for 'the man with the Crystal Cup.'

"I can never repeat the disappointments, the trials, the sorrow I have been through, but in the face of everything, somehow I could never give up. The thing which seems so strange to me is, while I have grown old in outer appearance, my energy and strength are as great as ever, sometimes I think greater, than in my fullest youth.

"In years, I am seventy. Today I just wanted to follow this trail, and praise God I have found you. My desire was so great, it was almost irresistible."

"But my good man," I asked, "what am I to do for you?"

"You will know," he replied, "for I know I have made

no mistake. In the heart of this majestic mountain is a Great Power. I feel it. Ask God to show you what to do."

Suddenly, I felt the "Mighty God Power" surging forth so strong, it almost lifted me from the ground. Making the sign Saint Germain had taught me, I called to God for "Light," and raising my hand in salutation said:

"Mighty God in man and the Universe! We seek Thy Light! We seek Thy Wisdom! We seek Thy Power! Let Thy Will be done in and for this, My Brother, who has sought and found me to do for him I know not what. Thou knowest! Manifest Thy Will through my mind and body, and let whatever is to be done for this Brother—Thy Son—come forth."

As my hand came down, it held the Crystal Cup filled with "Living Liquid-Light." I offered it to him, and my Mighty God Self spoke again.

"Drink without fear. Thy search is ended."

He drank the contents without a moment's hesitation. I stepped forward quickly and took both his hands in mine. Slowly and steadily every vestige of age disappeared from him, and the God in me continued:

"Behold! Thou art forever *free* from all earthly limitation. Ascend now unto the 'Great Host of Light' who await Thee."

Very slowly, he began to rise from the ground, and as he did so, his human garments disappeared, and he became clothed in raiment of glistening white. I let go his hands. Then in a voice of deepest Love, he said:

"I shall return to thee, Beloved Brother. Well shalt thou be repaid for this Transcendent Service. Thou wert the only one through whom this could be done for me. Someday thou shalt see why." And with a happy smile, he disappeared on a Radiant Pathway of "Light."

As the Mighty God Power within me receded, I was so astounded, I fell on my knees and offered the deepest prayer of my life in grateful humility and praise for the privilege of giving such service.

I rose and the Master Saint Germain received me into his wondrous embrace.

"My Beloved Brother!" he said, "I am greatly pleased. Noble and faithful was your attendance upon the Great God within you. Beautifully did you receive your Mighty 'God in Action.' I do indeed congratulate you. You will ever be held within Our Embrace, even though outwardly you may not always be aware of it.

"You have become a worthy 'Messenger' of the Great White Brotherhood and the Ascended Host. Hold close to your Mighty God Self. Thus, you will ever be ready for service wherever and for whatever is required. My Love enfolds you until we meet again. I will keep you informed."

Slowly, I wended my way back to the lodge, every step praise and gratitude to the "One Mighty God" that molds us all into "Eternal Perfection."[1]

The story of the crystal cup is your story and it is my story. When we contemplate the naturalness of the miracle, we wonder, Shall I be the one who gives the cup or shall I be the one who receives it? Well, in giving we receive and in receiving we give.

Today the crystal cup is the chalice of communion. That communion is the teaching of the ascended masters. I come to you with a crystal cup of the message of the ascended masters for your individual ascension. As you take the cup of light and the cup of the teaching and you drink all of it, as Jesus said,[2] you become filled with the light and thereby you may call forth the cup and give it to another.

This actual tangible experience shows the uniqueness of the

single lifestream. For years and years until he was seventy years old, David Lloyd wandered the mountains of North America until the attunement of his heart was so great that it irresistibly drew him to the heart of Godfré. Godfré, the obedient chela of Saint Germain, was at the nexus of the cross, the point in time and space where he was supposed to be. And so the meeting of the two was a very distinct initiation for each one—the one to be the instrument, the other, the day and the hour of his ascension.

You can see from the record of his life that he had a single final initiation to pass, that he had earned that ascension in many previous incarnations. Evidently an adept arranged for him the supply necessary so that he could spend an entire lifetime searching for the crystal cup.

The Record of Each Ascension Is Sealed in Every Heart

The point of that ascension on that mountain leaves the record in time and space. The record of the ascension is always sealed in the heart of every person on the planet. Each time someone ascends, it is recorded in your heart because it is the great victory of life, and that recording says, "One life has ascended to God, you may also ascend." Every ascension is the call, the promise, and the word that you, too, can reunite with your Great God Self.

There is a determination that seizes the heart and the soul of the initiate who will ascend, and he says in his heart, "I will ascend to God." He says that not as that proud boastful one Lucifer who fell; he says it in the humility of his God Presence. The use of the word "I will" is lawful when that which you will is the will of God.

Godfré himself was the crystal cup and Saint Germain commended him for being truly a messenger of the Great White Brotherhood. I know of no greater calling. I know of no greater commendation than the commendation of Saint Germain. Saint Germain has commended the chelas in this very year for their tremendous work in preparing the written books and the tape recordings of the teachings, in giving the lectures and letting the light shine and transferring that liquid elixir.

I think that one word of praise from Saint Germain that lets us know we are on the right path and that our service is worth something to life could not even be balanced in the scale with a thousand or two thousand words of praise from unascended beings. The commendations of the ascended masters are few and far between because it is not their desire to make their chelas feel too sure of their attainment. Every day on the ascension path is an intense challenge to be more light than you were yesterday; and each time you go up a niche in the ladder of the ascension, when you take that new position of light, because you have more light, you have to defend that position.

The Challenge of the Fallen Ones

Every new step on the path means another assailant, someone on the left-handed path who has misused the light in black magic or witchcraft who says I will not allow you to stand in the position of your attainment. And so there are many stories of ascended masters who were challenged by fallen ones.

The fallen ones refuse to acknowledge your light and your attainment. Therefore, you and you alone must affirm it, must be convinced of it, must not doubt or fear it. You must know that the light in you *is* the light of God that never fails.

Think of this: Godfré had been just that moment the instrument, the means, the indispensable hand for the transfer of that light, that ascension current that passed through that liquid light. Saint Germain embraced him and said, "You will always be in our care and always in the presence of your mighty I AM Presence although you may not always be fully aware and conscious of it."

That shows you that you can be an advanced chela on the path and not necessarily experience every single moment the tremendous descent of light rays of your Presence. That means that you walk by faith, you walk by the memory of the inner initiations. You walk by the memory of the joy that you know in the master's presence. And then when you go forth in the world you are expected to walk on your own feet, by your own bootstraps, by your own insistence of the acceleration of the wheels of light.

And so the mountaintop experience, even the experience of the witnessing of an ascension, is followed by your descent to the valleys of life where your karma is left unbalanced. Suddenly you find yourself in the midst of old vibrations and old conditions. And at that very moment you are called upon, *remember* the light, *remember* the Word of the Ancient of Days, *remember* the descent of the Holy Ghost within your temple. *Keep* the flame, *keep* the watch, *keep* your word, *keep* your honor. Invoke the light and transmute it and move on.

Karmic Requirements for the Ascension

The path is exciting. It leads you to the place through initiations and testing where you fulfill the requirement for the ascension of balancing 51 percent of your karma.

This was not the requirement in past eras. When Enoch walked with God and he was not, for God took him,[3] he had balanced 100 percent of his karma. He had given back to God 100 percent of the energy that God had given to him in the beginning and throughout all of his incarnations, with interest. Think of that!

God gives you your inheritance, just as David Lloyd received his inheritance. It is a certain sum of light. You go forth with that sum of light and you sow and you reap and you sow and you reap. Some of it you misqualify, so it doesn't cycle back to God day by day.

That energy starts building an anti-forcefield—we call it the electronic belt, the subconscious mind. It starts building up a momentum of that which is not in a state of flow with the mighty I AM Presence. Whatever passes through you that becomes discord or nonaligned energy accumulates around the physical forcefield, and each time you return to embodiment it is there. So you have this sum of light, which you could represent as a white cube, and then you have that little pack on your back that represents the misqualified portion, and that is the recording of the subconscious.

Long before recorded history, people began to misqualify more and more of their energy. Eventually, earth's evolutions had misqualified nearly 100 percent of the original allotment of their lifestream. With so much misqualified energy, they forgot their source, ceased to give adoration to the light within the heart, and the entire purpose for the evolutions of the life upon earth was lost.

It was then that the Cosmic Council decreed the dissolution of the planetary body and its evolutions because it became, as you might say, a bad debt of the cosmos. The people were no longer capable of balancing their karma because they had misqualified so much energy that they could no longer contact the threefold flame within the heart, and without that contact you cannot begin the path.

The Physical Ascension

Enoch was an initiate of light sent to earth with Sanat Kumara. He walked the earth and he was not, for God took him—exactly in the same manner as he took David Lloyd. The physical ascension comes when 100 percent of one's karma is balanced.

In fact, 100 percent of one's karma is not balanced until the moment of the ascension. A certain portion of karma must remain, otherwise there would be no way that the lifestream could be anchored in the earth plane. The physical body, the gravitational pull to the earth must be sustained, and therefore the portion that is usually retained by those who have balanced their karma is between 7 and 8 percent.

Jesus incarnated in his final embodiment with only that portion remaining. His life, then, became the great rehearsal for the finale of the public example of the initiations that before that time had been taking place in the inner retreats of Luxor and in the Great Pyramid. In the final hours of his mission, the crucifixion and resurrection, more light came into his body, more of the karma was transmuted, until the final moments when the ascension flame itself consumed the remainder.

Now the individual may have already balanced 100 percent of his karma, and therefore some substance involving the dharma, involving the tie to other lifestreams, is retained.

The New Dispensation

When the 100 percent balance of karma was the requirement, very few people made the ascension. With the coming of the Aquarian age and with the sponsorship of Saint Germain and many cosmic beings, the Lords of Karma announced the edict from the Cosmic Council that because of the acceleration of light in the earth, because of the great service of Sanat Kumara, and because of the new dispensation of this age of freedom, they would accept candidates for the ascension who had balanced 51 percent of their karma.

These souls would be allowed to take the ascension at inner levels. Their physical bodies would not make the ascension. They would be, if at all possible, cremated. The soul would go into the etheric retreat at Luxor and there make the ascension from the inner planes. The soul would then function as an ascended master in ascended master octaves, but the soul would be required to remain with the earth until the remaining 49 percent of karma had been fully balanced from the ascended octaves.

It is difficult to balance karma from the level of the ascended masters unless you have left a means to contact those in embodiment, because the way that earth karma is balanced is through service in the earth. This is why we all need physical bodies. This is why we need to be in embodiment. We must balance our karma here; we cannot do it out of the body in the etheric temples or on the astral plane or in the mental plane except there be a very small portion remaining.

If you balance 50 percent of your karma, you might be able to balance the remaining 1 percent in the etheric temple, spend perhaps five or ten years there and then make your ascension. This has happened recently; it continues to happen. So the balancing of karma from the ascended master state requires that the ascended master in some form be able to contact life on earth and influence that life and transfer the message of the path.

Helping people who cannot see, hear, feel, touch, smell, or identify your presence is sometimes difficult. You might think about that if you're planning to make your ascension with 51 percent. Our beloved Lanello has challenged us all to balance 100 percent of our karma, and he said that it is entirely possible and it will begin to set the matrix of excellence and to give once again the public example after the year 2000 of physical ascensions.

The ascended masters have spoken of Mighty Victory's Temple, which is a dispensation of the building of a three-tiered temple, the first, the second, and the third tiers representing the threefold flame; the lowest tier represents the great multitude, the next tier the saints, and finally the inner initiates preparing for the ascension in the top level. The masters have said that when that temple is built, the top level should contain an ascension chair.

An ascension chair is a focus that is in the Cave of Symbols, and there is also such an atomic accelerator in the Cave of Light, the Great Divine Director's retreat in India. That forcefield of acceleration helps those at inner levels to accelerate their light and their consciousness and to pass their final initiations for the ascension.

Diagramming Your Ascension

I would like to tell you that the path of your ascension can be diagrammed, it can be analyzed, it can be studied from the standpoint of the cosmic clock, which is the teachings of Mother Mary on your astrology—which is always the outpicturing of your karma. The calling for the violet flame for the balancing of your cosmic astrology by the cosmic clock is an exciting way to see how day by day your initiations come under certain vibrations that correspond with the twelve solar hierarchies and their initiations. Their initiations are key to your path. It is important to know what they are.

I have given a lecture on the karmic clock that shows the clock divided into four 25 percent sections, showing you what is the karma of the etheric body, the mental body, the emotional body, and the physical body—understanding that all of these interact.[4]

When you decide to do something, you must go about it scientifically, mathematically, and always in God. When you look at a challenge and the challenge is too great to swallow all at once, you dissect the problem. You look at your expected lifetime, and you see how if you make the best use of the remaining days and cycles, you can accelerate and invoke enough violet flame to transmute the past, engage in service, and you can actually realize, if you take your life step-by-step, that it is indeed possible, given the gift of the violet flame and the science of the Word, for you to make your ascension in this life.

It is not something that happens suddenly, unexpectedly,

without planning, or without warning. It comes by a conscious concentration of your lifestream. It doesn't matter how old you are or how little you have known of the teaching, it's purity of heart and love that makes a candidate for the ascension. You don't have to be an adept, aware of the most complex formulas. I have seen very humble people whose love alone and light and constancy in service and in the giving of decrees fulfilled all of the requirements of the Law.

Love Is the Fulfilling of the Law

Remember that love is the fulfilling of the Law.[5] And if love is the fulfilling of the Law, then you'd better know what love is and what love isn't. This is the age of Aquarius, and its sign is love, its sign is the Holy Spirit. And the Holy Spirit is a fierce white fire that consumes in us all unlike itself—all self-sympathy and self-pity and all of those drippy emotions that we have thought to be love that are nothing but personal possessiveness.

Real love is that which supports the light and is willing to wrestle with all that opposes the light within you. Having the courage to support the individual on his path—even when that individual thinks that by that support you are not his friend—is something you must remember. To be a friend is to be a friend of the soul and to take sides with the Christ even when the soul is siding with his own carnal mind.

Let us now hear the words of David Lloyd as he describes the process of the ascension, the process of the transfer of the flame on that mountainside in that moment when he received the crystal cup. This is a dictation of David Lloyd that he has delivered through Mark Prophet.

CHAPTER EIGHT

From Glory unto Glory, Even as by the Spirit of God

David Lloyd

O wondrous, effulgent, liquid light, how beautiful is this diadem, diamond-like, sparkling, yet flowing crystal stream, the elixir of life—the radiant fashion of the tides of heaven come again to the panting, thirsty heart and soul.

I come, then, to you tonight, mindful of the glorious appearing in my own life of the victorious achievement of the ascension. The ascension, unknown by many, is the foundation and beginning of the kingdom of heaven for every man. The example set by the Master Jesus, almost in the fashion of the prophet Elijah going into heaven in a chariot of fire,[1] is the radiant end (or beginning) of every lifestream's opportunity for cosmic service.

We who serve at higher levels in our outpouring of service to humanity upon this planetary body do give our energy and the fruits of our service and attainment unto embodied humanity as a bequest of infinite love. Yet our service is not all-engrossing unto humanity, but it is also about our Father's business in that realm of the Spirit that is considered by many to be fictitious but by others to be a heavenly but unknown state; and still by others it is considered to be a heavenly and known state.

For there are varying degrees of attainment here upon the planetary body in the hearts and beings of man. And in these various, diverse measures of attainment we do see and witness how one individual differs from another at a given moment, yet all will one day come to the selfsame crowning achievement of those cosmic goals of the Spirit that are the birthright of every man.

The elixir of life—the flowing energy of the sacred fire immortally brought forth into the consciousness of those who are imbued with the power from on high to accept their high calling of God—is bequeathed to all. Yet all do not at a given moment accept it, one being taken and another left.[2]

My own experiences with beloved Godfré are to me a source of infinite joy—infinite joy and compassion for those who have not yet attained but are still awaiting attainment.

Take heart, beloved ones. *Take heart.* I give to you and pledge to you my sacred word this night that the love of God has programmed for you all a similar opportunity, a victorious overcoming of the vicissitudes of life and the darkness of this world.

The Divine Search

Over land and sea, over mountains that lay before me as mountains of stumbling, I journeyed in my search to find attainment. Imagine, then, my startle as at an unexpected moment the joy and victory of that search culminated in the beautiful experience of which you have heard—the experience of attainment. The hopes of all the years were then brought to a fruition of the Spirit.

Calmness and the certitude of knowing are beneficial to the soul of man, for these enable him to recognize that after a considerable search he will at last be rewarded.

Do not be overconcerned, beloved hearts of light, simply because you have failed to attain in previous moments of struggle and search. Be not dismayed. Be not affrighted nor consider yourselves as an offcast from the gates of heaven, for heaven beckons and comes very close.

Many times, as I journeyed throughout the realm of experiences in the earthly life, I also found that the struggle seemed to overcome me, and discouragement aimed directly at dissuading me from the search caused me, momentarily, to pause. The wise do it not, and yet I do not think of myself in that former state as always acting wisely. But I acted persistently, for I was persistent to storm the very gates of the citadel of heaven and I continued to pursue the spiritual path even when some around me sought to discourage me. And many circumstances that are unrecorded, still, occurred in my life that prevented me from enjoying at all times the fullness of the divine search.

The Gift of the Ascension

Yet, the eye of God beckoned. The perception of God continued to call me, and I knew that it was a matter of divine and infinite destiny that one day I should receive the gift of the ascension. Yet when the moment came, I knew it not. And scarcely as it was happening, did I know it.

Yet so wondrous was it when I began to feel that buoyant joy, that caress of the Infinite upon my finite being that dissolved it altogether. And in its place, almost as the sea, there spewed forth the beautiful, compassionate experience of molding me in cosmic form into the infinitude of God's thought.

The perfect body appeared. The perfect mind appeared. The perfect soul ruled the world of my being. A surge of infinite strength came forth and I rose into the air, into the arms of a similar dissolvement as had happened previously to beloved Jesus.

For a cloud, too, of infinite, cosmic love received me out of the sight of men. And in the bond of cosmic compassion, I expanded my knowledge into the Infinite as cadences of loveliness receding into a far and distant future, which appeared before me then as a mountain of hope. And I entered into the joy of God, and the joy of God filled my soul and darkness vanished altogether.

And in the mystery of being, I understood that others like me would also follow in the wake of my experience and would come to realize at last that the infinite lamp of God was always lit, awaiting the return home of the prodigal child and the lifting up of each individual who passed through this magnificent gift of attainment with the vestments of immortality.

Oh, what joy filled my being! After all these years, Home at last! At first I was impelled to shower the universe upon my benefactor. I felt such compassion for him that I almost did not utter praise unto God. And yet almost in an instant, praise unto God swelled up within me, and the passions of holy prayer, even from this higher state, began to peal—first like distant thunder and then with increasing cadences and power, until my soul could scarcely stand the completeness of this joy as it cascaded within me.

The Light of the Eternal Presence

O beloved hearts, I urge upon one and all a faith and sense of response to the purposes of God, which abide in you all. I urge upon you the infinite grace and understanding of life and the life of the soul.

Be not affrighted, as I have said. Be not of fear, but be of faith. For then one day, that of which you have scarcely dreamed will become for you, as for me, a tender reality, an infinite gift —the gift of Infinity.

And yet our point of contact in service is also meshing with the gears of time as we come forth from time to time to admonish, to teach, to express, and to shower our love upon mankind. The darkness ought not to be. Only the light ought to endure. The doubts that assail mankind ought to vanish in a burst of faith. Beauty ought to replace ugliness, and mankind ought to understand that the pseudo-image must cease to exist in the light of the face of the eternal Presence.

For the Presence has power and glory and strength beyond the ken of your imaginations, of your thoughts, even at first, of some who enter the ascended state. For there is also a required development after the ascension, and the process of learning continues from glory unto glory, even as by the Spirit of God.[3] And the hopes of the ages find fulfillment in the dawn of individual realization, and then the purposes of God become reality to each soul.

The Father Has Intended This Victory for All

O tender hearts, hearken unto the words we speak. But above all, hearken unto the Spirit behind these words. Understand that it is the loving plan of God for each of you to be raised into the ritual of your ascension in due process of time, when the fullness of the time has come. Then each of you will also suffer* this experience as a tribute to the joy of God within you.

Realize that many circumstances that appear now as shadows upon your path are only that—the clouds betwixt the sun shining in her strength upon the mountaintop. And even at the mountaintop man sees the clouds as reflected in the shadow. But one day there will be no more clouds because man will have climbed in consciousness to those mountain heights of spiritual experience brought to him by the Holy Spirit, which will lift him up high upon the mountain into that realm, that cloudless realm where he can at last see the fullness of the sun shining in his strength.[4]

Waiting the elixir of life and the crowning joy of all of your experience, you will find one day that each breath is a prayer, that each thought is a thought of compassion to humanity.

*to undergo, to keenly feel

Godlike in its extensions, it continues to radiate out into the world the newness and flower of hope—hope to the ages, hope to the nations, hope to all races and kindreds and tongues—that they may realize at last that the Father, in his infinite love, has intended for all the victory of attainment and for none the demolition of their opportunity.

Will you, then, tonight, fastening your faith upon the living God, be content to rest upon the laurels of divine love within you, to realize that it is love that moves and impels all of you together to create the ritual of joint attainment, that it is love that enables you to transcend individualized experience and to rise at last into those infinite arms of love whereby the joy in you will become complete because it is the completion of a divine and infinite experience?

The Gift of the Transfiguring Experience

O magnificent, ascended joy, convey thyself unto humanity! Convey thyself unto the students of the light and enable them to rejoice at last that the power of attainment is coming their way, that that power will annihilate all that is less than the perfection of the light, that that light itself will engulf them as a swaddling garment, as the newness and renewal of all life and all strength and all love, that then their chief concerns will be that they will continue to remain in that infinite light of contact, as in the experience of Peter, James, and John upon the mountaintop in the crown of the transfiguration.[5] For these experiences precede the experience of the ascension.

And therefore those of you who will, if you will it strongly enough and if it please Divine Providence, shall also receive prior to your ascension the gift of the transfiguring experience whereby your body, mind, and whole being are aerated by the Holy Spirit and given that stroke of infinite compassion, that majesty of the heavenly gift that enables you to taste, even ahead of time, those cosmic experiences of divine bliss that will one day be yours for all ages and all time immemorial. For there shall be no darkness there, but only light.[6] For the Christ of every man will be the light within the city, the citadel of his being.

I, David Lloyd, pledge to all of you who are serious about the ascension the bequeathing of my momentum according to your own dedication and the measure thereof. As you shall give, so shall you receive.[7] This is the promise of God. It is the promise of your Holy Christ Self. It is the promise of your mighty I AM Presence. It is the promise of life unto life, the speaking and the echo and the reception.

For joy and peace and love in the Holy Spirit abide forever. As a mantle, they shall cover the earth. As a mantle, as you will, so shall they cover you with the gratitude and grace of God for man, his creation. We are also his servants.

Peace be upon you.

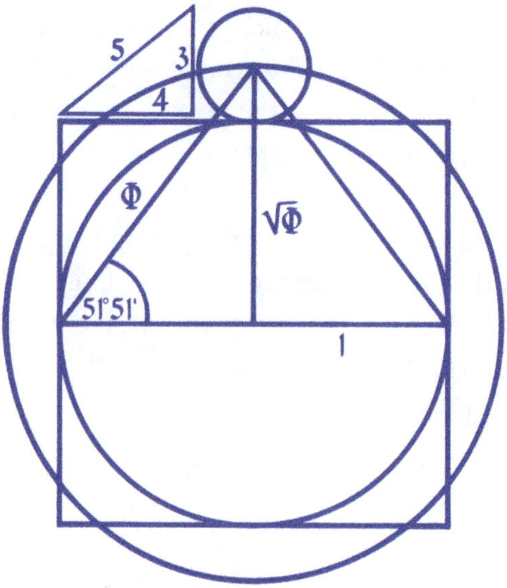

The geometry of the Great Pyramid

CHAPTER NINE

The Geometry of the Word in the Great Pyramid

Many people have studied the Great Pyramid, and many people offer great wisdom and a very organized set of knowledge concerning the Pyramid. I have not sought to make myself in my outer mind an expert on pyramidology.

I have rather considered that to become the Pyramid should be the goal of my life and to be able to transmit the vibration of the flame that is burning in that upper chamber of the Great Pyramid. That is my calling and that is where I must concentrate my life—because this, in itself, is a major challenge. To have that flame in my heart and to be able to transmit it at any hour of the twenty-four when a call for help is given, this is the Father's work that he has given to me.

However, there is a diagram of the geometry of the Great Pyramid that has appeared here and there, including in a book by John Michell called *City of Revelation.* I find it interesting for what it reveals. It portrays some of the advanced mathematical and astronomical knowledge of the architect of the Great Pyramid, Serapis Bey.

I want to reiterate to you that Serapis was and is the architect of that Great Pyramid. That information was given to me by him in recent weeks. Just meditating upon Serapis Bey's meditation upon the Great Pyramid is an explosion into cosmic consciousness.

Long ago we were told that El Morya was the master mason of the Pyramid. Thus Serapis Bey, the architect, designed every line and every form, and El Morya was the one in charge of executing the form. We begin to realize that the blessed chohans of the rays had a very intimate part in the building of that pyramid, and perhaps we dare to think that they placed it there in anticipation of the golden age of Aquarius and our coming and that they left that record in stone for you and me very personally.

I think we should take personally the statements of the immortal gurus and realize that they are made personally for their chelas whom they hold in their heart for thousands of years before they come to their own individual God-realization.

The large triangle in this diagram represents the Great Pyramid and its sides, which ascend at an angle of fifty-one degrees, fifty-one minutes. The angle of that triangle within the pyramid is the writing in stone of the requirement of the law of your balancing 51 percent of your karma. That is an astounding revelation inasmuch as the old dispensation of karmic law was such that it was required for you to balance 100 percent of your karma.

We see that the proportion of the dimensions of the pyramid are in a harmonious balance. When you drop a line from the apex and bisect the base, and you assign a value of one to the base of each resulting triangle, then the perpendicular is the square root of phi, which is the golden ratio number.* The hypotenuse of each triangle has the value of phi.

We know the golden ratio to be the very foundation of building in nature and in life. The golden ratio is the relationship and

*See pages 161–62.

proportion of energy within a spiral, and Serapis Bey says the golden ratio is the very principle of the ascension flame itself.

The Earth and the Moon

The diagram shows two concentric circles with a smaller circle on top. The inner concentric circle represents the earth and the smaller circle on top is the moon. They are shown here in their true proportional relationship.

When the base of the pyramid is inscribed within the earth circle, its apex perfectly intersects the center of the moon circle.

We are seeing, then, that the relationship of the relative sizes of the earth and the moon can be illustrated in the Great Pyramid.

The Squaring of the Circle

The square that represents the base of the pyramid has the same perimeter as the circumference of the larger circle.

The circle is always the symbol of the Trinity—the Trinity of life. When the Father, the Son, and the Holy Spirit determined to manifest the Godhead in the Matter spheres, they lowered the flame of the Mother, and it was the Mother flame that became the fourth principle. The fourth principle, then, is the squaring of the circle.

Another name for the squaring of the circle is the materialization of the God flame, or the crystallization of the God flame. The squaring of the circle is the flame of God holding the Matter crystal. So the larger circle is symbolical of the threefold flame in your heart, and the square is the symbol of the fourfold foundation of your own pyramid of life. In order to be in Matter, those four components—Father, Son, Holy Spirit, and Mother—must be present.

The circumference of the larger circle perfectly intersects the center of the circle representing the moon, showing the interrelationship of the Great Pyramid's proportions with these celestial bodies.

In addition, in the upper left we see that the triangle formed by the moon circle and the square is a perfect 3, 4, 5 right triangle, which is the most common representation of the Pythagorean theorem: $A^2 + B^2 = C^2$.

A Diagram for the Ascension

This diagram is a very simple example of just some of the vast scope of geometrical, astronomical, and spiritual knowledge embodied within the walls and the chambers of the Great Pyramid. I am certain that if a chela determined to become an initiate of Serapis Bey and to balance his karma, if he prepared himself scientifically and mathematically, he could meditate upon the Great Pyramid and write down therefrom every step of the path of initiation unto the ascension.

The Golden Ratio

The golden ratio is a specific mathematical proportion that is so omnipresent that many philosophers, artists, mathematicians, and scientists have considered it an essential component of beauty, perhaps integral to life itself. Plato considered it the key to the physics of cosmos. The Egyptians thought it more than a number and believed it symbolized the creative process and the fire of life.

This magical golden proportion is found by dividing a line (AC) at a particular point to yield two unequal sections, where the smaller one (AB) is proportionate to the larger one (BC) as the larger one (BC) is to the entire line (AC). The ratio is expressed as AB/BC = BC/AC.

There is only one such point (B) on any line. The ratio between the two sections is always the same on any length line: 1:1.618. . . , represented in mathematical symbolism by the Greek letter phi, φ.

The numbers after the decimal point are endless. Phi is what is called an irrational number—a number that cannot be expressed as the ratio of two integers. Man can only approximate the exact figure for phi. This is because this number represents a divine ideation—an etheric formula for transcendence and beauty superimposed by the Creator upon the physical plane. The essence of this ratio operates in a higher dimension, and so finite numbers cannot perfectly contain this infinite principle.

The Parthenon was designed to fit a rectangle where the ratio of the length to the width is phi (a golden rectangle). Renaissance artists also made abundant use of this ratio. Da Vinci's famous conception of man within the squaring of the circle describes man's body in terms of phi—a fact of human anatomy known since Egyptian times. Phi proportions fill the works of Raphael, Titian, Luini, and Veronese, defining both the architectural designs and the living figures in their compositions.

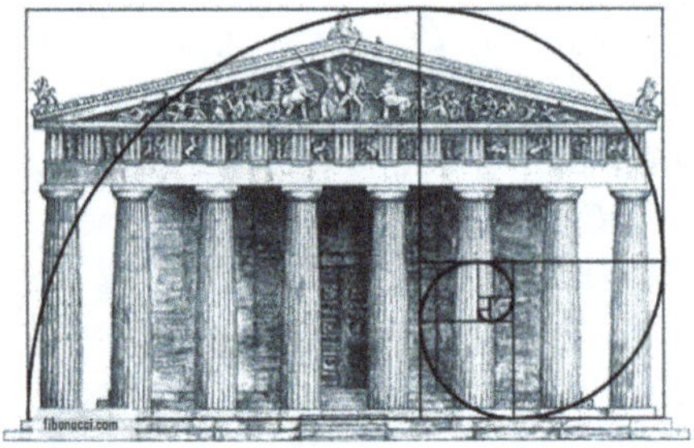

But it is more than coincidence that phi endures as a symbol of life and beauty in art and architecture. The golden ratio describes with numbers and geometry the universal formula for growth. Its resulting pentagonal symmetry (using phi angles) is not naturally found in inorganic, "inanimate" forms like crystals or snowflakes but only in "living" forms.

CHAPTER TEN

The Flame in the Heart of the Great Pyramid

Serapis Bey

Hail, legions of light!

I salute seraphim of Justinius' bands. I AM Serapis. I am come to claim you for ascension's flame. I am here in the blazing glory of that light of our retreat that you will one day enter.

The supreme light waits. The light is the inner calling of the soul. The light is the flame that burns on. The ascension flame waits. And it has waited for you, my beloved, for many aeons.

And so you have come to this outer retreat to learn the first footsteps of the Path and to accelerate light. I desire that this contact with our flame should be the open door for you to make that God-determination which will catapult your soul night after night to the temple of Luxor, to the ascension retreat. For we desire to place in the earth body, concealed within the garment of souls who yet walk the physical earth, an extraordinary light of ascension's flame.

You have heard that the pyramid is built in the very center of the earth, the land mass thereof. This was our design that the Mother flame might rise again upon the landed surface of the earth in this era. The white light of the Mother must rise out of Egypt. And that which was death must become eternal life. And all of those evolutions and crosscurrents of lifewaves that meet at that point must ultimately submit to the Mother flame.

There are challenges that we face—we the Brotherhood of Luxor—as we look to place increments of light as a tiny white cube, an electrode of ascension's flame, within your forcefield.

First, we must reckon with the balance of light of your own karma, and we must predetermine what will be the response of your being to this accelerated fohat*—a new experience indeed to be a walking electrode of ascension's flame.

Holding the Balance of Light

Therefore, you have heard of the fourteen-month cycle[1] of walking the fourteen stations of the cross[2] with ascension's fire. Now in the seventh dispensation of that activity of light, you learn the path of the heart under the hierarchy of Leo. And therefore, in the heart, we come midpoint in the seventh cycle of these stations, the stations of the cross. Each walking of them is intended to give to you an accelerated opportunity to carry a portion of planetary karma and to balance it.

Our son Jesus Christ set the example for the holding of the balance of the light of the Trinity in Mater. The age of Aquarius is rightly the age of the Woman and her seed walking those stations, carrying the Mother light. The Aquarian water-bearer carries the golden-liquid light—the elixir of sacred fire. The bearer of the cup is the lightbearer, the Aquarian. And therefore, the line of Aquarius in Leo marks the sign of the soul that becomes endued with the light of the heart by self-discipline in the principles of the Mother flame. Hence, we begin at Luxor and with a flame in the heart of the pyramid.

**fohat:* a concentration of sacred fire released from the chakras of an ascended master or an adept

Now that you have for many a year sustained the violet flame and made those mighty invocations to the Elohim Astrea,[3] now that you have cleared a certain level of being—saturating the heart with light—we desire to open the way for the rising, pulsating Mother flame to be within you a fervent force of acceleration unto all the earth. This acceleration is to be the resurrection of all of the seed of Christ unto the eternal resurrection, of the resurrection of them that sleep and of those who are dead until they are quickened, and the resurrection of the seed of the wicked that their works that are not of the light may be flushed out, brought to the fore, and they and the children of light may look upon those works and choose the pathway of truth.

Therefore, when the Mother flame rises from the depths of Lemuria, from the Great Pyramid, from your own citadel of light within your temple, you may anticipate that all that remains in each man's portion of the 100 percent of the allotment of the increment of light—all that remains that is not balanced—will also come to the surface. The Mother light brings to the surface all that is within consciousness.

We, then, are certain that our methods and our training are such that no one will be given the increment of light in whom that light will cause a disturbance that the individual will not be able to deal with.

We Know the Power of the Mother Light

We know the power of the Mother light. We know the Mother light intimately. We know that earnest initiates of the flame are those who will come to Luxor and deal realistically with the light of God and with the portion of that light that yet requires balance.

If you are told to go back and accelerate your service and

your invocation to the violet flame, be encouraged and be of good cheer. For you are being guided by adepts, ascended masters, and some who might be ascended masters but are not by free choice, for they have chosen to remain as unascended adepts balancing almost 100 percent of their karma and holding that forcefield in Matter so that they might be present to train you in the requirements of the Law for the holding of the ascension flame.

We must also consider what the planet will bear, what its evolution will bear, when the light begins to increase. Verily, I say to you, the coming of the golden age depends upon the few willing to carry the light and to understand that the light will always bring joy. And it will always bring out that which is the anti-joy momentum of the earth, which must be transmuted before it colors the crystal clear stream of life flowing through the desire body.

I speak of your feeling world. How quickly and easily the feeling world becomes depressed or excited or enangered. How easily emotions become a tempest in a teapot. And suddenly, the sea begins to roar. This illustrates that the individual yet identifies with mass human emotions and with emotions that come upon the rock of his being, as it were, beating upon the rock of the lighthouse that is your mighty I AM Presence.

I say, be not moved by these conditions. The measure of your God-mastery must be your ability to hold the flame when all assails you, when riptides of human emotion, condemnation or persecution or outright lies assail you or this activity of light.

There is a calm center within the heart. And there is a center within the secret chamber of the heart. And there is a center within the solar-plexus chakra whereby you can maintain peace by the sacred fire breath and not follow the turbulence of the world's turmoil.

We, then, watch for those who do not allow the ego to be

carried away in being offended or disturbed by any word, any accusation or any injustice whatsoever. God in you is justified. And wisdom is justified of her children. And there is no need to go and attempt to solve any problem by emotional substance. Remember my word well. For we come to tell you of those points of the Law that are found wanting and that must be met if you indeed are to accelerate on the Path.

Guard Your Harmony

I have received many of you at Luxor. And you have sat in our retreat and contemplated how the energies of the earth body and how the transmittal of mass consciousness emotions is transferred to your own temple. And I have shown you, in diagrams and the most precise explanations, of the challenges that you would face on the very next day after your coming to our retreat. And some of you have gone forth and met very serious building-up of energy forcefields with a calmness and a poise that would equal that of an adept of our retreat.

But others of you have not carried to the physical octave the soul knowledge, and often it is a point of pride. And that pride that goeth before the fall[4] goeth before the fall of the feeling world as it descends to a point of inharmony because of someone's offense or someone's unkind word or criticism. And the sharp sting, as it stings not the Christ but the ego, then becomes a lashing back, and suddenly you know that you have lost that equipoise, that center—that place where the line of the pyramid is drawn in the very center of the earth itself.

Understand, then, that these are the testings that are repeated day after day after day until nothing—no thing in this world—is capable of moving you from the firm attention and joy and love upon your God Self. And what is the formula for this mastery? It is this, quite simply—that you love God and your oneness with him more than you love yourself and its pseudo defenses in emotional tirades, outbursts or mood energies; loving God and loving to be in his presence, waiting upon the LORD for the next initiation on the Path.

Watch, then. Is there someone in your life, someone who is capable of disturbing you? I say, praise that one. It is the guru in disguise. You will not be rid of that one until you learn to give the fiat of the living Christ: "Peace, be still and know that I AM God."[5] That fiat is not spoken to the individual but to your own four lower bodies.

Therefore, see how karma and its circumstance evokes the person from whom you learn the most—the one through whom you must conquer or be conquered. Harmony is the key. And when you can guard the harmony in the face of aggravation, irritation, even lies and calumny, then you will be ready for this acceleration of ascension's flame that must be carried into all the earth if this earth is to accelerate and begin a spin that throws off the greatest darkness and the remaining evil forcefields of those fallen ones.

Acceleration Is the Key to the Judgment

Acceleration is the key to the judgment. You have asked, "Why does the judgment not come upon those who have sworn their anti-God consciousness to be their life and to unseat the little ones? Why has the judgment not come upon them?" It is ever so simple. Not enough lifestreams hold the equivalent of light to counterbalance the darkness that must be removed.

Darkness is a heavy weight and a forcefield. Light, then, must replace every erg of darkness that is removed from the earth. If we are to remove the strongholds of the wicked and the seed of the wicked themselves, then we must have forcefields of light and sons of light instantly ready to fill the vacuum. For when you remove a large cancer such as a beast or a dragon from the astral plane, instantaneously you have an open space.

And it must be filled with the Holy Spirit, else a multiplication of greater darkness will occur by the remaining elements of the fallen ones who will multiply to occupy that given space.

This law may not be entirely understood by you or understandable, but I tell you truly, it is a law. And if you would clean out the Augean stables with Mighty Hercules,[6] you must, then, be ready to fill them with light. For nature abhors a vacuum. And we will not allow the further proliferation of darkness. Therefore, let light increase.

The Coming of Maximus

I invoke the being Maximus. And Maximus comes forth out of the octaves of light with legions of light. For he has been called by Alpha and Omega to speak to you this evening.[7] And therefore, I announce to you his coming that you might prepare this evening to be in the presence of one who is given the calling and the office in cosmos to maximize good, to multiply the light of Alpha and Omega within you.

His is the outpicturing of the mathematical formula of the Great Pyramid. And when I meditated upon the form of that pyramid within the heart of God, I found it in the Great Causal Body of the being known to you as Maximus. To maximize the light of the Mother within us is the meaning and the calling of his name.

Soldiers of the light, enlightened ones, you who would be illumined on the path of the ascension, you who desire the ascension in the desire to give love and freedom to all life, I AM Serapis. I have come because you are ready for an increment of ascension's flame. I have come because the seven Holy Kumaras and the Goddess of Purity have determined to fill this city with light and to increase that light that will flush out darkness and will also accelerate the path of initiation. San Francisco, here I come!

I AM Serapis. I will not leave you as I have found you. *All hail,* children of the light! *All hail,* Justinius! We are one in the God-determination to implant ascension's flame here and now within this earth and within the brow of our chelas of the flame.

All hail, we are one.

Amen.

CHAPTER ELEVEN

Meditation on the Crystal of the Self

Psalm 108

A Psalm of David

O God, my heart is fixed; I will sing and give praise, even with my glory.

Awake, psaltery and harp: I myself will awake early.

I will praise thee, O LORD, among the people: and I will sing praises unto thee among the nations.

For thy mercy is great above the heavens: and thy truth reacheth unto the clouds.

Be thou exalted, O God, above the heavens: and thy glory above all the earth;

That thy beloved may be delivered: save with thy right hand, and answer me.

God hath spoken in his holiness; I will rejoice, I will divide Shechem, and mete out the valley of Succoth.

Gilead is mine; Manasseh is mine; Ephraim also is the strength of mine head; Judah is my lawgiver;

Moab is my washpot; over Edom will I cast out my shoe; over Philistia will I triumph.

Who will bring me into the strong city? Who will lead me into Edom?

Wilt not thou, O God, who hast cast us off? And wilt not thou, O God, go forth with our hosts?

Give us help from trouble: for vain is the help of man.

Through God we shall do valiantly: for he it is that shall tread down our enemies.

Let us sing to beloved Sanat Kumara.

In the name of the I AM THAT I AM, I invoke the light of Sanat Kumara. Light of the Ancient of Days, shine forth, shine forth now in the hearts of these thy children. Blaze forth thy light, O flaming one! Blaze forth thy light by the power of the Great Central Sun.

Seven Holy Kumaras, come forth. Come forth in the name of the flaming Word. We invoke thy presence in each heart. Quicken the heart. Let the light be the explosion of the God consciousness, and let it consume all unlike thyself.

In the name of Mother Mary, we pray, and we command light to go forth and obey the Word that is spoken within us as the acceptable Word of thy will, O God. Amen.

Our Beloved Sanat Kumara

(sung to the tune of Finlandia)

Sanat Kumara, Regent, Lord, and King
  To thy great Presence praises now we sing
Off'ring our gifts of humble service true
  Reverence and honor to God for you
Thou art God's glory, majesty, and grace
  Thy patient care for earth held her place.

All through the ages that have gone before
  Thy love has been for earth an open door

Held in thy Light, sustained by thy great pow'r
And in thy wisdom guided each hour
We feel thy peace in love's own God-control
As thy great wings of love now enfold.

Glory and honor unto thee belong
Let all adore thee now in grateful song
As all that live upon this planet raise
Heart, soul, and spirit—thy name we praise
Great Central Sun, thy gifts of love we call
For our dear friend of Light, Lord of all.

As for dear Venus, Goddess from the Sun
Bless their dear planet, all life thereon.

The Crystal of the Self

We're going to meditate upon the crystal of the self. The crystal of the self is created to house the flame. The crystal of the self is an opportunity for great gain. It is a multiplication of consciousness.

The self that discovers the crystal that is to house the flame is the enlightened self. When you discover the self to be the crystal, and then you recognize that the crystal is a fire mist crystallized and a crystallized fire mist that is created to contain the crystal fire mist, then you begin the path of your ascension.

So the temple is built, but the flame must be invoked. And how we hurry around the earth, building temples and shrines and all sorts of houses to house the temple that is already built. If we knew that the temple was already built, we could do away with all of that and concentrate upon the flame.

We see in the world today many churches empty, tall buildings where business is conducted. We enter churches or buildings or homes and we find no flame. We feel no welcoming light. The angels feel no welcoming light. And so we find typically what has happened at the end of the Piscean age seems to happen at the end of every age.

The Ritual of the Seventh Ray

The conclusion of an age is intended to be the fulfillment of the seventh ray. The seven rays are for our outer manifestation. Over the approximately 2,100-year period of each age, there is a spacing, according to the golden ratio, of the seven rays. And so in the end of the cycle, all that has been externalized by the seven rays is intended to move in the ritual of the seventh ray of freedom.

The seventh ray ritual of freedom is reflected in the orders of priests and priestesses of the sacred fire, those who are committed to the sustaining of creation in the day of rest.[1] The day of rest is the day of rest in motion. It is the going over and reconfirming by the power of the Word of all the good that has been accomplished. By the seventh ray, all that has been brought forth in the creation may transcend itself, and thereby the action of the seventh ray is seen to be the instrument for the creation to go through the self-transcending process.

The ascension is the self-transcending process. It cannot be won without the communion with the seventh ray. This seventh ray action, then, is a part of the crystal fire mist and a very necessary part of your endowing of your crystal with a flame.

What happens, however, at the end of the ages is that people do not mount the spiral of the first six rays, so that when it is time for the seventh ray, they descend into the level of rote, of a letter of the law, of the repetition of cycles, with no apparent awareness of why they are repeating cycles.

And all of a sudden, we find in the last decade, especially in the United States, a generation of New Age children who have said, "Wait, stop, what is all of this round of making money to spend money to merely exist?" Seeing this, many have forged out on their own to carve out a life that is meaningful—because they see no meaning to the ceaseless round of an existence that is only lived to perpetuate the outer form and not endow it with the inner flame.

The Dawn of the Seventh Age

So many of this generation are pioneers, pilgrims who have come to begin a New Age, and the age is sprung from the seventh action of the last. The order and the ritual that brings the previous dispensation to the peak of its manifestation, making it the acceptable offering upon the altar of the LORD, is the springboard into the next dispensation.

It so happens that the next dispensation is the seventh age, so that all of the bringing forth of the seven rays in this age will have the coloring and the covering of the violet flame—the seventh age containing all of the seven rays.

At the end of the previous age, there was the same descending to rote, to a dead ritual that had not the spirit. Gautama Buddha came as the great revolutionary to challenge this dead ritual of Hinduism, this codification of the letter of the law. Jesus Christ came with the same mission to challenge those rituals that were dead to the letter in Judaism. It is the teaching that no longer has a flame but is repeated for the sake of repeating it instead of being repeated for newness of life.

So we are here at the end of the Piscean age. And what do we see? When I travel around the world, I see tired electrons. I see tired atoms, tired molecules. They have been spent. If they are not soon endowed with a living flame of the Holy Spirit, they will go into the disintegration spiral.

When you see a building decaying and falling apart, it is because it is no longer endowed with a flame and the components out of which it was created have given the content of their energy. If they are to endure, they need a new infusion of light. If they don't get it, we build again with new materials.

But I also see souls who are tired. Many souls are tired of living the same old rote patterns, the same existence lifetime after lifetime. They know that there should be a new infusion, a new energy, a new consciousness, something more worthwhile than the way we are living. And they are waiting for the coming of the Mother.

I can feel it in their souls. They have been so long separated from the Mother flame that they don't even remember that it is the Mother after whom they long. All of the various psychological complexes, all of the crime, all of the perversions, it's almost a screaming of the soul: "Mother, notice me, come to me, do anything. Spank me, if you will. But at least let me know that you know that I exist." That seems to be the very deep crying out of the souls of our people.

The Mother Flame Is Rising Again

America is a Mother nation. It is Lemuria come again. It's the wilderness land that John the Beloved saw for the appearance of the Woman who gives birth to the Manchild.[2] It's the place of her seed, which is the seed of Sanat Kumara.

Sanat Kumara is the Mother in disguise, and the Mother is Sanat Kumara in disguise. The presence of Sanat Kumara in our midst is the presence of the Great Guru, and he comes truly in our midst. He comes into our heart. He quickens a flame, and he shows us that after all, it is the flame that will endure after the temple has served its usefulness.

The path of the ascension is the path whereby the soul recognizes that flame and determines to live in it. When you determine to live in the flame, it is true—you no longer live as others live. But that should not be a pain. It should be a joy, a realization that you are setting the pattern that others will follow.

David Lloyd told us that he had the recognition that many others would follow him on the path of the ascension. Yet if all the people in the world started wandering around mountains looking for a man with a crystal cup, the foundations of civilization would be no more. So there are different levels to the pyramid of life, and there are different initiations, and within a given age, there are some people who will be working on the first ray or the second, the third, the fourth, the fifth, the sixth or the seventh simultaneously.

So within the age is a spiral upon a spiral, and we are most grateful for people who find the challenges of life in carrying on with civilization. We, however, cannot be grateful for those who abuse the foundations of the temple, but we have none other to look to than ourselves.

If we see a job that is not being conducted properly in Congress or the state legislature or in the dealing of our economy, we have no one to blame but ourselves. If we are not there doing the job, then we understand that the job is occupied by whoever has the attainment, whether it's the left-handed path or the right-handed path, to be there.

Why Are the Wicked Not Judged?

Serapis Bey gave us a very important teaching today. I was wondering if you heard it. He said, "We ask, 'Why are the wicked not judged?'"

David asked God, psalm after psalm, "When will you deliver me of mine enemies?" He had a great deal of opposition because he was incarnating the Christ consciousness.

The soul of David is the soul of Jesus Christ. David reincarnated as Jesus Christ for the perfectionment of his lifestream. He already was holding the flame of Christ in the midst of Israel, and he already had to deal with the Antichrist. The Psalms are full of his concern, "God, what are you going to do about the enemies?"—the enemies of him personally and of the kingdom of Israel.

Serapis Bey told us that God cannot remove the unrighteous or the seed of the wicked or their works until their space would be instantly filled with light. And so there is a certain type of individual, not a chela, not a devotee, situated in the political and economic structure of our nation today. And there are those to the left and those to the right in this relative human spectrum of the human consciousness, and upon their platforms, they war with one another, vying for position. It is neither the right nor the left nor the middle of the road but it is the universal Christ consciousness that ought to be in those positions.

Lightbearers Are Called to Leadership

The Darjeeling Council and the World Teachers are raising up a generation of lightbearers who will become educated in the things of the Spirit and the things of the Matter pyramid and who will be prepared to take their positions, understanding that the government and the economy is upon the shoulder of the inner Christ.

When these come to the fore and take their places, then it will come to pass that the prophecy is fulfilled, that the government shall be upon his shoulders,[3] and that the true shepherds of the people will lead the people and that the false pastors will be removed.

This is the calling of the ascended masters. They can do very little with the earth and the things that are happening in it until devotees of the flame come to realize that unless it is the hour before your ascension, it is not the moment to be wandering on the mountain for any longer than it takes you to realign your consciousness with your God Presence and go forth. And that shouldn't take more than a few moments, sometimes a few days, sometimes a week.

But the here and now action of making a golden age physical means that adeptship must be taken up by those who will not leave civilization or society, though it be dense and heavy and full of vibrations that are contrary to the path.

We Must Finish the Spiral of Pisces

The seven chohans of the rays stand with us at the end of the age now, and they challenge us to finish the spiral of Pisces. The Piscean age, the last two thousand years of history, is full of war. War is the Antichrist attempting to destroy the flame of the Prince of Peace within us all.

It is not enough for us to raise up the violet flame to finish the Piscean age. Saint Germain says, "Go back in history and transmute the past." Begin with the Christian era. Invoke the violet flame into that history and go into your own past.

All of us have had numerous incarnations in this two-thousand-year period. The ascended masters want us to balance the karma of that period with the violet flame. And if in the first part of our incarnations we did not wholly fulfill our purpose in the first ray, we must perfect that ray in our words and our works today, and then the second ray and the third, the fourth, the fifth, the sixth and the seventh.

If we will do that, we will be the microcosm of a laboratory for the Great Pyramid to appear, person by person across the earth. The seven levels of the pyramid are the seven chakras of your being. The central flame is the heart, the King's Chamber, the replica of the secret chamber of your own heart. You are the living pyramid. But because we have builded incorrectly, we must go back and rebuild, set the age aright and then build upon the foundation of that attainment.

The Piscean age was given to us all to perfect the Christ consciousness. Jesus Christ set an example, and he gave us two thousand years to become what he became and what he was. Summit University was founded by Gautama Buddha for the sons and daughters of God to catch up on the lost years of unfruitful lives, to catch up on the initiations that have been missed, especially in these two thousand years, but also in the ages prior.

The Violet Flame Is the Foundation of Aquarius

All of this, then, becomes the foundation for Aquarius. The key dispensation that makes possible your ascension is the knowledge of your mighty I AM Presence and the violet flame. The meditation upon the crystal that is you is for its endowment with the flame. This you accomplish by taking your decrees daily and turning to the violet-flame section.

Saint Germain once told the messenger Godfré the requirement of the Law for that ascension: thirty minutes each day of violet flame. With that you can transmute your past and leave a record that it is possible for all to achieve the same goal. I challenge you in the name of Saint Germain to prove, as God has said, "Prove me now herewith, saith the LORD, if I will not pour you out a blessing that there shall not be room enough to receive it."[4]

He said that when he called for the bringing in of the tithes. The tithes are the lawful offering of one tenth of our portion daily. When we give our energy to God in dynamic decrees, it is multiplied by ten and returned.

A Six-Month Challenge

I challenge you then to experiment with the Path, to take a six-month cycle of your life and to give thirty minutes in concentration, not five minutes here or there, but thirty minutes in concentrated action of the violet flame, and write down the new exciting things that happen in your life day by day.

Keep up your violet-flame decrees and keep a violet-flame notebook, because in six months you won't remember where you were when you started. You will be so many miles from the point of your origin, and the alchemy of your life can be the equivalent of six hundred or six thousand years wandering in the miasma of your karma without the violet flame.

I say that to you directly from the heart of Saint Germain. If you really want to accelerate, experiment with his law. Experiment with the violet flame and find out why the God of Freedom to the earth and the hierarch of Aquarius has considered the violet flame to be the greatest single gift, the key to America's destiny, to the ending of war, to the bringing together of the lightbearers of all nations.

I'm going to make the commitment to do it with you. And so I'm going to make the call when I give it each day to reinforce your violet-flame decrees, and I'm going to keep a notebook and I'm going to tell you what happened as the result of my six-month novena.

So now we're going to meditate upon you in the center of the violet-flame crystal.

Meditation on the Violet Flame

(over music)

O light, light, light I AM! Light I AM!
Light, I AM, I AM, I AM.
Light within my heart,
Now start, start that fire, that sacred fire.
Blaze in me, O sacred fire.
Live and learn to be
The fullness of eternity.
O my soul, expand, expand the violet flame.
Saint Germain, now command, command all life free.
Send violet flame from my heart
    to every heart and every soul in every land.
Violet flame expand.
Violet flame expand and set the people free.
    Set the people free. Set the people free
    in the name of Christ.

I invoke the science of the Word, the lost Word.
All my centers, all my life, all my being.
Let it be now an electrode of light
from out the Great Central Sun.
We are one. We are one. We are one, O God.
Every soul of light on earth, return now to
power, wisdom, love.
Release the sacred fire in thy Word, O God.
I speak thy Word.
It is thy rod of living flame.
The spinal altar is thy rod of light.
Rise, O sacred fire, Mother light
from the base unto the crown.
Fill me with thy light.

I AM the living church.
I AM the temple.
I AM the place of refuge and the lighthouse.
I AM a light and a beacon to all souls
seeking the homeward way of light.

O, violet flame, come violet flame,
Now, blaze and blaze and blaze.
O violet flame, come violet flame
To raise and raise and raise!
The earth and all thereon,
The earth and all thereon,
The earth and all thereon.

O violet flame, come violet flame,
Now blaze and blaze and blaze.
O raise and raise and raise
The children and their teachers,
The children and their teachers,
The children and their teachers.

The plants and elemental creatures,
The plants and elemental creatures,
The plants and elemental creatures.

Light expand, light expand, light expand,
expand, expand.
Light I AM, light I AM, light I AM, I AM, I AM.
I AM a living flame.
I AM a freedom flame.
I AM, I will be free, I will be free.

I will serve to set all life free and let my people go,
let my people go.
I will stand in the midst of the
congregation of the righteous.
I will challenge all evil, the energy veil
by the power of the Lord Christ.

I will use the Word.
No more helpless or hopeless,
I will forge my God-identity.
I will fire that fiery destiny.
I will be *God, here and now, in the understanding*
that by his flame, I live.
By his will, I AM.
And in his Word, truly, I forgive!
I forgive seventy times seven,
seventy thousand times seven.
I AM the forgiveness flame.

I walk a pilgrim nation unto nation,
A witness of this light that I AM, that I AM, that I AM.
I AM THAT I AM.
I AM THAT I AM.
Father, Son, and Holy Spirit, I would hear it in thy name.

Come and speak thy Word,
Amen. Amen. Amen.
AUM. Sacred fire, blaze!
AUM. Sacred fire, blaze!

The call compels the answer.
I AM the answer.
I AM the call.
I AM a son of God.
I AM a daughter of God.
No more, no more do I descend to the darkness of death.
No, I rise because He is risen.

I AM one.
We are one.
We are one.
We are one.
We shall overcome.
We shall overcome.
We will overcome.
We will overcome.

Light expand, light expand, light.
Light, set me free. Light, set me free. Light, set me free.
Light command, light demand,
Light expand, light I AM.

I AM a being a violet fire.
I AM the purity God desires.
I AM a being a violet fire.
I AM the purity God desires.
I AM a being a violet fire.
I AM the purity God desires.

God in You Is Worthy of the Full Cup of Life

Let us take our decree books and turn to the prayers for purity.[5] The white section in the decree book is your work with the ascension flame and the Mother flame.

The "Decree for Purity" was dictated by the Goddess of Purity, who established a healing flame at our retreat in Colorado Springs when she gave this dictation.

The Goddess of Purity sponsors San Francisco, together with Archangel Gabriel. So we will give this invocation to Purity together.

Decree for Purity

In the name of the beloved mighty victorious Presence of God, I AM in me, my very own beloved Holy Christ Self, Holy Christ Selves of all mankind, beloved Goddess of Purity, beloved Jesus the Christ, the beloved Elohim of Purity, beloved Lanello, the entire Spirit of the Great White Brotherhood and the World Mother, elemental life—fire, air, water, and earth! I decree:

Open the door to Purity!
Open the door to Purity!
Let the breezes blow and trumpet Purity
Over the sea and over the land;
Let men understand
The voice of Cosmic Christ command.

I come to open wide the way
That men without fear may ever say:
I AM the Purity of God
I AM the Purity of Love
I AM the Purity of Joy
I AM the Purity of Grace
I AM the Purity of Hope
I AM the Purity of Faith

And all that God can make of joy
and grace combined.

LORD, I AM worthy of thy Purity. I would have thy Purity surge through me in a great cosmic burst to remove from the screen of my mind, my thoughts, and my feelings every appearance of human vibratory action and all that is impure in substance, thought, or feeling.

Replace all that right now with the fullness of the mind of Christ and the mind of God, the manifest power of the resurrection spirit and the ascension flame, that I may enter into the Holy of Holies of my being and find the power of transmutation taking place to free me forever from all discord that has ever manifested in my world.

I AM Purity in action here, I AM God's purity established forever, and the stream of light from the very heart of God that embodies all of his purity is flowing through me and establishing round about me the power of invincible cosmic purity which can never be requalified by the human.

Here I AM, take me, O God of Purity. Assimilate me and use me in the matrices of release for the mankind of earth. Let me not only invoke purity for myself, but also let me invoke Purity for every part of life. Let me not only invoke Purity for my family, but also for all the family of God neath the canopy of heaven.

I thank Thee and I accept this manifest right here and now with full power as the purity and authority of thy words spoken through me to produce the instantaneous manifestation of thy cosmic purity in my four lower bodies, intensifying hourly and accelerating those bodies until they attain the frequency of the Ascension Flame.

Isn't it wonderful to be able to say, "LORD, I AM worthy of thy Purity," instead of saying, "Lord, I'm a miserable sinner." At last we can affirm the self-worth of God within us. God in you is worthy of the full cup of life.

The Golden Pink Glow-Ray: Essential Agent of Your Ascension

Now we'll take up our decree to beloved Helios and Vesta. Helios and Vesta release the golden pink glow-ray, and the song to Helios and Vesta draws forth the golden light of wisdom and the pink flame of love. And when these fuse as one ray, it is called the golden pink glow-ray.

This ray is a very essential agent of your ascension. The golden pink glow-ray is for the clearing of the physical body, as well as the other bodies, and the balancing of Alpha and Omega, or the balancing of the body and blood of Christ.

We're going to invoke this ray from the heart of Helios and Vesta, who are the twin flames who sponsor this solar system. Their retreat and their heart is the sun of our system.

The physical sun is the physical expression of the Sun behind the sun that is the spiritual Sun of our system. So there is the spirit Sun and the matter sun, and Helios and Vesta govern the flow of life at the nucleus of the atom that is our solar system.

> *In the name of the light of God that never fails, I call to beloved Helios and Vesta for the light to flow in the very center of the being of these souls who would be candidates for the ascension, who would receive the accelerated light of Serapis Bey, who would have the light and energy of the Mother flame to hold and to be in the earth electrodes of the ascension flame.*
>
> *Helios and Vesta, prepare these hearts and souls and minds and temples for the coming of our beloved Maximus. Fill us with thy light, Great Central Sun Magnet. Come now and magnetize the Christ consciousness in our hearts, and demagnetize from this city and nation and earth all that is Antichrist in every child.*
>
> *So we pray in the name of the Father, the Son, the Holy Spirit, and the Mother. Amen.*

Father-Mother Light Mantra

Helios and Vesta!
Helios and Vesta!
Helios and Vesta!
Let the light flow into my being!
Let the light expand in the center of my heart!
Let the light expand in the center of the earth
And let the earth be transformed into the New Day! (3x)

Your decree book is your handbook for your ascension.

We're going to take now the decree for the golden pink glow-ray. Please visualize this light streaming into your body temple the great gift of love and wisdom.

Decree for the Golden Pink Glow-Ray

In the name of the beloved mighty victorious Presence of God, I AM in me, and my very own beloved Holy Christ Self, I call to the heart of beloved Serapis Bey and the Brotherhood at Luxor, beloved Lord Gautama, beloved Saint Germain, beloved God and Goddess Meru, beloved Sanat Kumara and the Holy Kumaras, the Cosmic Being Harmony, the seven mighty Elohim, the seven beloved archangels and their archeiai, the seven beloved chohans of the rays, beloved Lanello, the entire Spirit of the Great White Brotherhood and the World Mother, elemental life—fire, air, water, and earth!

1. I AM calling today for thy golden pink ray
To manifest round my form.
Golden pink light, dazzling bright,
My four lower bodies adorn!

Refrain: O Brotherhood at Luxor and blest Serapis Bey,
Hear our call and answer by love's ascending ray.
Charge, charge, charge our being
With essence pure and bright;
Let thy hallowed radiance
Of ascension's mighty light

Blaze its dazzling light rays
Upward in God's name,
Till all of heaven claims us
For God's ascending flame.

2. Saturate me with golden pink light,
Make my four lower bodies bright;
Saturate me with ascension's ray,
Raise my four lower bodies today!

3. Surround us now with golden pink love
Illumined and charged with light from above;
Absorbing this with lightning speed,
I AM fully charged with Victory's mead.

And in full Faith I consciously accept this manifest, manifest, manifest! (3x) right here and now with full Power, eternally sustained, all-powerfully active, ever expanding, and world enfolding until all are wholly ascended in the Light and free!

Beloved I AM! Beloved I AM! Beloved I AM!

A Living Chalice

Let us give "I AM Thy Chalice." I'd like you to stand for this. When Mark Prophet taught us to give this decree, he taught us to raise our hands and form a chalice and to visualize the light coming into the chalice. If you're going to offer the crystal cup, you have to become the crystal cup.

I AM Thy Chalice
by Lanello

I AM the true life of the flame,
A focus of God's I AM name,
Descending cycle from the Sun,
My radiant source, thou lovely One!

I AM thy chalice ever free—
My purposed aim like Thee to be,
A ray of light's expanding love,
A focus for God's Comfort Dove.

Thy ray now anchored in my form
Does my divinity adorn:
Thy flame, a rising sacred fire,
Each moment takes me ever higher

Until at last made purer still,
Eternal focus of thy will,
I AM thy crystal chalice pure,
An anchor of thy love secure.

A healing fountain to the earth,
I AM real proof of life's rebirth,
Which by the power of thy name
Ascends today thy love to claim.

I AM thy radiance crystal clear,
Forever pouring through me here.
Thy living joy fore'er expanding,
I AM with Thee all life commanding!

CHAPTER TWELVE

Surya: A Being from the God Star, Sirius

Surya is a great being known to the ancients. There is a great statue erected to Surya—a massive piece of sculpture. It reveals a being of cosmic consciousness whose seat of authority is the God Star, Sirius.[1] And he amplifies the light of the seven Holy Kumaras out of the Pleiades.

Beloved Surya has offered his Electronic Presence, which is the duplicate of his auric forcefield. He has offered that Presence to be manifest in the earth many millions of times, wherever he is called. He has said that wherever the Judgment Call is given, the call from Jesus, that he will place his Electronic Presence, which is the duplicate of himself, there where the judgment is required.

When we call for the Electronic Presence of Jesus, we can see Jesus multiplying himself a million times and manifesting himself in the body of the earth. So we can also visualize Surya, this mighty being of intense blue aura, Buddha-like in appearance. He has this cosmic immensity, and he places it in the earth to accelerate God consciousness.

Statue of Surya at the Sun Temple at Konark, India

Beloved Surya

Beloved mighty victorious Presence of God, I AM in me, my very own beloved Holy Christ Self, Holy Christ Selves of all mankind, beloved Surya, legions of white fire and blue lightning from Sirius, beloved Lanello, the entire Spirit of the Great White Brotherhood and the World Mother, elemental life—fire, air, water, and earth! In thy name, by and through the magnetic power of the immortal, victorious threefold flame of Truth within my heart and the heart of God in the Great Central Sun, I decree:

1. Out from the Sun flow thy dazzling bright
   Blue-flame ribbons of flashing diamond light!
   Serene and pure is thy love,
   Holy radiance from God above!

Refrain: Come, come, come, Surya dear,
By thy flame dissolve all fear;
Give to each one security
In the bonds of purity;
Flash and flash thy flame through me,
Make and keep me ever free!

2. Surya dear, beloved one
From the mighty Central Sun,
In God's name to thee we call:
Take dominion over all!

3. Out from the heart of God you come,
Serving to make us now all one—
Wisdom and honor do you bring,
Making the very soul to sing!

4. Surya dear, beloved one,
From our faith then now is spun
Victory's garment of invincible gold,
Our soul's great triumph to ever uphold!

And in full Faith I consciously accept this manifest, manifest, manifest! (3x) right here and now with full Power, eternally sustained, all-powerfully active, ever expanding, and world enfolding until all are wholly ascended in the Light and free!

Beloved I AM! Beloved I AM! Beloved I AM!

The Path of Your Christhood

The path of the ascension is the path of your Christhood. At Summit University, we mark the steps of the path by keeping a notebook that is called "My Christhood." Jesus set the example of the initiations. As we meditate on the steps of his path, we can begin to feel the swelling of his flame within our temple. Because we believe on him and on his name, we should go forth and do the works that he did. And as he promised, "greater works than these shall he do; because I go unto my Father."[2]

This meditation is upon the going unto the Father of Jesus Christ, his ascension and the steps that it involved. Place yourself in the scenes of his life as the person of Christ—Jesus Christ, the guru of Pisces. Love him and desire to be with him in each moment of his life as the celebration of the ritual of his becoming God.

It happens that as you join him on the path and he initiates you in that light, by and by you discover that you are truly working out the same salvation of being that he worked out. You begin the path by joining him on his pathway, and you end the path in discovering that he has joined you in your initiation in this your hour of victory.

[Meditation on scenes from the life of Christ from Gustave Doré's Bible illustrations accompanied by "Christos," by Franz Liszt]

CHAPTER THIRTEEN

I AM Maximus, I Drop a Sound, I Maximize Light:

1) To Multiply the Judgment of Love, 2) To Multiply the Resurrection, 3) To Multiply the Preaching of the Word

Maximus

Ascend the ladder of light with me, my children. I come to take you by the hand and to show you a vision of the Promised Land. A ladder of light my angels have let down. And all of you I take by the hand and we climb together. I show you a perspective of life. Let us ascend these steps together as a dress rehearsal for your own life waiting to be lived—oh, waiting to be lived as surely as you wait for the crystal cup to be given.

Therefore, come, and have a look, a peek at the place where angels look and peek-a-boo with each other and one another, and find together that life from loftier heights gains newness of perspective. Come, then, we mount. We mount the stairs and do begin to see earth recede as you mount to the stars.

And you look upon life below as though it were a lilliputian world and a portion of yourself is vested in that life. And when you become centered in that life, all things loom large, even gnats and flies and little petty problems. But in the perspective of the vast teeming millions of stars and sun centers and all of the places we have been together, you can easily see with me that the segment of time and space that you occupy and call your life is but an inch in a cosmic inch of measurement. And therefore, you say, "Can I not give an inch to God for all the inches that I have taken for myself?"

This Is the Age of Your Ascension

What seems to be the intense struggle to overcome is but episode upon episode of a preordained drama of the path of initiation. Your soul has known from the beginning the great turmoil that would be in the beginning of this age. Your soul has known that this is the age of your ascension.

I AM Maximus. I sound the sound of the inner memory and the sound of the great cathedral and the sounding of the bell that is rung by Jesus Christ, the sounding of the sound that initiates the spiral whereby you will surely mount this ladder. And when you mount it on your own, you'll find your footsteps not so lightly, easily mounting as we do together this night. For I take you over a thousand rungs of this ladder so easily—as easily as the angels ascending and descending.

And from your vantage point, you see with me other stars and evolutions and shining worlds and hierarchies of light and brothers and sisters you have known. Behold the vastness of space and the immensity of light positioned within space. Behold above you the legions of light, all of whom have their attention upon all that is taking place within the earth, within your life, within your community and on the path.

You see millions of mankind untethered to any light at all. You see a great multitude arising out from among them with a certain self-awareness. You see the saints leading the multitude to the Great Pyramid. And you see the Two Witnesses witnessing unto the vastness of the Solar-El.[1]

The Ladder of Hierarchy

I AM that El. I have come to tell you of the great sign of the cross that marks the telling of the El. Sanat Kumara bids you,

"Go, tell them. Go be with Gautama what I AM THAT I AM." And the Witness writes the poem "Tell Them."

And you are bidden to descend the ladder and to tell the saints and to tell the multitude of a light from far-off worlds. When you see the vast spiral of a golden ratio, burning—burning its way through a cosmos—and you see lifestreams unending, themselves forming the ladder that becomes the chain of hierarchy; all of a sudden, the All-Seeing Eye zeros in on the point on the ladder that you occupy. You have been positioned there by Sanat Kumara.

With angels attending, you hold the flame for a level of initiation. Sometimes you think that life is humdrum or you are bored with sameness. But in actuality, you ensoul a light for all who are on the same wavelength of your consciousness. And were you to vacate your position, there would be a vacuum easily seized by fallen ones whose strategy is to unseat the lightbearers from their niche in the ladder of life and then to take those positions and from them to unseat others.

For life is not a single ladder but many ladders crocheted by the Cosmic Virgin. And you climb the ladders of her crocheting, and you form a vast antahkarana that drapes a cosmos like a golden net that is cast into a golden sea. And the niches of light—the knots that are tied—are the points of light that you carry. And by the holding of the net, it is a strong net. And the Lord of life casts down that net to draw in the great multitude of fishes who will see in the sign of Pisces the twin arcs that form the mounting caduceus—a caduceus fashioned of lives victorious in the ascension flame.

How beautiful it is to be in the temple beautiful of the universe, to sense one's self a unique cell in the body of God. How beautiful it is to be one in the universal flame. How beautiful it is to breathe the breath of life. And he who said, "Occupy till I come,"[2] has assigned to you, each one, a situation beautiful to be magnified.

There Are Many Holes in the Net of Life

Now, then, look at the reflection of this golden net. Look at the sea of lives in the earth. Look at the multitudes who are the sheep gone astray and see how the wolves have come to unseat them and to occupy their positions. Beloved ones, there are millions of positions in the great net and network of life that have been abandoned by the sheep who have followed the pied pipers of this age.

O my beloved, the result is many holes in the net of life. And the children of the light do not know how to uphold the standard—the inner blueprint of the net. And therefore, much is gone awry. Much is out of the way of the inner blueprint. And you breathe a sigh as you look from exalted heights with angel bands and you see the gaping holes. And when that net is cast for the harvest of souls, many will pass through, for there are all too few who have taken up the light.

Yet the standard was so strong that he brought. And the ascended masters have set a flaming proof of the Word by example. Have you not heard how often the messengers have wondered how so many, many could be led astray when the truth has been so plain these thousands of years.

But suddenly, the loud ones, the proud ones are all that is heard in the land. Their voices are amplified and multiplied.

I Withdraw the Power of the Fallen Ones

But I, Maximus, withdraw the power they have taken to multiply and amplify their cacophony that has naught to do with the soundless sound and the intensity of the Word. No longer will they be heard, for they have abused the power to multiply the Word. Watch and see.

You think that the monolith of power that they have built cannot come tumbling down in a day. I say to you, the Lord God Almighty has not done it for the very reason that Serapis Bey gave to you—for want of souls to take the place in this race of life, for want of souls who know the name I AM.

But coming to the fore are many angel bands and souls of great worth. And therefore we have deemed that some of that which has been misused may be taken down. For I AM Maximus. And I have descended from the Great Central Sun to come to be among those who have determined to invoke the Word, who have seen through the Mother's eye the great injustice that has been wrought against the children of God.

I have waited long for your call and for your call to reach such a resurgence, a resurrection, a spiral, a spire. For Alpha and Omega promised me aeons ago in the very hour of the Great Rebellion that when certain sons and daughters of light should so accelerate and so expose that rebellion, when certain bands of saints should commune and sound the Word, and when that Word should be heard in far-off worlds, and when the power and the thrust of that Word should reach a certain intensity; then I would be sent to follow the sound back to the source and there to undo the misuse they have made of the light of Maximus.

I Drop a Sound

Therefore, I come. It is yet a limited dispensation.

I show you from the very top of the ladder how I drop a sound. Did you ever think of dropping a sound to the earth and then hearing the reverberation of the sound—a sound that none can hear save the Elohim and the elementals in the thicket and the tiny cricket. Elemental life respond to the sound of the Word while humans do not hear. Their senses are dulled, but the inner sound does sound.

Now with me, watch the earth and its body. Watch for the quivering of the aura of the earth as I drop the sound of the tone of Alpha and Omega.

Ommmmmm

Did you see the quivering of the aura of the earth? [whispered] I sound the sound again. Watch and see by the eye of the Great Silent Watchers.

Eummmmmm

The sound descends. It is a rippling of light. It will accomplish its work.

Now, my beloved, we descend together, for we must be in the earth to catch the reverberation of the sound. It is the sound of love. I smile because I know what is the ultimate ending and beginning of the sound. I know how it will resound in hearts and strike a chord of love. I know, for I am Maximus, and I have been Maximus for a long, long time and space and for a wide, wide eternity. I know, for I have sounded the sound of the Word in other systems of worlds.

By the Word, the Worlds Were Framed

By the Word, the worlds were framed. By the Word, the worlds are unframed.

By the Word and only the Word is the Luciferian creation no more. They know me even as they know you. They have succeeded in postponing the sounding of the sound by casting out their nets—dark nets. They do their fishing at night while children sleep,[3] and they catch the souls and draw them through the astral plane, programming souls asleep to their own net gain.

But it is no more, for with the awakening of the Buddha Gautama, with the awakening of the light of the Cosmic Christ, with the point of contact in the hearts of the few, the cycles roll and the appointed hour is struck. Hear the striking of the bell of the cosmic clock. Understand the timing and the spacing of light.

The self-assurance of God is in the rhythm of the wave, and the cosmic wave is indeed oncoming. It breaks upon the shore of life. And all things are in a state of change. It is the hour of victory and we are at peace. We transfer that peace unto you—peace that is the certain knowing that our God is in the earth in the flame of Sanat Kumara.

The eye of peace is the point of release of the sound. I have sounded two words, syllables of light. The sound will never end. And it will take a million years for that sound to fulfill its cosmic purpose. Immediate effects are noted in the planetary homes. But life is vast, and many evolutions will come and pass through and ascend by the sounding of that tone. You have heard an outer sound, but the inner sound is the sound behind the sound.

Use My Name

I AM Maximus. I maximize light. Now I come by dispensation only. My gift to you—access to my name to multiply the judgment of love, to multiply the resurrection, to multiply the preaching of the Word—these three. Use my name and you will understand the cosmic multiplication of the geometry of the Word. And when this sound has reached again Alpha and Omega by the golden ratio of light, then I will come to tell you of the dispensation that may follow upon the foundation that you will have laid.

I enter the sphere of light. It is tiny by your sight. In cosmos, it is infinite. Within the sphere that I AM, I disappear to earth's evolutions, but I am always here in the sphere of light in the heart of Mother.

Elizabeth Clare Prophet:

Let us remember that Maximus has said we may use his name for three purposes: to maximize or to multiply the judgment, the resurrection, and the preaching of the Word—a tremendous opportunity for our calls and invocations with the promise that when that sound from our hearts has reached a certain increment of light and intensity of sound, he will come again to give us his name to multiply again light dispensations in the earth.

Benediction

Light expand from the heart of the sun.
Light expand from the heart of the earth.
Light expand from the soul of great worth.
Light expand from the heart of the angel.
Light expand from the heart of the elemental.
Light expand from the heart of Maximus.
Lo, I AM THAT I AM.

In the name of the Father and the Mother, in the name of the Son and of the Holy Spirit, be sealed in the light of ascension's flame, and hear the Word, "Lo, I AM made whole. Lo, thou art made whole."

In the name of Sanat Kumara, Amen.

Tell Them

Lanello

Tell them,
Ancient Fires,
How the strata of the rock
Cooled and formed the surface
Of a verdant sphere to be.

Tell them,
Ancient Waters,
Of the coolants of the deep—
Mighty cycles of perfection,
Marine world now we see.

Tell them,
Mighty Atmosphere,
Of blue inspired veil,
Of lacy white cloud cover
Curtained Cosmos does unveil.

Tell them of Creation
That like clockwork telling time
Shows the intricacy of nature
In a network so sublime.

Tell them of a seedling
Filled with patterned destiny.
Tell them of a cedar tall
That through sunshine was to be.

Tell them of a whisper
That was heard within the soul.
Tell them, Ageless Wisdom,
Nature's blessed goal.

Tell them of Reality
That plays hide and seek with men.
Tell them of a Golden Age
That cometh once again.

Tell them of the Buddha
And of Christ upon the hill.
Tell them Truth, Reality
That hungry souls do fill.

Tell them of electric spark
That flashes 'cross the sky.
Speak of Immortality that cradles our humanity—
That one day none shall die.

Speak of Truth
That out the mouth of Christ did manifest,
That Pilate heard and questioned,
That now in truth is blessed.

Speak it loud and speak it long;
Tell in poetry and song
That tall upon the hills of time
An ageless wisdom now does chime—

Carillon bells from celestial towers
Rung by other hands than ours,
Angel voices chiming in
Raise an anthem now to win.

Tell them how that we who read
Can in faith plant vital seed,
Watch them push their shoots right through
Soil and rock and obstacle too—

Thrusting roots into the earth,
Seeking vital essence' worth
And reaching to the sun to claim
That I AM real in God's own Name!

Tell them, then, that darkest night
Waits the first dawn's early light,
That man may see and catch the thought
That God in truth has to us brought
An opportunity so fair—
An answer to a child's own prayer.

Our Father, help us now to be
Selflessly engraft' in Thee—
That our nature then shall be
Like a father's heart of love;
Seeds from heaven up above
Scattered here in garden fair—
Sun and rain in falling there
Can assist the planned delight
And the victory for the right!

Tell them, Father, Ageless One,
Of Thy Nature's Golden Sun.
Tell them of Thy Name and Spirit!
Tell them so that all may hear it!
Tell them so that none may fear it!
Tell them so that all revere it!
Tell them so that none may lose
Life or gift—that all may choose
Now and without fail to see
That only Truth can ever be
Clad with Immortality.

CHAPTER FOURTEEN

The Initiation of the Eighth Ray

The Maha Chohan

And I saw in the right hand of him that sat on the throne a book written within and on the backside, sealed with seven seals.

And I saw a strong angel proclaiming with a loud voice, Who is worthy to open the book, and to loose the seals thereof?

And no man in heaven, nor in earth, neither under the earth, was able to open the book, neither to look thereon.

And I wept much, because no man was found worthy to open and to read the book, neither to look thereon.

And one of the elders saith unto me, Weep not: behold, the Lion of the tribe of Judah, the Root of David, hath prevailed to open the book, and to loose the seven seals thereof.

And I beheld, and, lo, in the midst of the throne and of the four beasts, and in the midst of the elders, stood a Lamb as it had been slain, having seven horns and seven eyes, which are the seven Spirits of God sent forth into all the earth.

And he came and took the book out of the right hand of him that sat upon the throne.

> And when he had taken the book, the four beasts and four and twenty elders fell down before the Lamb, having every one of them harps, and golden vials full of odours, which are the prayers of saints.
>
> And they sung a new song, saying, Thou art worthy to take the book, and to open the seals thereof: for thou wast slain, and hast redeemed us to God by thy blood out of every kindred, and tongue, and people, and nation;
>
> And hast made us unto our God kings and priests: and we shall reign on the earth.
>
> And I beheld, and I heard the voice of many angels round about the throne and the beasts and the elders: and the number of them was ten thousand times ten thousand, and thousands of thousands;
>
> Saying with a loud voice, Worthy is the Lamb that was slain to receive power, and riches, and wisdom, and strength, and honour, and glory, and blessing.
>
> And every creature which is in heaven, and on the earth, and under the earth, and such as are in the sea, and all that are in them, heard I saying, Blessing, and honour, and glory, and power, be unto him that sitteth upon the throne, and unto the Lamb for ever and ever.
>
> And the four beasts said, Amen. And the four and twenty elders fell down and worshipped him that liveth for ever and ever.
>
> Revelation 5:1–14

I AM the Maha Chohan. I am the movement of the Holy Spirit and the sponsor of the seven chohans. Together we stand within this city. And I am the sealing of the eighth ray.

I come with the seven chohans to impart a light. We come determined to cut free those souls who are our own, those who are here and there—the nonaligned ones yearning for alignment yet not knowing the way to go. This is the moment of the opening of the scroll of the decade of the eighties.

We come in the name of Almighty God, for we have a work to work and it is the flame of cosmic integration. It is the light of the eighth ray[1] that by the power of ten does initiate that cycle of initiation unto all souls of light in 1980. Thus, this decade will see those souls who are of the light integrate with the Great God Self.

The process of integration is the flow of God-harmony of the elements of being into the single identity fused in God. Now when the energies of the individual begin to flow according to the flow of the Buddha and the Mother, all elements of the self flow—as when the northern rivers melting in springtime begin to flow with giant pieces of ice, and in the flow these are broken up and the swiftness of the waters comes from the momentum, the intensity and the downward movement.

Thus, the flow of your life brings with it all that is accumulated of the four seasons. And this is the moment of the springtime when the resurrection fire directs and dictates the moment of the flow for integration.

Therefore, the movement of the internal waters of the soul brings the hour when all must come to resolution, for the debris and the blocks of ice and all that comes down the channel of consciousness must be transmuted. For in the moment when the flow arrives at the nexus of the figure eight—which is the cosmic cross of white fire[2]—in that moment, only the crystal clear stream of the river of water of Life[3] may pass through. And if there is untransmuted debris, you see, it will block the orifice and temporarily, then, stop the flow of that fusion of the heart of a soul with the heart of God.

So much so, for the initiates of the path we are not so concerned. For they possess the elements of truth and the wisdom and the science of the Law whereby they can navigate those waters and within those waters, for they are goal-fitted and goal-minded. We are more so concerned with the great multitude of the sheep upon the hillsides who yet move in flocks seeking the Good Shepherds. We are concerned for they, too, must flow with the movement of the initiation of the eighties.

It will be an unparalleled experience. And you might know that the angels are almost breathless in anticipation of the victory and summoning cosmic forces to roll back the fallen ones in their courses who would take advantage of mass flux, all in a state of change, and use it to their own devices.

The Challenge of the Initiation of the Eighth Ray

Beloved ones, the fallen ones know the challenge of the initiation of the eighth ray, and there they go. And they go to confuse and create disorder. And for this purpose the fallen ones have, for a number of decades, been training the youth in guerrilla warfare and in social upheaval and in the takeover of societies and nations. And, therefore, the criminal attitudes of those who do not believe enough in their own goals and ways to work for them within the legitimate structure and framework of cosmic law go outside the Law and attempt to tip the scales out of balance.

They, then, imitate the Lord Christ, who chased the moneychangers out of the temple and overturned their tables.[4] This he did by the action of the Law and by the light of Shiva. And he held the flame for the continuity of the temple and its truth. But those who come to overturn civilization here and there in the nations, they keep no flame of life or order or God-harmony. The living Christ, when throwing the wicked out and pronouncing their judgment, holds the entire planetary balance for the children of the light—not so with those who imitate the great revolutionaries of our Brotherhood who have come with their revolution of light, ages upon ages.

Therefore, I say: Watch and pray, for the treacherous waters come. The water of Life[5] must be the water of change. For transmutation and acceleration and the law of self-transcendence dictates that from the seven rays to the ninth ray—the power of the three times three—there must be self-transformation and the self succeeding the self.

This is the purpose of the eighth ray. It is the ray of integration in preparation for the cosmic consciousness that is to be given as initiation in the 1990s—beloved ones, all of this laying the foundation of Aquarius.

The Word Must Go Forth

Therefore, I am come. I am come with design, with wisdom, and with love. For we are determined that all souls who are tied to the seven chohans of the rays, to the Holy Spirit, and to the World Teachers shall hear and know our summoning. Therefore, we have directed that the Word should go forth as the published Word, as the spoken and the printed Word. Therefore, we have commissioned you to go forth and to speak that Word—to teach it and to preach it, to convey it and to confront all that opposes the mighty truth of life.

The saturation of the planetary body with the light of harmony occurs on many planes—seven rays, seven ways, seven gospels that are to be preached and the coming of the Lamb and the light of Sanat Kumara. Therefore, we are here that you might receive of our Body and of our Blood, of the light of Alpha and Omega, of a nucleus of Great Central Sun energy representing each of the seven rays.

The Lamb and the Lamb's Wife

Therefore, I have come today, myself, to serve you Holy Communion through our messenger. I come to embrace the Lamb and the Lamb's wife. The wife of the Lamb is the soul who is chela of the embodied Lamb. The wife of the Lamb is the light of the ages, sealed in the souls of the hundred forty and four thousand.[6] The wife of the Lamb is the one who walks the path of the alchemical marriage—the union with the Great God Self.

Worthy is the Lamb. Worthy is the Lamb. And the strong angel who cried, "Who is worthy to open the seven-sealed book?"[7] is the angel of the fourth place, the angel of the fourth race—your very own beloved Serapis Bey. He has cried out unto Sanat Kumara, who sitteth upon the great white throne,[8] calling for the opening of the seven-sealed book.

Therefore, in the dispensations of the centuries and the ages, the Lamb worthy is the Son of God who descends out of the great heart of Alpha and Omega into the Matter spheres—spheres that are unredeemed, that are requiring redemption.

The Lamb descends and the Lamb is slain from the foundation of the world of maya. The Lamb who is worthy is the Lamb who ascends, returning to the heart of God, victory fulfilled. The Lamb who is worthy is the one who comes for that initiation of the Lamb that is given to the Son of God who ascends with 100 percent of his karma balanced.

The ascended master, then, who fulfills all initiations of the path, after numerous ceremonies and rituals in the various planes of the four cosmic forces, presents himself before the Ancient of Days, presents the report of the mission—even as the knights who went forth to bind the dragons, to bind the forces of witchcraft returned to Camelot and gave accounting of their deeds and also confessed their sins, received honors and penance and then rest and recreation and back on the next mission of light.

Thus, the ascended Son stands before the Ancient of Days and the four and twenty elders and the four living creatures. And when he is found worthy—worthy in all points of the

Law—then the four and twenty elders and the four beasts bow before that one in recognition that he has become the allness of God and that the allness of God given unto him has returned to God, multiplied by the light of Maximus. And millions of souls in the Matter spheres have been touched by the mission of the Lamb.

The Opening of the Seven-Sealed Book

The one who, then, is worthy to wear the mantle and the crown of the Lamb may take from the hand of the Ancient of Days the seven-sealed book.[9] And the seals are the sealing of the seven rings of the causal body[10] and the seven days of creation and the seven chakras. And the opening of those seals for the transfer of light unto the children of God may come only through the hand of the one who has balanced that 100 percent portion of light and who is found not wanting in all points of the Law.

Therefore, the seven chohans standing before you are the representatives of the Lamb worthy to open the seven-sealed book on the seven rays for the initiation of their chelas. Therefore, the Lord Jesus Christ is pronounced the Lamb who is worthy. And all of Christendom worships the Lamb and sings hosannas and the new song of that Lamb. And indeed it is true—the Lord Jesus Christ is become the Lamb.

My beloved, the name Lamb is the name of the office, then—the office that signifies certain initiations before and after the ascension in the light. Thus, the hour has come for the opening of the seven-sealed book and unto the lightbearers of earth is given a portion—but a portion of the teaching of that book. And that which is allowed in this dispensation is given by Sanat Kumara.

These teachings given so tenderly to you in the *Pearls of*

*Wisdom** are your manna, are your strengthening, are for your path of preparation when you would reinforce the entire planetary initiation of the eighth ray.

Serapis Bey, the strong angel who cries "Who is worthy?" cries that cry by way of summoning candidates for the ascension who will make themselves worthy. Serapis Bey urges candidates within his retreat to fulfill all points of the Law prior to the ascension. And he shows the goal of the initiation of the soul unto the office of the Lamb.

And all who assemble there in the upper classes are eager to qualify. And they are not summoned to the upper classes until they have balanced the seven rays fully and their cup is overflowing with the love and the presence and the soul-identification with the seven chohans. Therefore, simultaneously at Luxor there occurs the initiation of the light of the seven chohans and the advancing spiral moving through the figure eight for the resolution of the Macrocosm within the microcosm.

I AM the Maha Chohan. I have entered this hall carrying the seven-sealed book. I bear it that you might be in the presence of the forcefield of that book and its writing and its wisdom and the recording of Almighty God of the initiations that may come to be given to the embodied saints by the heart and the hand of the embodied Lamb.

The Opportunity of This Decade

I AM here in the fullness of the glory of the ascension flame that is upon the Two Witnesses. Together they stand where I stand and they are the focus for the flow of the figure eight in the holding of the balance of this decade. Mark you well, my beloved, for it is the hour when there can be, if you will it so, the complete flow and the cycling of the light of your causal body through the nexus of the heart of your Christ Self to the

*These are now published in *The Opening of the Seventh Seal: Sanat Kumara on the Path of the Ruby Ray.*

lower spheres of your consciousness.

The light of your causal body directed in its descent by your I AM Presence will come only as swiftly as you can contain the light, tolerate it, assimilate it, become it, and use it effectively as you wield your sword Excalibur in Morya's name.[11] Thus, within your great causal body is light enough to allow you to glow and to glow until the white cube becomes the glowing fervor of your soul in the earth.

Let each individual hold the key to the decision of how much light he can contain within his chakras. It is, after all, neither Sanat Kumara nor Gautama nor Maitreya nor Jesus Christ who will determine what initiations you will receive. But it is always your free will measured by the Law, measured by the reed that is given into the hand of John the Beloved for the measuring of the temple and those who worship in the temple of God.[12]

This is the hour for the measuring of the ability of the soul to contain light. It is the prophecy of the eleventh chapter of the Book of Revelation. And before the prophesying of the Two Witnesses goes forth abroad in the world by every means of communication, there is the moment when John the Beloved moves within the inner court, coming and measuring with the rod, like unto the reed, measuring the light quotient of every soul committed to the seven chohans, to the World Teachers, and to the Holy Spirit.

The angels walk the earth, angels of John the Beloved. And there is a moment, almost, as it were, a silence in heaven for the space of half an hour. And the moment is the interval of light for the preparation of the transfer from the initiations of the seven rays to the eighth ray.

If you have newly found the path and the teaching, it does not matter. For cosmos accelerates. You may pick up all of the stitches of the crocheting of the seamless garment. You may yet weave the deathless solar body.[13] You may yet pass through the halls of the retreats of the seven chohans even while there is abuilding in your temple the outline of the mighty figure eight of the Spirit-Matter cosmos.

I Summon You to the Path

I AM the Maha Chohan. I hold in my right hand the seven-sealed book. May you be worthy and may the Lamb who is worthy be the Son of God who elects to be the elector of the four and twenty elders.

The Path! The Path! To the Path, I summon you! At last! At last, to rise from the morass of earth! At last, to hear the certain voice. At last, to know that there is a way to go, that I AM the way, that the I AM in you is the Word, that the Word in you is personified in the embodied Lamb and that the Word in the messenger is indeed the Word of God, is indeed the Person. At last, at last, souls of earth can know the homeward path is open.

Open the way! Open wide the way, for we have come to San Francisco today to announce the procession of light! And all who have graduated from earth's schoolrooms under these seven chohans, the World Teachers and myself have gathered here in a mighty demonstration of light to say, "*See!* We are here. We are the ten thousand times ten thousand and the thousands of thousands robed in white who sing the hosannas and the praises unto the Lamb and the Ancient of Days. For we have come up through the school of hierarchy. We have passed through the retreats of the seven chohans and we witness unto the Path—the certain path of life victorious over hell and death. We are here as the Lord Jesus Christ places in the hand of his vicar[14] the keys of hell and death that they may be bound in the earth as they are bound in heaven."

Understand the meaning of the binding of hell and death.

It is the final initiation of the one ascending—the binding of the power of the entire astral plane to intrude itself upon the children of the light. Therefore, the summoning of the Word and the Word that is manifest and the key of the Word is the binding of hell and death as the entire hierarchy of God ascended holds back the astral sea and it is parted, and the children of the light pass through unto the Path, the path of victory!

I Warn of Danger

I AM the Maha Chohan. I warn of the treacherous waters of the astral sea. I warn of danger lurking that surely is overcome in the presence of the Lamb and the saints. I warn of a path filled with light and glory opposed by all who are threatened by that path.

Therefore, walk—not with head tilted back or head tilted down, for in too much heaven-gazing you will lose your ground, and in too much earth-gazing you will lose your balance and your perspective. Therefore, look straight ahead. Look into the eyes of God who is before you in the person of the Faithful and True.

Look before you and look on the line of the horizon where the setting sun and the rising sun show the cyclic flow of the figure eight glowing with the light of the nexus. Thus, at the dawn and at the dusk is the celebration of the hour of the soul's daily ritual of passing through the nexus of the solar light consciousness.

I AM the Maha Chohan. By the application of all that you know, you will pass through the initiations of the eighties God-victorious. But apply you must and trust you must in the light of the ascended masters, your own God Self, your own Christ Self and in the nexus of the figure eight who is Sanat Kumara, the Eternal Lamb incarnate in the embodied Lamb. For the nexus is the key to this victory.

And you have heard of psychic forces hurling their psychic spheres, hurling their psychic predictions into those years. You have heard of astrological signs and portents and the Jupiter effect[15]—all of this—and the prognostications of war and the rumors of war and the massive buildup of power East and West and all of the manipulations. All of this, all of this is destined to be dissolved in the white flame of the fourth plane. And the fourth plane is the seat of Sanat Kumara. And the sign of the emerald is the sign of that plane.

Let Shepherds Rise

Therefore, if it is destiny, and fiery destiny at that, then, in the earth, positioned as the strong pilasters,* are the souls of light who will be the fulfillment of that destiny. Let shepherds rise from among you.

Rise, shepherds, and *seize* the Book of Life! For the Book of Life is the Everlasting Gospel and the angel flies in the heaven to preach that gospel to the men who dwell upon the earth.[16]

Take the teachings of the Maha Chohan. Take the teachings of the seven chohans. And as a mother feeding her children, take the teachings crumb by crumb, morsel by morsel and place them in the mouth of the little children. Learn as you go and go as you learn, for there is no time to wait.

Take the books. Be armoured with the tapes and listen to the Word and then speak the Word. For that Everlasting Gospel is the composite of all of the teaching of the Great White Brotherhood delivered by the witnesses in many forms and in the lesser gospels.

So it is come. So the mighty angel flying in the heavens is indeed the flying eagle.[17] And the flying eagle is your very own beloved Sanat Kumara who comes on time, ahead of time, on schedule in the nexus of the hourglass to deliver the Word

***pilaster:* a rectangular column, especially one projecting from a wall

whereby the evolutions of earth are saved to the uttermost in the eighties.

I AM come. *Rise,* O shepherds of the people! For now I would feed you my manna of light, and therefore I would bless the bread and the wine. Let it be brought to me.

[16-second pause]

Blessing of Holy Communion

Hail, O Elohim! Hail, O seraphim! For I AM come for the sealing of the light of these souls. I invoke the light of Victory. I invoke the light of the legions of Archangel Michael.

I AM the Maha Chohan. And with this ritual and with this consecration, I seal every heart of light who will carry my vibration to the ends of the earth. I summon my angels as guardian spirits of the life, the temple, the soul, the mind, the heart, the consciousness of you who have the courage to be the shepherds of the people of earth.

O tender sheep upon the hillsides, I send you love and comfort and promise that the true shepherds are coming. O tender sheep, feel my love, for in this hour it is love that you understand. And when you receive my shepherds and know the voice of the Son of God in them, you shall indeed hear the voice of the Almighty One and follow it. And then wisdom will crown the love that you are and that you have.

O my beloved, if it were only love that were necessary. I tell you these sheep have much love, but they are lacking in the balance of wisdom. And therefore, in order to balance the threefold flame, they must first have the wisdom of the Law, and therefore by the balance of wisdom and love receive the initiation of power and with power, the resolution of life and with the resolution of life, entrance into the halls of Luxor.

Therefore I transfer my Body and my Blood that none shall be able to pluck one of these out of the hand of the Father or out of the hand of the Son. I make the sign of the cosmic cross of white fire that none of the true children of God may be lost to the false gurus and the wolves in sheep's clothing. By the authority of our Word, we bind them in earth and in heaven.

> *Be bound* by Alpha, by Omega! I AM the Maha Chohan. I *tear* from you your garments this day! I *tear* from you your garments! Be *exposed* unto all the world and unto all of the lightbearers! Be *exposed,* ye fallen ones! I *tear* from you your garments!
>
> I AM the Maha Chohan! You shall no longer defile the light of the Holy Ghost nor the person of Sanat Kumara in the Mother flame nor the person of the Father or the Son nor the person of the witnesses, the saints or the great multitude. I *tear* from you your garments!
>
> Now receive the initiation of the station of the cross. Be stripped of your garments! Stand naked as you had him stand before all the world. He stood naked and he was not found wanting. Now you shall stand naked and all shall see the defilement of your being and the being of God, for thou art the abomination of desolation standing in the holy place where it ought not.[18] I *tear* from you your garments, ye fallen ones! Be *exposed!* Be *bound* in the earth and in the heaven!

In the name of Sanat Kumara, in the name of the cosmic cross of white fire, it is done! And I charge this Body and this Blood of Christ with the full impetus of my Word that you might witness unto the Holy Spirit's judgment in this hour of those who have defiled love—the true love of the Guru and the chela, the true love of the Lamb and the Lamb's wife, the true love of twin flames and of the Almighty for his own.

I AM THAT I AM, and the LORD God is come into his temple and he will not be moved. I will not be moved. You will not be moved. Therefore, come. Come to this altar now and receive of me and mine own. For I AM here to atone because I love you.

[Holy Communion is served.]

I Announce Your Names before the Throne of the Lamb

My light body you are and you are become myself. Portion by portion is the Holy Spirit granted unto the soul. You have stood and you still stand.

Before the throne of the Lamb, I announce your names, each and every one. I speak your given name in this life and I speak the new name.[19] And the recording angels have written that you have stood to be the shepherds of the people. Now all of heaven will converge upon that soul who says, "Here am I, Lord, send me."[20]

Therefore, watch and wait, for by many means will the teaching come—by our teachers taught and our books that we have wrought. We will raise you up in proportion as you raise up the light of the Son of man within you.

I AM the Maha Chohan. I have come to embrace you as of old. I hold you in my arm of light. I hold you to my heart. Now be with Sanat Kumara, the eagles that take flight to carry with the angel the Everlasting Gospel.

Lo, I AM Who I AM. Lo! I AM come and it is sealed.

CHAPTER FIFTEEN

The Opening of the Door to the Octaves of Light

Archangel Gabriel

So Jesus came again into Cana of Galilee, where he made the water wine. And there was a certain nobleman, whose son was sick at Capernaum.

When he heard that Jesus was come out of Judaea into Galilee, he went unto him, and besought him that he would come down, and heal his son: for he was at the point of death.

Then said Jesus unto him, Except ye see signs and wonders, ye will not believe.

The nobleman saith unto him, Sir, come down ere my child die.

Jesus saith unto him, Go thy way; thy son liveth. And the man believed the word that Jesus had spoken unto him, and he went his way.

And as he was now going down, his servants met him, and told him, saying, Thy son liveth.

Then inquired he of them the hour when he began to amend. And they said unto him, Yesterday at the seventh hour the fever left him.

So the father knew that it was at the same hour, in the which Jesus said unto him, Thy son liveth: and himself believed, and his whole house.

> This is again the second miracle that Jesus did, when he was come out of Judaea into Galilee.
>
> John 4:46–54

Hail, O infinite fire! I AM Gabriel of the Sun! I AM come to stand in the midst of the congregation of the righteous!

I AM the Angel of the Annunciation, and I come to seal you in the promise of love's victory won. I come to seal you, and I touch you now upon the brow. My hand is upon you, O soul. I AM here and I touch you, that you might be made whole within the inner matrix of thy life. This wholeness is the light that is unto the ascension. For you have decreed it, God has decreed it, and I have come to confirm, to ratify that decree.

I AM known as the Angel of Consolation, therefore I bring consolation to the soul of the seed of the Woman in the very heart of the earth. I bring consolation in the hour when souls are yearning to be free and yet know not the way to go. I bring consolation to the lightbearers who see the great harvest and know that the laborers are few. I bring consolation from the LORD, and I AM here. And my legions of light come bearing the banner of divine friendship, for legions of Gabriel come forth to befriend the souls of light who will walk as bearers of ascension's flame.

You have a message to trumpet over the plains, over the mountains, the lands, and the sea, into the very depths of the souls of the earth. The message of the ascension is the message that you bear—the goal of life. It is the garment that you wear. Not only do you speak it but you are examples of the ascending souls. Therefore, let thy life come into conformity with the principles of the Word.

I AM Come to Reinvest the Earth with a Certain Knowledge of the Goal of the Ascension

The living example of the ascending one is what the world needs. For I have walked up and down the world this week.

I have walked in the streets, in the little towns, and in the large centers of population. I have gazed into the eyes, the hearts, and the souls of the people, and I have scarcely found even less than a percentage of the entire earth body who pays any attention to the ascension in the light with an awareness that is adequate even to approach the sword of the ascension flame, the person of the ascension in the hierarch Serapis Bey.

I find *wanting* the basic knowledge of the law of the Path! I find *wanting* even the spark of desire! For mothers have not implanted in their children the desire for eternal life and the certitude that eternal life can be won here and now. And the mothers have not transferred that hope, that dream, that all, because they have not been God-taught.

Therefore I am come to reinvest the earth with a certain knowledge of the goal of the ascension, and I place my light and my aura, impressed with the light of Alpha and Omega, here in this city. I hide it not, yet I seal it in the hearts of devotees. I place it in the hills, in the high places. And where there is a certain monument of light, I will place that forcefield and that hope. Let this flame of hope burn. Let it increase. Let the light of hope burn on.

The ascension flame—twofold light, Alpha and Omega—consumes all imbalances and all challengers of the pure stream of the living flame. And all who pervert that flame have already been served notice by emissaries of the Goddess of Liberty. Let them repent! Let them come into alignment in the service of the light of the Mother, which they long ago betrayed!

The Requirement of the Hour

I AM Gabriel, and I bring the Word of Alpha and Omega to you. It is the requirement of the hour that souls of humanity *pay attention to the ascension fire as the goal of life!*

For this is the moment when many shall move into its

currents and others shall step into the flame and pass through the second death.

We are at the end of an age! We come to teach, to preach, and also to admonish. We admonish that those who have gone out of the way swiftly return to the light and become true servants of the light, and we bring our love and we penetrate your soul and we reveal to you the footsteps of the Path.

You have heard the Mother say that Serapis Bey could not allow all of his works to be published in this year, the year of the publishing of the *Dossier.* For he said that if all of his dictations were to be published in the same year, the amount of light penetrating the earth could cause cataclysm. Understand, therefore, that he has required the carrying of the light of the *Dossier*—its teaching, its transfer—to many hearts. And he has promised to review with the Brotherhood of Luxor the publication of others of his teachings in the coming year.

Understand, then, what it means when a single book of ascended masters' teachings have widespread dissemination. It means that the earth must change, for better or for worse. For that light stirs up all, and all must come to the surface. And therefore, transmutation is required. And we the archangels are watchful, lest the imbalance that might occur be too much for the bearing of the lightbearers and even of those who know not of the light.

Therefore we hold our conferences, but these seminars and retreats into the living flame are for a multifaceted purpose. They are for the increase of the light of the devotee and for the sealing of the guru-chela relationship. They are for the clearing of the cities. They are for the binding of millions of discarnates in the very body of the earth itself, which must be taken to those secure places in the octaves of light where their evolution may be accelerated. And those other discarnates that are of the form of mass entities, they then must be consumed by the flame.

Gather Together and Unite in the Living Flame

Mankind are daily in the process of creating more and more psychic effluvia. Therefore it becomes the work of devotees to gather wheresoever the Lamb goeth,[1] there to give the Word. For the multiplication of the dynamic decrees by those present creates the great geometry of light whereby the worlds are sustained.

We have told you that without the circle of the Guru and the devotees, all of cosmos would not be sustained, and therefore here and there throughout the universes the Lamb is gathered with a nucleus of lightbearers. And the hundred and forty and four thousand is the alchemical number of those who are required to contain the light of a single Lamb, the single forcefield of the one imbued with light.

Therefore it is our desire to increase the numbers of devotees upon the planetary body. It is our desire to fill the slots in the great chain of hierarchy. It is our desire to see that number—that number of Maximus himself—become the great leaven that the woman took and hid in three measures of meal,[2] that the whole leaven of these planes of consciousness might be leavened by those gathered in the etheric consciousness within the Lamb, within the retreat.

Therefore did Saint Germain secure freedom of worship, freedom of the press, freedom of religion, and above all, the freedom to assemble. Without the freedom to assemble, beloved ones, we could not fulfill this principle of the Law. And therefore let it be guarded, for in many nations it has already been cut off. For the fallen ones and the seed of the wicked, who know that their judgment is come, understand the power of the people when the people unite in the living flame.

Therefore value your meetings and your services, and know that because you are able to gather together in twos and threes and hundreds and thousands, therefore is the flame multiplied.

And do not neglect this most important aspect of community wherever you are in your towns and cities.

Let it be at least two and three, and let it be that you suffer inconvenience to come together several times a week to reinforce the violet flame. For you do not know, beloved ones, how important it is for the souls who are coming into embodiment and for the little children that these discarnate entities be cleared in our ascension services and that the healing light go forth.

The Ascension Is the Process Whereby All of Life Is Lifted Up

So much is accomplished that I, Gabriel, must come as the Angel of the Annunciation and the Angel of the Consolation to tell you that though your eyes see not all that is done, the cities of this nation, even in this hour, would not have continued in the balance in which they hold were it not for the dynamic decrees of the students of this activity. And over the years of our service there have been numerous ascensions of chelas who have graduated from these very ranks. Some of you have not known them. They kept the flame sure and strong. They remained well into the years of their eighties and their nineties and then took their leave quietly, almost unobserved.

Your own Clara Louise Kieninger left a forcefield of ascension's flame in Berkeley, California. And by that forcefield and that flame there is anchored there a light of purity that has guarded many souls from going down the wrong path and straying away from the light—that path of drugs and anti-light and anti-America and all that has come forth out of the pit through certain individuals who have begun their anti-revolution there.[3] It is a revolution "anti" the living light of the Word in you all. And though freedom goes by many banners, the freedom to deny the light of the soul and the upholding of it is not freedom but is the license taken by the fallen ones.

But, beloved ones, you do not see how much worse conditions could be were it not for the ascension of that single soul. And there have been many more and some beyond the folds of this activity. The ascension is the process whereby all of life is lifted up, and your decrees have cleared the way for many innocent lifestreams to be tethered to their God Self and to be spared untold burdens of karma and of disease and of the breaking down of the great wheels of life in this nation.

You have only to journey beyond the United States to realize how accelerated, how high the astral waters are where there are not forcefields of light. And thus Saint Germain has called in his Mission Amethyst Jewel for that focus in Vancouver and Mexico City.[4] And we cannot wait through another solstice. We must have the light of those forcefields anchored, and we yet call forth recruits.

Some have volunteered and more are needed, for the teaching centers are the veritable wellsprings of life. And therefore I speak to all devotees: When you enter the teaching center, you enter an outer focus of El Morya and of Saint Germain. It is a great privilege to tend the flame, but some have come and become bored with the keeping of the flame, for they have not seen the true vision of what is given to the cities—all of the cities of the earth—by the multiplication of the dedicated souls.

Therefore, Camelot is come again and again wherever there is that teaching center and that study group. And these nuclei of light are for the setting of the matrix for communities of the Holy Spirit to light up the planet for the beginning of the golden age. There must be many communities, but they must be under our hierarchy. For unless a person of the Holy Spirit anointed by the chohans be in the position of leadership, there is but an amalgam of human consciousness and a degeneration of the inner purpose.

There must be the sacred-heart chalice within each center.

Therefore, we seek shepherds. For with those leaders able to carry that flame, we can begin again. And Morya and Saint Germain have their eye on other nations where the light must go forth. For the rising of the astral plane through human creation does definitely threaten nations that are destined to hold the light of freedom in this decade and for the fulfillment of this century.

I speak of India and of Chananda's call long ago for a teaching center there.[5] Well, it is not in the distant future. But I say that those of you who would carry the light there must become strong and true. You must become Excalibur,[6] sharpened and ready to do battle with the Indian false hierarchy and the false teachings and to bear a light unto a people who know the Mother intimately.

India is the home of the Mother and the home of the great adepts, and therefore the light comes out of the West and goes unto the East for the completion of the squaring of the circle. There are souls here who will not ascend until they see their day fulfilled on that land of India, for you have a mission and you have a work to complete. And if you sense this in your heart, come to our retreat, come to Camelot and to the Ashram of the World Mother. For we will not send you forth without proper preparation, for we know what goes before you. Legions of angels lead the way and answer your call, but you must face untold darkness as well as light, all telling.[7]

Serapis Bey Places His Electronic Presence in the Teaching Centers

Therefore, we would dot the earth swiftly with centers of light. And therefore we bring you the message of joy, of holding the flame, of ascension temples around the world. For in this retreat Serapis Bey announces to you, by my Word and by my flame, that he will now join El Morya and Saint Germain and set his forcefield of ascension light in every teaching center. And therefore he will place his Electronic Presence wherever there is a teaching center, wherever there are those who are willing to dedicate their life to the opening of the door to the octaves of light in the name of Sanat Kumara.

My beloved, it is a privilege and an honor to be called to serve in the teaching centers, and the Darjeeling Council depends on chelas of the will of God to extend all of the teachings, principles, activities, life, and love of Camelot to those centers.

Beloved ones, those who are the manipulators of World Communism, those who aid and abet it through world capitalism, they have determined to destroy the cities of the free nations. They have set about that destruction by many avenues to corrupt the youth, to demoralize the people, to break up the families and the homes, to introduce new lows of materialism and greed, to corrupt the governments of the cities and to make of them a mass mechanization. They have sought to tear down the flame of life within the cities, and we have sent our chelas to build up that flame of life.

I will tell you that without this teaching center in San Francisco, the Goddess of Purity could not have diverted the center of the recent earthquake apart from this city[8] and there would have been much greater destruction in San Francisco, as has been predicted by the fallen ones and the psychics and as is due this city for the wanton misuse of the sacred fire. . . . That karma that was on Sodom and Gomorrah could well have fallen upon San Francisco in this very year but for the chelas of the flame who determined to keep that flame, but for the service of the light and the messengers coming here.

Beloved ones, I open your eyes that you may see that the value of life of the individual is tremendous to the cosmos. And therefore we look for quality and not quantity. The single heart that beats with the heart of Serapis twenty-four hours a day is the heart that is the Keeper of the Flame of Life for millions within a city. And that heart does counteract such infamy and degradations that I dare not even speak of them—those practices of Satanism and of blood ritual and murder that continue to the present hour.

Beloved ones, this abomination indeed upsets elemental life, and expiation is required by the Holy Spirit. Therefore the people know not the danger that is upon them as a Damocles sword, nor do they know the danger that is spared them by the humble chela unnoticed by the world and sometimes scarcely noticed by his peers—that chela who has the constancy to know that the power of Astrea and of the violet flame makes all the difference in the preservation of worlds.

Karma and Cataclysm

You who can see and hear and listen, you who with Hercules are accustomed to the saving of worlds, you then will know whereof I speak and receive the charge of life that I give to you.

Have not all the scientists and psychics predicted their earthquakes? Beloved ones, cataclysm comes only by edict of the Karmic Board as it transfers through elemental life the necessary adjustments in the earth.

Do you think that the LORD God withdraws his hand and allows accidents to happen in the earth? There is not a rain, not a hailstorm, not a tornado that does not come because of the necessity to expiate human karma and the misuse of the sacred fire.

Therefore the Law itself does act. And often when the great mercy of heaven would intercede on behalf of human life, we are not allowed. Therefore we stand back and our angels move in to bind up those who are burdened, who may lose their homes or even the life of family members. For we come, we minister, we love, we soothe, and we pray. But we cannot stay the hand of karma when that karma descends by the Law itself.

Astral Forces Must Be Bound and Removed

Therefore understand that there are forces abroad in the earth and in the astral plane who manipulate mankind's karma and attempt to use that energy to exaggerate the returning karma. And therefore the practice of voodoo is rampant against these United States, against the lightbearers, against the Mother herself.

Voodoo and witchcraft out of the Caribbean, out of certain forcefields in this nation, even in Central and South America and out of Africa, that voodoo that is practiced against the light would long ago have caused serious problems to your activity and yourselves. But the light of God that never fails in your dynamic decrees is the light of Elijah. And all of the altars of Baal torn down by the mighty Gideon of old[9] cannot equal the altar of the heart where the threefold flame burns, where the chela does worship fearlessly in fearlessness flame!

Therefore there is consternation among the fallen ones, for they have not been able to hurt or defile in all my holy mountain, saith the LORD God of hosts![10] For he is in the midst of Israel![11]

Therefore, *charge* in the name of Archangel Michael! *Charge,* and see how the rolling of the violet flame and the thunderous calls to Astrea send legions of demons into the very forcefield of Astrea to be bound and removed from the planetary body!

We clear from the within to the without, and therefore the signs and wonders that some seek as proof of our witness are not forthcoming. For the calls of our chelas touch to the very depths of the astral plane, and the work of the messenger is unto the clearing of the pit itself.

Therefore that which is removed by these invocations are the unseen forces of the entire subconscious, electronic belt of the planetary body. And therefore does life continue. For these are the very forces projected upon the screen of life, even by prophecy itself, and prophecy is the warning of Almighty God. And that prophecy that is the result of the projection on the screen of life of coming events, of coming karma, has often been set aside by the Word of the devotees.

Welcome to the Real Path of the Ascension

You who have come newly into our aura, welcome. You have had a strong cup to drink in this retreat. You have heard many teachings. You have seen how the real chelas of life are tutored for the real calling of defending the innocent. You have seen the demands of the real Gurus.

I ask you, do they compare in any way to the false paths that have led you astray? I see and I know that there is no comparison! There is none who can equal the light of a Serapis Bey, of El Morya, of Saint Germain, nor deliver the ultimate freedom of the path of the ascension!

Did you think that we would present to you a single formula and that you could write it down and keep that piece of paper and read it once a day and thereby know that you would ascend?

The ascension path, the path of the golden ratio, golden spiral, is an enigma until you grasp the flame of love and understand the person of the Lamb and the Presence of God—seen yet unseen, known yet unknown.

He humbled himself, fashioned himself as a man like other men, walked among them, was so like his disciples as to be scarcely recognizable.[12] Therefore the Lamb cometh, the Lamb goeth forth, and often disappears from the midst of his adversaries. For they do not see him as he is. They do not know him as he is. They see by their corrupt consciousness. They see only the corruptible one. They have no vision of the Incorruptible One! But the sheep of the Good Shepherd, they see and know the Incorruptible One. They understand the mysteries.

The mysteries that are told are not the mysteries that I tell. The mysteries that are told are the keys, and only those who are of the light can take those keys and turn the lock to the inner retreat.

The mysteries spoken in the parables of Christ, the teachings of the ascended masters, they are keys only to devotees. Did you ever stop to consider that fact? It is a living truth. To speak the mystery to one not quickened in the light, to one who is of the seed of the wicked, it makes no difference. He has not the vibration or the inner light to take the mystery and thereby open the door to the secret chamber of the heart.

The mysteries are always sealed except to the Lamb and the initiates of the Lamb. We fear not the publishing abroad of our Word, for only the souls of light can take that Word and live forever.

The Meaning of Divine Friendship

I AM Gabriel. I AM the friend of the Mother. I AM the friend of the Mother's friends. I AM the friend of all who befriend the ascended masters and their chelas. My legions bear the banner of friendship, for we desire that you should know the meaning of divine friendship.

Some of you have longed for a true friend, one to whom you could speak, pour out your heart, share every part of your soul. Some of you have been disappointed again and again. You have sought a friend in father and mother and brother and sister and associates through all of your life, but the friend whom you have sought you have not found.

Have you been betrayed? It is the story of every lightbearer. Have you been persecuted? Thereby you know you are of the light.

I come to communicate divine friendship. It is a cup for which you must reach. For when you seek limited friendship, in limitation, beloved ones, you receive what you seek. If you desire human comfort, now it will come; now it will be withheld. But if you reach up for divine friendship and divine comfort, the cup is given. But you must return the cup.

The ascended masters and angels are loyal friends to the uttermost. We are loyal. We share a trust. As we give our friendship, committing ourselves in loyalty undying, we expect the same. We expect our friends upon earth to shun evil and the ways of evil. We expect friends on earth to set their house in order and to seek companions of light and to not share our cup with our betrayers. When we give our cup, it is for our friend. It is not for the friend to give away to those who cannot be our friends, for they have not tarried with the Lamb or the Lamb's wife.

We do not give our light for it to be squandered upon those who will not get their own light on the path of initiation. It is not your privilege to give the ascended masters' light to those who turn and use it for their lusts, for their material gain, for their success, or even for their physical health, when they have not paid the price of devotion to Almighty God.

The Cosmic Honor Flame Is the Flame of the Ascension

I AM Gabriel. I AM the friend of God. I do not compromise my friendship with him for friendship with those who have betrayed him.

There is a cosmic honor flame! Live by it! Serve it!

And know what it means to have access to the courts of heaven! Know what it means to speak the name of Gabriel and to have Gabriel at your side. Consider the price. The cosmic honor flame is the flame of the Holy Spirit! It is the flame of the ascension!

All who have not the flame, I say of them, they shall not pass into the circle of our oneness, into the guru-chela relationship! They shall not cross over the line of the circle of our wholeness!

Therefore, search the soul. For I have one thing yet to say, and it is this: Examine your consciousness, confess your sins, wash your robes, and do not withhold from God or from the messenger any compromise of the Law or of the Path.

For when you entertain an untruth, a falsehood, when you withhold the knowledge that should be given, in that moment you have severed your tie to the messenger and to our Brotherhood.

It is the Law that is operable, and therefore the early Church set the practice of the confession of sins. You cannot compensate for falsehood, for deception, by violet-flame decrees or calls to Astrea. Let your house be aligned!

The Speck of Dust upon the Pane of Glass

There is a certain individual who passed from the screen of life out of this activity who had withheld from the messenger information concerning a serious breach of the code of conduct. Yet that individual appeared to be a sincere devotee and attended many conferences. That withholding and that compromise of the Law was not balanced by any other sacrifice made, for it became that that sacrifice was a substitute for obedience.[13]

Do not think that you can draw down a curtain of light and cover over those rationalizations of the mind. There is a flame! It is the cosmic honor flame! You must be at peace with your God, with your Christ Self.

I do not say that you should become the victim of the accuser of the brethren or the condemnation of the hordes of darkness. I do not say that you should somehow have a psychological complex. I do not threaten you. I speak the Law! I speak the law of purity!

If you would ascend, you must confess your sin, repent of your sin, then cease sinning and not go back and take the forbidden fruit and think that heaven will wink. It may very well be that heaven will wink—but don't count on it.

Heaven sees virtue. Virtue may very well swallow up vice, but don't count on it. For the Law is written that every jot and tittle must be balanced and settled.[14]...

The messenger is the representative of the Karmic Board and therefore should be apprised. Do not bypass the messenger, then, and fancy that by writing letters to the ascended masters and burning them, you can live by the cosmic honor flame.

When there are souls in the community who withhold the truth, they weaken the forcefield of the community and therefore carry that additional karma of sin against the community as well as against the direct relationship to the messenger.

John the Baptist did not come preaching repentance without a cause. And Jesus Christ, after he (John) was thrown in prison, took up the very same cause, saying, "Repent ye: for the kingdom of heaven is at hand."[15] They spoke of the consciousness of God at hand, at the very door. But it cannot be assimilated until you set your house in order.

This, therefore, is my message. Do not overlook and swallow, then, the whole whale while straining out the little fishes. Whether the great whale, whether the little fishes, whether a camel or a gnat, beloved ones, you never know what is the speck of dust upon the pane of glass that makes your soul no longer transparent.

Serve the Light, and the Light Will Serve You

I AM Gabriel. I was the friend of Abraham, who was the friend of God.[16] I AM the friend of prophets. I AM the friend of all who enter the path of the ascension.

I have spoken forthrightly! Would you not? Would you not seek to avert in souls on the Path the same fate suffered by the one I have described?

How will that karma be balanced? Will another embodiment be required? Perhaps. But the same individual in the same period of time could have made his ascension, as you would say, "hands down," but for the deception and the misuse of the light of God.

Let the heart's motive be opened, as the Book of Life is opened and the secrets of men's hearts are known. Let the desire body be purified.

If you desire to ascend, then I say, desire it with your whole being, your whole mind, your whole consciousness. Do not trifle with the Law, and the Law will not trifle with you.

Become the friend of the Law, and the Law will *work* for you! And the sails of your soul shall billow full with the Holy Spirit, and the earth itself shall rise up to propel you on your mission, and elemental life will serve you. Serve the light, and the light will serve you.

Now I command in the name of the living Word, let the foul and unclean spirits come out of the subconscious of these souls who would be free! *Bind* them, O living Word! *Bind* them, Almighty God! *Bind* them, Alpha! *Burn* through! You have *no power* to imprison these souls any longer!

I AM Gabriel. *Come out!* For I have lit a fire. Be *burned* in that fire! Be *burned* in that fire! Be *burned,* I say!

For I stand, and in the name of the LORD I bind you, and my legions bind you, and these souls of the light shall walk henceforth in the light and be free *if they will it so!*

Do you will it so, my souls? [Audience replies, "Yes!"]

I Love You unto the Finish!

I say, I love you unto the finish! Let us now fight the good fight and run in the race. For the race is unto the victors of the flame!

I AM Gabriel. I stand. I still stand. And I will be at your side until you no longer desire my friendship or until you compromise it so that the Great Law requires that I depart. So be it.

I have offered you my heart. I will not take it back except by the command of Almighty God.

I choose to kneel before the light within your heart.

[22-second pause]

I AM Gabriel, which standeth in the Presence of God![17] I kneel before Alpha and Omega, and I kneel before the company of saints.

> *LORD God Almighty, bless them that they might go forth in thy name. I worship the light! I worship God! And I succor the soul becoming the light!*
>
> *I implore the Godhead: Send thy legions for the guarding of these souls unto the Victory. And give them, O God, the courage to come clean before thy altar and to confess the truth and the error of life, and therefore to be free.*
>
> *Behold, ye shall know the truth, and the truth shall make you free!*[18]
>
> *Word of the living Christ, go forth as the two-edged sword and set my captives free.*

O my beloved, I AM always and always your friend, Gabriel of the light!

CHAPTER SIXTEEN

The Spirit Cup and the Matter Cup

When I saw Saint Germain's portrait for the first time at the age of eighteen, it was love at first sight. And from that time to the present moment I have learned what it means to love Saint Germain. It means to communicate his message and his Word.

Jesus said, "If you love me, keep my commandments."[1] Saint Germain has given us his message, and I have found that it is a very unpopular message. I have found that I could be far more popular among many more people if I didn't speak his message.

His message challenges what is popular in the world today. It challenges sloth and indulgence and everything from the free-love movement to the free-speech movement of Berkeley. It challenges World Communism, it exposes the manipulators of capitalism, the multinational corporations, it challenges the Watchers,[2] and it challenges the carnal mind within the individual.

When I was first being trained to be a messenger, Mark told me that it was very difficult to take a message from Saint Germain and I would have to go through much training before my mind could mesh with the complexity of his mind. I have learned that this is true, and I have also learned that the cosmic consciousness of Saint Germain has the handle on the whole problem of Light and Darkness on the planet. The problem of evil, its choices, its embodiment, is not simple; if it were so simple, men long ago would have discovered the solution, and we would be on our way.

I didn't understand the problem until Saint Germain explained it to me; and he has taught it to me over many years. He has brought to me people, research, information. He has taken me to the Royal Teton Retreat, he has shown me records. In all levels of consciousness he has educated my soul, my mind, and my heart to understand.

And the first thing you have to understand about the message is the reading of vibration—because many people come speaking truth or part truths, many people come supposedly with good will, wanting to help people, but their methods may be in error and they may lead to destruction. The motive behind the message is key. Because if men's motives are impure their message is impure.

Mother's Manifesto

On July 4, 1976, I stood on the platform at George Washington University in Washington, D.C., and I was commissioned by the Brotherhood to write *Mother's Manifesto*. A manifesto is a statement, a declaration of intent, of platform, of motive. What is *Mother's Manifesto?*

It is the presentation of the real teachings of God as pertaining to your identity, your I AM Presence, your Christ Self, and the homeward path. It is the whole body of the ascended masters' teachings that have to do with your spiritual life. That is the Spirit cup of the manifesto.

There is also a Matter cup. Once you are aligned with the Godhead, you know who you are, where you are going, you know the science of the Word, then you must also drink the

Matter cup. And so the manifesto on the Matter cup has to do with every perversion on the planetary body of that principle statement of the truth of being, of the I AM THAT I AM and the indwelling Christ and the flame of God, the path of karma, reincarnation, and the ascension.

There are many perversions of that statement of truth, the original truth with which our souls were endowed. The perversions run through every area and field of human life. Of course, that which is most important to life becomes education, government and the economy, science—and of course, religion is the Spirit cup. We find that the fallen ones have set themselves citadels of power in Church and State, and in the State they have manipulated government by manipulating the economies of the nations. They have come to control the wealth of nations, hence their leaders.

So *Mother's Manifesto* is being distilled, it's being stated, and I am stating it in numerous ways. In the last two years I've given lengthy lectures at conferences on these various subjects—a thorough examination of the entrenched forces of darkness that seek to undo the path of the soul. These have been published heretofore in the format of a "Confidential File."

The reason I published them as "Confidential Files" is to somewhat curtail their marketing to a wider audience. El Morya said to me the people of light and the Keepers of the Flame should first digest this material and begin to give their dynamic decrees on these issues, because the sudden thrust of this into the hands of the world would be too much upheaval and too much for me to handle as the rebellion to the message.

So for about nine months these messages have been published under the label of "Confidential File," and you have been sharing them.[3] They were on the subjects of Karl Marx, Jesus and Socialism, and the KGB; and in our last conference I gave a lecture on the Fourth of July on "The Manipulators of

Capitalism and Communism."[4] This has been a very key exposure on the destruction of the free market economy in the United States, the destruction of that system that is the foundation to the path of initiation.

The path of initiation on the abundant life was set forth by Jesus, and I explained that in my lecture entitled "The Economic Philosophy of Jesus Christ: The Religious Philosophy of Karl Marx." So we have this album of *Mother's Manifesto* under that title.[5] We're now taking off our gloves and getting into the ring and publishing it as the *Manifesto* for world distribution.

Other lectures that I have given—including the one on marijuana, which is a very important exposure of the fallen ones in their invasion of our youth—will be coming out under a similar format. All of this is part of the *Manifesto*.

You know, it's much more difficult to make a statement concisely than it is to make it at great length. The complexity of, for instance, the marijuana question or of capitalism or Communism, is great. I think it's very important for those who are leading the battle of light to come to grips with the many nuances within these subjects, and then for the ultimate paperback book to contain the distilled version for popular reading.

From my standpoint, you have to know a lot to make a few strokes of the pen and make them accurately. From your standpoint, you should know the extent of what I'm speaking on so that you can make the incisive calls. You need the information for your dynamic decrees. *Mother's Manifesto* is the message of Saint Germain and the one he comes to represent, who all of the ascended masters represent, Sanat Kumara.

I'm grateful that we together have the opportunity to come together in conferences to take the most vital subjects, to explore them, to give decrees on them, to give our Judgment Calls and watch the action taking place. We need incisive lectures on our economy, on the Federal Reserve system, on energy, on nuclear power plants, on the abuses of the environment, on women's liberation, on all sorts of activities that are happening where you see the combining of light and darkness, the tares and the wheat, and the people who are of the light cannot distinguish between the vibration of good, the vibration of evil, the vibration of the Great White Brotherhood and of the false hierarchy.

So I'm looking forward to studying these subjects, to doing research. And when the research is all collected and it's in order and I sit at my desk and I study it, Saint Germain will come and he will give to me his most incisive and dynamic comments on that material. That to me is a very exciting moment.

It is my responsibility to prepare, it is our collective responsibility together to join in the research department at Camelot, which Saint Germain has requested, so that the necessary research can bring to light the facts and the figures that we need to know, which the world needs to know, but above all that which we need to place before the masters so they can give us their feedback.

The Translation of the Word by the Messenger

You need to understand that a messenger is not a teletype machine or a typewriter or a psychic in a trance. If Saint Germain gave a dictation in Greek, it would be Greek to me. I can assure you that I could not take a dictation in Greek—at least, my present consciousness is not aware that I could take a dictation in Greek. I am not in a trance, and the Holy Spirit speaks through the forcefields that are in my consciousness developed in this life.

The Word often goes through many translations through the cosmos. The masters may speak in tongues. But the arrival of the message through the hopper of my mind arrives in the language that I speak, and the language that I speak is tethered to the education that I have.

So if Saint Germain releases a concept and the word that it comes through is not the precise scientific word, that has to do with the instrument—not with the accuracy of the message or the accuracy of the messenger; but the fact that if you blow air through a flute that has the fragrance of roses inside of it, the air comes out with the fragrance of roses. And so as the mind of the master meshes with my mind, the message is given in the available language and vocabulary mechanism that is within my consciousness.

Sometimes I behold with awe and wonder how God transcends the vessel. As I saw Gabriel and received that message, it was as though I was not there. I had to stand back and try to understand what had happened when Gabriel stood where I stood and delivered to you that message today.

That form of delivery is called *ex cathedra.* It is when the great being of light totally assumes the body of the messenger and speaks almost independently of the messenger's consciousness. But it is not independent, because free will is always the key. One always uses one's free will in becoming the instrument of God, and free will means complete consciousness.

Of course, there are many levels of consciousness. I'm explaining this to you so that you will understand that the masters recognize that we all should have the opportunity of making good karma, that the ascended masters don't do our work for us, that the ascended masters don't hand me a book and say, "Publish it."

If they want to publish a work on a subject that I am not educated in, they will let me know in advance and tell me to get educated because they are going to speak on that subject. And that is true of the teachings that come forth.

Sometimes I sit down and Sanat Kumara sits down with me and he teaches me the teaching that he is then going to dictate on. At other times he simply dictates it as I am in wonder of the concepts and the cadences as they flow through. So it is a process of the education of the messenger as well as the using of the messenger's vehicles.

Sometimes you'll notice that when I'm taking a dictation and the words are coming very quickly and my mind is following what is coming next while speaking what is there, that sometimes my tongue will stumble over the words because I'm speaking the words that are going by while I'm reading the next words that are coming. The master isn't making a mistake. I'm just getting a little bit tongue-tied. And it's just a simple problem of the mechanism of the instrument.

America Is the Keystone in the Arch of Planetary Hierarchy

I'm speaking to you about loving Saint Germain. "If you love me, love my dog." Well, if you love Saint Germain, you love his message—because Saint Germain *is* his message. He *is* the Word. So get to know his message.

He is very concerned about the tearing down of life in America and in every nation. He's just as concerned about the people of Russia and the people of China and the people of Africa. But he concentrates on the United States because he sees the United States as a deliverer nation. He sees the raising up of the sons of light who can do something about the problems in other nations.

America is the keystone in the arch of planetary hierarchy. If we don't save America, there won't be any other nation to save. And so many souls of light have been drawn here, have been given birth here. They are collected here by prophecy of all the prophets of ancient scripture. This is the wilderness land,[6] the Promised Land of the coming together again of the tribes of Israel, the seed of light.

We need to get educated. We need to understand the message.

We need to understand the Spirit cup and the Matter cup, put it together, become effective, have the courage to challenge darkness, have the courage to speak out and have the discrimination to know when to be silent.

You Don't Have to Agree with Me

If you are new in the teachings and you take up portions of the *Manifesto* in these albums or in our books and if you disagree with what I'm saying, please be at peace. It's all right with me if you disagree with what I'm saying. Write and tell me about it. Give me new information. Who knows? You might change my mind. I don't profess to have the final word on what's going on in this planetary body. The final word is the light itself. But how the light applies in specific conditions remains the challenge of every one of us—you and me and all of us.

The Word from on high as the dictations of light is the certain word of prophecy. The application depends on the genius, the attunement, the communion of every son and daughter of God. And we all know that when we're making decisions, the more facts we have, the more that comes to light, the better we are able to distill and weigh and come to a conclusion.

So life is ongoing. There isn't any one of us who has not evolved over the years that we have lived and perhaps changed our opinions on matters. What's important is that we have the courage to speak out with the gift God has given us to see and to understand. And if tomorrow I understand better, I'll tell you that I understood better. But today, this is my understanding on the manipulators of capitalism and Communism.

I have been very careful about what I have said. I have been very careful in studying what Saint Germain has taught me. It's a beginning. It's the threading of the eye of the needle. It's very important. I hope you'll go to the books that I have read and researched and look at them and go beyond and find more.

Maybe you'll find a lot of corroboration. It's very important to the final statement of the *Manifesto.*

I feel that I want to apologize that so much of our teaching is on tape and not in books. I would like to be able to say that we had the equipment and the staff to get these tapes right into paperbacks as soon as they're spoken. They would be cheaper and they would have a wider distribution. They would have greater availability to you. Our current facilities and staff do not allow this, but we're working very hard on making it possible.

A Message for the Entire New Age Movement

In the meantime, Saint Germain says that these messages on the Matter cup, on what's happening in the world and what are the greatest threats to our freedom, are here for the education of the entire New Age movement. The people who have the courage to come apart and to walk in the various paths of Aquarius, the enlightened ones wherever they are positioned, need the teachings. And you are the ones commissioned by God to take it forth.

The most excellent way to present the teaching is to listen to the tapes, learn the message, and then say it in your own words. But if you can't quite do that, take the tapes and play them for people. That's fine too. But people appreciate your personal message. And of course, you make the good karma of witnessing to the Word when you have your own message.

I wanted to tell you about this because it's a very important thrust. The manipulators of Communism and capitalism are one, and they are moving together at fantastic speeds to carve up the earth to their own designs. It's time that we did something about it, and we really can't do anything about it until we have these facts.

Our chelas Ralph and Lucille Yaney, with some wonderful supporting staff, have put together a book, *10,001,* on the subject of abortion.[7] It begins like a science fiction story with a certain soul who is about to embody, takes you through the deliberations of the Karmic Board, and then his eventual incarnation. Then the book has all kinds of teachings on the Law with the central theme being to understand why it is that the ascended masters teach the path for life. It has a marvelous appendix on all kinds of facts and figures of the Matter cup.

It's an important book because it's readable by people who are not on the path and especially these who are undecided about their stand. The 10,001 in the title refers to the 10,001 avatars whom Maitreya announced would be born in this century.[8] They're cosmic beings, Christed beings of great light. Some have been aborted—some of them numerous times.

We are living in the days when great souls of light are appearing, are trying to get into embodiment, and there is a dearth of alert parents—and of course so much abortion that it does come to pass that numbers of them are cut off from life before they get here. Jesus, in his last Christmas message, said it was the most important single issue of his concern.[9]

The path of the ascension is a path you walk challenging these injustices. Unless you are willing to challenge them and speak out and be active in your community, you are not fulfilling the path of the ascension. And this I must tell you in our concluding meeting this evening.

You Cannot Withdraw from Action in the World

You cannot withdraw. Withdraw for a time, come to Summit University, retreat to study the teachings—but ultimately you have to get in the very midst of what is happening. Jesus said that, and Mother Mary has told us that something must be done and swiftly.[10]

We have used the subject of pro-life as a means for Summit University students to learn the art of public speaking. The ascended masters want every one of you to become a public speaker, just to have the ability to stand up and speak on the truth that you know. That means taking courses in public speaking, joining a Toastmasters club or doing what Summit University students are doing.

You can go and join a pro-life group in your city and they will come and teach a group of you how to give the presentation on pro-life, which becomes an education in public speaking with a message and a content. Our students have done tremendously with this. Our high school students have taken that course and they've gone into the high schools in Los Angeles and stood up before these high schools and lectured on pro-life and answered the questions of those high school students.

It takes a lot of courage. And of course, once you begin that training—and especially if you begin at an early age—you get very much at ease before larger and larger audiences. You start speaking to one or two people in your living room in a relaxed way and then five or ten. Pretty soon you're advertising a meeting and twenty or twenty-five people come. You're speaking the Law and you know how to organize your notes and you know how to make a presentation. And then you're not nervous when it's a hundred or five hundred.

But you have to begin. There is no other way to overcome that first fear of talking before people not knowing how to present yourself or present your information. It's something that can be learned. You can learn it if you try. That seems to be Serapis Bey's byword: TRY. And I don't think anyone worthy to be a representative of the ascended masters should allow himself to be tongue-tied or to feel that he cannot speak before a group. It's something you *can* do. And if it is a fear, work to overcome it.

I think it's important to get ready, and it's important to begin in small ways, talking to one person or two people, and learning to express yourself. And then when you try it and play the recording back and listen to yourself, you find out what are your weaknesses and you sharpen up on them, that's all.

The Holy Spirit Is Waiting to Initiate You

The Holy Spirit is waiting to initiate you in the delivery of the Word. And when all is said and done, you've taken all the courses, and you've exercised and practiced and you've come to be able to do it well, you'll put it all aside and forget everything you learned, and the Holy Spirit will just pour through you. It's just the way it is. You go to school, you learn, you practice an instrument, or you learn something, perhaps an art, and when you have all the technique down, then you don't need it anymore. But if you never have the technique in the first place, you probably don't have the full orchestration that the Holy Spirit needs to work through.

So I'd like you to look at the ascended masters' teachings and our lectures in their totality as our manifesto. Right now, there is tremendous teaching available to you. There is enough for you to take and run with. There is the challenge to organize it, to join with study groups, to lecture on it.

And the thing you always have to remember is this: if you've just concluded your first two-day seminar with me, right now you know more than most of your friends about the path of the ascended masters. So you don't have to wait until you get smarter; you've already got a message right now. And you keep on building on the message.

Your Impostor on the Left-Handed Path

The reason that we brought to your attention in this conference the Ritual of Exorcism is because of our responsibility on the path of the ascension to call forth the judgment of all conditions and consciousnesses that are anti the light in the people.

I want to tell you another reason why you need the Judgment Call. When you enter the path of initiation under the ascended masters, you soon find out, as they will tell you, that on the left-handed path you have an impostor. For every one of you there is at least one individual, if not many, who at some point in your evolution were one with you, were with you as a friend, and at some point on that evolution that individual chose the left-handed path.

That point on the path is called the "Y." We all come to the "Y," and the "Y" is when you have a full awareness of the teachings, a full awareness of the consequences of its misuse, you have had certain initiations with the ascended masters themselves, and then you make the decision whether to take the light you've been given, take the teachings you have received, and use them for the glory of the ego. Therefore, those of you who are beginning or are already on the ascension path must reckon with the fact that you have an impostor—someone who is in the act of countering every move you make for freedom.

Sometimes I make calls for Saint Germain on various individuals on the planet who are thwarting his every move for freedom, and on a number of occasions when I have done so he has said to me, "That individual, lifetime after lifetime, has opposed every move I have made for freedom." That is the definition of an impostor.

An impostor may look like you, imitate you. An impostor is indeed extremely jealous of you, because you have the light, you are on the path, and he is cut off from the path. He wants to excel without obedience to the I AM Presence. It is necessary, if you would be free to accelerate, for you to call forth the judgment of all impostors of your path of initiation and of your soul.

I counseled someone recently who is a twin. She has a twin brother, and she has not seen her twin brother in many years. That twin brother chose the left-handed path quite a long time ago and subjugated her on that path, imprisoned her in the matrices of darkness, so that the karma came that they were to be born as twins, to be together in the womb, and coming out from the womb, she to gain her God-mastery, to separate herself from that individual, and to manifest enough light so that he would no longer have power over her.

I was recently making invocations for her, and what did I see interfering with her health? The extreme jealousy of this brother on the left-handed path. He can no longer control her actions or her life, because she has made such advances on the path of the ascended masters. And jealousy and envy is an energy that when projected at you drains you and makes you feel tired and even ill.

Much illness is caused by the projection of jealousy alone. Other things also cause illness, like hatred or condemnation or other forms of black magic. But the fallen ones always envy the children of God, and that jealousy is a ray that zaps your energy unless you are conscious of it and you reverse the tide.

You Have to Defend Your Position in Hierarchy

So decree 7.05 is used to reverse the tide of all opposition to you personally, to the light for which you stand, and to your path. And the Judgment Call is for the binding of all impostors of your soul and of your niche in hierarchy.

You occupy a position in hierarchy right now; every chela does. You have to defend that position; and there are people who are jealous of it, in embodiment and out of embodiment. You may not know these people or you may know them—it doesn't matter. You have to guard your position, your key point of light.

So in conclusion this evening we are going to give the Judgment Call. And that will be the final statement of this ascension class that you are making, your feet firmly implanted in the earth, that they shall not pass, they shall not cross your path, they shall not cross over the circle of your oneness with the mighty I AM Presence, and they shall not interfere with your victory and your love of Saint Germain.

You love Saint Germain so much you will deliver his message. And you will call for the binding in earth and in heaven of all those forces, persons, personalities, principles that are seeking to thwart what you must do for him because you love enough. Let us stand and I will make the invocation.

> *In the name of the I AM THAT I AM, I call forth the light of God that never fails. I demand the binding in earth and in heaven of all impostors of the chelas of the light. I demand the binding of the impostors of the Holy Spirit. I demand the binding of the principalities and powers and spiritual wickedness in high places of Church and State that are thwarting the path of the lightbearers upon this planetary body and the incoming golden age of Saint Germain.*
>
> *I demand the binding of all impostors of Saint Germain, El Morya, Lanello, and all ascended masters of the Great White Brotherhood. I demand the implementation now of the judgment of Almighty God of the false gurus. I demand action now for the binding of all that would attempt to cross the way in the path of these chelas of the light. I demand the reversing of the tide of that energy and forcefield. I demand the binding of the Antichrist, the False Prophet, the Dragon, the Beast, the Great Whore, and the beast that cometh up out of the earth and the beast that cometh up out of the sea.*[11]
>
> *I demand the binding of the beast of World Communism and the beast of World Capitalism. I demand the binding of the dragon of the international bankers.*

I demand the binding of the entire hordes of fallen ones, and especially those interfering with the incarnation of the mighty avatars. I demand the binding of the impostors of the light who are seeking to expand the practice of abortion, who are advising people on abortion, and who are cutting off therefore the incoming lifewave of the souls of Almighty God.

By the flame of the ascension from the heart of Serapis Bey, by the mighty sword Excalibur, Archangel Michael's sword, and Mighty Astrea's cosmic circle and sword of blue flame, we demand the instantaneous intercession of all of the hosts of the LORD *and the implementation of this our Word, and to that end we give the Judgment Call.*

[Give the Judgment Call, pages 124–25.]

In the name of the I AM THAT I AM, I invoke the light of Mighty Surya and Cuzco. I call for the mighty confirmation of the judgment by the Great Causal Body of Surya and Cuzco everywhere within the planetary body and this system of worlds where the Judgment Call is required and is the manifestation of the living Christ.

Stand forth for the entire Spirit of the Great White Brotherhood and the chelas of the light, and let the judgment sound forth, and let there be the binding on earth and in heaven of all those whom it is the will of God to remove, then, and bind in this hour.

In the name of the Father, the Son and the Holy Spirit, in the name of the Mother, we decree.

[Give the decree to Surya, pages 192–93.]

CHAPTER SEVENTEEN

Light!

Surya

Light! Let light echo in the chamber of your heart. Light is the essence of your life and your path and your ascension. Apply thyself to the study of light.

Light is the intelligence of the I AM whose geometry, by the power of the Holy Spirit, is manifest as the cross of Alpha and Omega, the Spirit-Matter spheres. I said light, l-i-g-h-t.

We seal in the heart of the Word the nucleus of its energy and intent. The study of the Word is the study of the science of creation.

I AM Surya. I AM the light of Sirius. I AM the Sun behind the God Star. I AM the Sun of light. I emit light. You also may emit light if you choose. But the fusion of the heart and the echo of the light within the heart is the science that you must learn.

If you are not a suitable instrument, the light will not pass through. If the light does not pass through you, then you will not be nourished of the light. If you are not nourished of the light, then you cannot be of the light, for the light transforms, creates, re-creates the soul. In order to sustain light, you must be an instrument of light—as water passing through a pipe, so light passing through a vessel. Light passing through the vessel keeps the vessel clean and in tune with its origin.

Light, then, is the intelligence of God, the intelligence of God that moves in the cloven tongues of the Holy Ghost and precipitates in the cross of Matter.

All of creation is light. How is it that we say that some are not of the light? Some are not of the light because the light that is in them is darkness.[1] From whence did the darkness come? It has come as a misstatement of light, as a misqualification of light, as the mystification of the science of light.

We, then, stand at the fulcrum of life to deliver pure light, that the pure light that we give may flush out impure light—light made impure by an ungodly matrix.

Receive the Gift of Those Who Have Gone Before

In actuality, life and its science is simple. And all of the science of life may be learned by you through meditation upon the Great God Self. But other men and women who have become the immortals have meditated upon that Self before you and written books and set forth their instruction.

Therefore, to take their word is to take their compressed energy of light, a coiled spring. Sometimes the gift of a single book is the gift of an entire lifetime or ten lifetimes and the distillation of the individual's meditation upon God.

Those who boast and say, "We need not the ascended masters; we need not teachers—we will go to God, because we are God," are the very ones who rebelled against the Word incarnate. They have gone forth in the land with their complex philosophies of undoing the path of light. Those who renounce the Great White Brotherhood while calling themselves God are fraudulent in all points of the Law, for this is the undoing of the blessed tie that binds the soul to light.

There is a light that you are not capable of assimilating.

It is the light of far-off worlds and cosmic beings. Therefore, that light is stepped down to other ascended beings and angels. And through your mighty I AM Presence, the light of the white-fire sun, which you also are not able to assimilate, is stepped down through the blessed Son, the Mediator, and then passed through your chakras, again stepped down for the assimilation of physical matter and physical cells. Thus, you see, hierarchy as a principle is inherent in the transfer of light.

The fastest way to the Great Central Sun is to take step-by-step the messages of the angels and those nearest you in the ladder of life. Understand light and its meaning and its purpose, and take the proffered cup of crystal light.

We Will Allow Only One Miracle for Those Who Seek a Sign

The ascended masters' teachings are charged with light. And the miracle we bring for those who seek a sign before they will believe in heaven and the One Sent from heaven[2] is the miracle of the soul converted to light and the path of light. This is the miracle we bring. This is the purpose of our coming. For the gift of miracles indeed belongs to the messenger, but only one we will allow for the proof of heaven here and now—the miracle of souls converted to light.

Where can you go across the face of the earth and find so many ardent chelas? Have they pulled themselves up by their own bootstraps or by their intellectual awareness of the teaching? I tell you, they are filled with light by the miracle itself, the miracle of conversion—the literal turning around of the soul and the polarization of the soul to its mighty God Self. And when that soul has been turned to God, if that soul is a living soul of light whose origin is in the seed of Christ, none can undo that soul.

But those who come into the flame for self-gain, who are the seed of the Wicked One, though they be converted for a season, they are not converted by the Holy Ghost, but their conversion is by their own seeking of the light that they have not earned. Therefore, they tarry for a while and linger for a while and soon discover they are not comfortable among dedicated hearts, constant hearts, serving hearts. And they find that neither the messenger nor the ascended masters will give to them light or its glory without honest participation in the disciplines and the initiations of the path.

Thus, those who are converted because they began in light and will finish in light, they stay with the light not by might or by power or by self-will but by the magnet of the Holy Ghost and the miracle gift of light itself, which we transfer in our dictations and our lectures. This light is an arrow that knows its mark in the very heart of the lightbearer.

And do you know that this dispensation of the ascended masters is ordained for key individuals upon earth whose names are written, whose souls are numbered, and who are known by every angel? And those who are called, those who have elected to be of the light, are already sealed in that light but require the physical contact and the physical transfer of the Word and the light for the realignment of forces and the realignment of a selfhood that has become a part of misqualified light, and therefore knows not the way to go.

The Science of Light

Light and its appearance in the earth has a geometry and a certainty. And the science is so beautiful to contemplate that those chelas who serve on the fifth ray of science with Hilarion meditate upon the science of light and on the flame in the heart of light. And they easily enter into exalted states, samadhi and beyond, by the very contemplation of the Spirit-Matter science of God.

Light in its appearance in each of the seven rays is a vastness all of itself. Learn of the light of the will of God and learn of the power locked in the diamond. Learn the secrets of the violet flame and follow the flame back to the light and learn what is the real source of transmutation. Follow wisdom's ray back to the Sun and you will contemplate the unique meditation of Alpha and Omega upon the light that manifests as the mind of God, that turns and in turning gives birth to cosmos.

I AM light. I wield light. Do you think that perhaps the ascended masters are not able to deliver the light to save the earth or a single soul? It is not a question of ability or capability. It is a question of the law of light and the curve of light in space and the line of light in time. It is a question of the Law.

We transfer light. We implement all the light that is allowed by the law of each individual lifestream connected with a lifewave of a planetary home. That law includes the law of karma of the soul, of its blueprint, of its divine plan. And we release each day the maximum light for each individual in the lifewave of earth. And the total of that light is the increment of each given day. And by Law it may increase only if the individual in the application of the law of selfhood expands selfhood by the law of light and therefore increases his capacity for light.

Each individual is a capacitor of light. Each individual has the capacity to multiply light when the individual is in contact with the flame in the heart and when the spheres of the chakras are free for the expansion of light.

Why do we come and speak on subjects of self-discipline, morals, ethics, love, the path, decrees? All of this is our way of teaching you the law of light so that you may arrive at the point of self-discipline whereby you discover the inner key to increase light within your temple. This discovery must be made by each individual.

All That We Have Given Contains Keys

We have given all that we can give up to this moment of the dispensation of the Two Witnesses. And all that we have given contains keys. And beyond the words are cadences and even formulas. And if you knew the formulas of the words, you could go to the Word behind the words and the numbers behind the words and discover right there in the printed books keys to light beyond your imagination.

Why, beloved ones, sometimes it is as though the ascended masters were hiding the thimble and making it so obvious as to almost be a source of amusement that people walk by day after day and read the words and hear the dictations and somehow not yet do they cross the barrier where all of the wisdom for the mastery of the seven rays is contained.

Take the volumes of *Pearls of Wisdom*. They seem simple, obvious. Each *Pearl* is a masterpiece of a mathematical formula for the release of light. When you drink the cup of that *Pearl* as your communion before you depart your body temple in sleep, your soul takes with you the inner formula though the outer mind may not have penetrated.[3] And you follow that wavelength back to that master.

And by and by, you increase in your God consciousness that awareness that grows and grows and grows like the unfolding of a thousand-petaled rose. And then, you see, the dawning light and its inner key comes to the consciousness. And often when it comes, it comes in a pre-assimilated form so that it comes as awareness to do, to be—as awareness, "I AM."

The light is. It is no longer a mental process. Light is. Is, is. And Isis is unveiled as the Mother flame. And the Mother flame is seen to be the way Home, eternal life—ascension's flame, its mighty sword.

Your joy in singing and in giving dynamic decrees and in reading and listening to the teachings is the joy of the soul's assimilation, veil upon veil, of filigree patterns of mathematical matrices.

Sometimes you meet a friend who has been away from the teachings for several years. You notice something a little bit different, a different vibration. The difference is that the friend has missed several years of daily and weekly transfers of light to increase the God consciousness. Those who leave the light and then desire to return are like those who are crossing a cosmos and step off a meteor, a spaceship or a shooting star. It is difficult to catch up, as those who go on have crossed vast reaches of space.

Space is the habitation of the Holy Spirit. Space is a coordinate of time. And time and space are the distillers of light into your consciousness. Cycles consisting of the measurements of time and space transcend time and space and become increments of infinity.

Do you know when you cross the line from time and space to infinity? It is a matter of consciousness. Mortals live in time and space. Sons and daughters of God live in cycles. And the adepts live in infinity while moving in and among both.

When the adepts put on the full garment of the ascension flame, there is scarcely a ripple of consciousness. For them the ascension is but a modicum of light from the former state. For they have so expanded light, even in this octave, that the transition becomes minute. And then again, by other standards it is indeed cosmic.

Guard the Light You Have Received

I AM Surya. I converse with you while I implant electrodes of light in the earth. It is good to be with you, to be together again in these moments, for we have shared other moments.

I am grateful to seal this *Retreat on the Ascension* as a sphere of light. You have become one and classmates. From this moment, you will be a bursting sun and each one a ray of light precipitating light in a unique vibration with your personal stamp of love and truth. Therefore, rainbow-colored hues and manifold flowers of light will grace the earth where you pass and walk.

Take care, then, that you guard the light and garner the light. Take care that no man take thy crown.[4] Let this energy remain sealed within you. Do not remove your vibration from this moment of harmony. Will you not make an experiment, consciously and determined, to note well the guarding of harmony that no one, no thing, no circumstance can cause you to alter the moment of your vibration with me? Beloved ones, it is possible.

The great teaching that Saint Germain gave to Godfre was the fixing of the attention upon the I AM Presence. Sometimes you are so unaware and so undisciplined that you lose harmony, without even realizing that you have lost it, by engaging in unnecessary human conversation about subjects so far removed from light, by being disturbed about world conditions or a remark that someone makes. Fatigue levels may increase your absence of self-discipline.

Many of you have great light and have manifested great light in other lifetimes and even planetary bodies. And I perceive that you have gotten yourselves into a rut of the non-measurement of light and harmony. Light and harmony, *light* and *harmony—harmony,* the sealing of light; *light* emanation, the harmony of the seven rays.

Beloved ones, I would give you a key to immediate acceleration in self-mastery. Learn to recognize the levels of your individual vibration. Summon will and determination to guard the flame and the harmony of light and to sustain a certain level of being. "Hold fast what thou hast received" is the command of the Maha Chohan, the Keeper of the Flame. If you would only hold what you have received and not allow it to pass through a sieve consciousness, you would see how much more quickly you would fulfill your divine plan.

After all, if you are going to ascend in this life (and there is certainly a very good possibility that a number of you will) would it not be enjoyable to attain to that ascended master level—and then have a quarter of a century or a half a century to live your life in a state of self-mastery where you could go forth into the multitudes and be such an example of the Law, as Jesus and Gautama were, that people would begin to believe the Law by your living proof of it? Would you not desire to bring comfort to life and the healing of the nations, not for pride but for the inner joy of seeing people fulfill their life in God? All this is possible to you if you will learn the law of light and light emanation and begin to notice the disparaging forcefields that attempt to take over your harmony.

Yes, you have heard any number of dictations on this subject and read and studied. How about beginning to take seriously this message of harmony in the feelings and the law of light? Why not accept that in the twinkling of an eye you can be free? Why hear the Word and say, "It doesn't apply to me," or, "It does apply to me," and then forget it on the morrow? It is a question of human habit patterns, human thinking, human feeling, and somehow coming to the point of God consciousness in our presence, then leaving and going back down to certain levels by sheer habit and for no other reason—not because you particularly enjoy those levels, but you have not retrained your lifestream.

I impress upon you now the ascended master consciousness of dignity, self-worth and discipline. God-mastery is sheer joy. To be able to do what you do and do it well is worth the effort. There is nothing like self-mastery to build self-confidence—confidence in your soul's oneness with your Higher Self, confidence that where'er you go the Higher Self is and will bestow through you light and love and all that is necessary to balance your karma.

Life Need Not Be a Struggle

Life need not be a struggle. You need not be fretful or worrisome. I am saying that by the law of light, here and now, you can make a decision to take dominion of your life as you have never made it before. I say you can make that decision because I am here. I AM Surya. And the full God consciousness of the God Star surrounds you and bathes you in the self-awareness of your Higher Self and the vast reaches of your life in God that you have lived long before you became entangled with this planetary sphere.

You may not be desirous of contemplating a million years or more of existence. But ask yourself this: Was there ever a time when God was not? Was there ever a time when you were not? Do you have a beginning and an ending? Or do you have infinity?

A portion of yourself has never left the golden age or the octaves of light. Do you not long for that portion of yourself and to be reconnected and reinvested with the fullness of it? Do you really feel complete in your outer mind? Often your memory fails you. Often you feel you would like to extend your mental faculties, for you grapple with subject matter and cannot understand it. And your physical body will not do what you tell it to do, and your feelings have not the capacity to enjoy the vast music of a universe. Do you not long for wholeness enough to be diligent in a few things and to take the keys we give you and liberate an entire lifewave?

Of all of the avatars you have heard of, have you not noticed that it has only taken one—*one* to convert millions? Such is the magnitude of *your* star, *your* I AM Presence, *your* causal body and the God that you now know only in increments.

God is revealed in nature. God is revealed in the ascended hosts. But the God that you know is limited by your capacity to know—is it not so? Would you not increase the capacity? You can. You may. You are able. God has ordained it. There will come a moment, and the moment can be the *now,* when the meshing with the mind that I AM will be your springboard to eternity.

Sons and daughters of God, I *challenge* you to this path of the ascension.

I AM Surya. I AM one in the God flame that you are, that I AM. I seal you in your fiery destiny. I seal you in your divine plan. And I greet you, soul of light whom I know, whom I AM, whom I will be.

CHAPTER EIGHTEEN

The Sealing of the Seminar

I want to express my gratitude to each and every one of you who has lit your candle to make this retreat a wonderful experience for us all, for this city, our country, for the masters. I want to thank you for giving the masters the opportunity of using your lifestream to advance the cause of light in the earth. I want to thank our musicians and all who have been a part of making this conference a success in every part of our service here.

It's very heartwarming to know that the ascended masters can call for a retreat and we have the resources and the people and the willing hearts and hands who bring it all together and make it possible for the new chela to walk in off the street and find that the marriage feast is prepared and waiting.

I look forward to seeing all of you at Camelot as soon as you can get there. Remember that when you wake up after you sleep, the first thing you're going to do is give your "Heart, Head and Hand Decrees" and your "Violet Fire and Tube of Light Decree." Keep your momentum, keep your light. It is daily application that will take you Home and see you winning all the way.

Be Sealed in the Light of Your Ascension

In the name of the I AM THAT I AM, I seal you in the heart of Nada. O mighty pink flame of the heart of Nada, O blessed presence of the Lords of Karma, chohan of the sixth ray, guide each one in the outpicturing of his Christhood that he may follow the Saviour all the way, and in following him discover the path of the ruby ray and Lord Maitreya and Gautama, and Sanat Kumara, and Saint Germain, and the saints and witnesses and all the great multitude.

Beloved hosts of light and beloved Nada, I pray that the children of God upon earth might find one another and the path swiftly, and that we might have the joy of being together on this path and of helping each other to help our dear earth.

In the name of the Father, the Son, the Holy Spirit, let the entire Spirit of the Great White Brotherhood assembled seal you in the light of your ascension. Amen.

Notes

Books listed here are published by Summit University Press unless otherwise noted.

CHAPTER 1 • The Path of Reunion with God

1. Acts 1:9.
2. II Kings 2:11.
3. Rev. 14:4.
4. Gen. 37:3.

CHAPTER 2 • The Story of Serapis Bey: The Squaring of the Circle

1. For a detailed account of Jesus' journey to the East and his studies in India, see Elizabeth Clare Prophet, *The Lost Years of Jesus.*
2. Dan. 7:9–13.
3. In his first sermon, Gautama Buddha taught the Four Noble Truths: (1) Life is *dukkha,* "suffering." (2) The cause of this suffering is *tanha,* "desire," or "thirst." (3) There is freedom or cessation from suffering: nirvana. (4) The way to this liberation is through the Noble Eightfold Path.
4. Matt. 21:44.
5. R. A. Schwaller de Lubicz, *The Temple in Man: Sacred Architecture and the Perfect Man,* trans. Robert and Deborah Lawlor (New York: Inner Traditions International, 1977), p. 24.

6. Ibid., p. 33.
7. Herodotus *History* 7.225 (trans. George Rawlinson, pp. 151–52).
8. John 10:18.
9. Matt. 16:25; Mark 8:35; Luke 9:24.
10. I Cor. 3:16.
11. Based on the accounts of authors of antiquity, including the Greek historian Herodotus, the building of the Great Pyramid was traditionally attributed to the Egyptian Pharaoh Khufu, who reigned sometime between 2700 and 2500 B.C. Radiocarbon dating of mortar used in the construction of the pyramid gave a date between 2620 and 2484 B.C., consistent with it being constructed during the reign of Khufu.

    However, that may not be the last word in dating the pyramid. In 1872, a cedar plank was discovered in a previously sealed shaft off the Queen's Chamber. After having been lost for many years, this fragment was rediscovered in 2020 and radiocarbon dated to 3341–3094 B.C., more than 500 years earlier than the supposed date of construction of the pyramid itself.

    Some historians propose even earlier dates, claiming that Khufu, if he was connected with the pyramid, was only making repairs or modifications to a structure that was already ancient during his reign. See, for example, Graham Hancock, *Fingerprints of the Gods* (New York: Three Rivers Press, 1995). Some date the construction of the Great Pyramid to more than 12,000 years ago, at the time of the last days of Atlantis.

    In *The Stairway to Heaven* (New York: St. Martin's Press, 1980), Zecharia Sitchin proposes that the Great Pyramid was constructed by the fallen angels described in Biblical texts as *Nephilim.* However, it is also possible that the Nephilim themselves were only making use of a structure that existed before their arrival.
12. Rom. 8:17.
13. One account of Lucifer's Fall is found in the early Christian text *Vitae Adae et Evae.* In chapters 11 to 16, we read: "And she [Eve] cried out and said: 'Woe unto thee, thou devil. Why

dost thou attack us for no cause? What hast thou to do with us? What have we done to thee? for thou pursuest us with craft? Or why doth thy malice assail us? Have we taken away thy glory and caused thee to be without honour? Why dost thou harry us, thou enemy (and persecute us) to the death in wickedness and envy?'

"And with a heavy sigh, the devil spake: 'O Adam! all my hostility, envy, and sorrow is for thee, since it is for thee that I have been expelled from my glory, which I possessed in the heavens in the midst of the angels and for thee was I cast out in the earth.' Adam answered, 'What dost thou tell me? What have I done to thee or what is my fault against thee? Seeing that thou hast received no harm or injury from us, why dost thou pursue us?'

"The devil replied, 'Adam, what dost thou tell me? It is for thy sake that I have been hurled from that place. When thou wast formed, I was hurled out of the presence of God and banished from the company of the angels. When God blew into thee the breath of life and thy face and likeness was made in the image of God, Michael also brought thee and made (us) worship thee in the sight of God; and God the Lord spake: Here is Adam. I have made thee in our image and likeness.'

"And Michael went out and called all the angels saying: 'Worship the image of God as the Lord God hath commanded.' And Michael himself worshipped first; then he called me and said: 'Worship the image of God the Lord.' And I answered, 'I have no (need) to worship Adam.' And since Michael kept urging me to worship, I said to him, 'Why dost thou urge me? I will not worship an inferior and younger being (than I). I am his senior in the Creation, before he was made was I already made. It is his duty to worship me.'

"When the angels, who were under me, heard this, they refused to worship him. And Michael saith, 'Worship the image of God, but if thou wilt not worship him, the Lord God will be wrath with thee.' And I said, 'If He be wrath with me, I will set my seat above the stars of heaven and will be like the Highest.'

"And God the Lord was wrath with me and banished me and my angels from our glory; and on thy account were we expelled from our abodes into this world and hurled on the earth. And straightway we were overcome with grief, since we had been spoiled of so great glory. And we were grieved when we saw thee in such joy and luxury. And with guile I cheated thy wife and caused thee to be expelled through her (doing) from thy joy and luxury, as I have been driven out of my glory" (R. H. Charles, *The Apocrypha and Pseudepigrapha of the Old Testament* [Oxford: Clarendon Press, 1913]).

14. Phil. 4:13.
15. Jer. 31:33.
16. Isa. 55:11.
17. Matt. 24:35; Mark 13:31; Luke 21:33.
18. Col. 3:3.
19. I Pet. 5:8.

CHAPTER 3 • Serapis Bey and the Founders of the Theosophical Society

1. *Letters from the Masters of Wisdom,* Second Series, letter #7.
2. Ibid., letter #3.
3. Ibid., letter #27.
4. Ibid., letter #17.
5. Ibid., letter #15.
6. Ibid., letter #10.
7. Rev. 7:9.
8. *Intermediate Studies of the Human Aura* is published as part of Kuthumi and Djwal Kul, *The Human Aura.*
9. Rev. 5.
10. *Pearls of Wisdom* are weekly letters of instruction dictated by the ascended masters to their messengers Mark and Elizabeth Prophet for students of the sacred mysteries throughout the world. To find out more about the *Pearls,* go to www.SummitLighthouse.org/Pearls-Wisdom.
11. Elizabeth Clare Prophet, *The Opening of the Seventh Seal: Sanat Kumara on the Path of the Ruby Ray,* p. 122.

CHAPTER 4 • The Call of Serapis

1. San Francisco is sometimes referred to as being built on seven hills, which are usually listed as Telegraph Hill, Nob Hill, Russian Hill, Rincon Hill, Twin Peaks, Mount Davidson, and either Lone Mountain or Mount Sutro. The seven hills of San Francisco in the days of Lemuria held focuses of the seven Holy Kumaras.
2. On August 6, 1979, a magnitude 5.7 earthquake occurred on the Calaveras Fault near Coyote Lake, in Santa Clara County, California. Although the shock was felt in the San Francisco Bay area, the damage was limited to the nearby towns of Gilroy and Hollister, and no deaths were reported.
3. Matt. 10:38; 16:24; Mark 8:34; 10:21; Luke 9:23; 14:27.
4. Matt. 11:30.
5. The Lords of Karma serve as the spiritual Karmic Board, which dispenses justice to this system of worlds, adjudicating karma, mercy and judgment on behalf of every lifestream. All souls pass before the Karmic Board before and after each incarnation on earth to receive their assignment and karmic allotment for each lifetime beforehand and the review of their performance at its conclusion. See *The Masters and Their Retreats,* pp. 153–55.
6. Marxism: The political and economic theories of Karl Marx and Friedrich Engels, later developed by their followers to form the basis for the theory and practice of Communism.
7. John 21:16, 17.
8. These teachings by Sanat Kumara are published in Elizabeth Clare Prophet, *The Opening of the Seventh Seal.*
9. Paul the Venetian quotes from "Bedouin Song" by American-born poet Bayard Taylor (1825–1878).

CHAPTER 5 • That Every Man Can Realize Christhood

1. John 12:44–49.
2. See, for example, Romans chapters 3 and 7. This is also a major subject of the Epistle to the Hebrews.
3. Mark 16:15.

4. Matt. 8:26; 14:30; 16:8.
5. Rev. 1:4; 4:5; 5:6.
6. Rom. 3:23.
7. John 14:2.
8. I Cor. 15:40.
9. John 5:35.
10. Luke 12:49.
11. Mark 10:30.

CHAPTER 6 • **The LORD's Ritual of Exorcism**

1. Mark 16:15.
2. Godfré Ray King, *The Magic Presence* (Schaumburg, Ill.: Saint Germain Press, 1963), p. 243.
3. Isa. 9:6.
4. Matt. 18:18.
5. Matt. 18:20.
6. Matt. 18:19.
7. Matt. 10:34.
8. John 5:30; 14:10.
9. Mark 5:9; Luke 8:30.
10. Acts 4:12.
11. Isa. 43:1; 45:4; 56:5; 62:2.
12. Matt. 21:21; Mark 11:23.
13. The Two Witnesses are twin flames sponsored by the Brotherhood in every age, messengers of the Word incarnate, who witness to the cycles of Alpha and Omega, the beginning and the ending, the Father-Mother God. Those who serve in the office of the Two Witnesses write down the law of the Manus, the guardians of the race and sponsors of each 2,000-year dispensation. They are the prophets of the LORD who stand as the representatives of the World Teachers to the chosen people and to the multitudes.

    The messengers Mark L. Prophet and Elizabeth Clare Prophet received the anointing by Saint Germain to occupy the office of the Two Witnesses, which were foretold in the Book of Daniel 12:5 and Revelation 11:3–12. "And they shall prophesy a thousand two hundred and threescore days [i.e., cycles whose length is unknown], clothed in sackcloth. These are the two olive trees, and the two candlesticks standing before the God of the earth," the Lord of the World, Gautama Buddha.

In 1973 Mark L. Prophet took his ascension and is now known as the ascended master Lanello. Thus, the messengers continued their service as the "other two, the one on this side of the bank of the river and the other on that side of the bank of the river," as Daniel described in his vision.

14. John 5:30; 14:10.
15. Matt. 18:19.
16. Matt. 18:20.
17. John 14:6.
18. Isa. 55:11.
19. John 14:26.
20. Matt. 17:4; Mark 9:5; Luke 9:33.
21. Rev. 19:20; 20:10, 14, 15.
22. Gen. 1; 2:1–3.
23. Exod. 32.
24. Ezek. 1:10; Rev. 4:7.
25. In a dictation given on November 19, 1978, Saint Germain inaugurated Mission Amethyst Jewel. In this dictation he called for centers to be established in Vancouver, British Columbia, and in Mexico City as "that point of light for the bulwark of freedom" and for the "guarding of North America." On April 14, 1979, Elizabeth Clare Prophet explained Mission Amethyst Jewel as "Saint Germain's commitment to send chelas to the nations of the earth, beginning with the most important cities. . . . Mission Amethyst Jewel is based upon the principle of the violet flame burning within the heart of the chela. The chela is the jewel, and as chelas place themselves together as atoms that become molecules that form outer centers, the Mission Amethyst Jewel becomes crystallized."

    On January 14, 1979, Archangel Gabriel said, "The Darjeeling Council sets forth its solution to world problems. It is

Mission Amethyst Jewel. We stand in a vote of confidence around the Darjeeling Council table in honor of Saint Germain and all servant sons and daughters who embody the great spirit of freedom as a mystery of the Holy Grail."

26. Isa. 45:11: "Thus saith the LORD, the Holy One of Israel, and his Maker, Ask me of things to come concerning my sons, and concerning the work of my hands command ye me."
27. Matt. 17:14–21; Mark 9:17–29; Luke 9:38–42.
28. John 7:24.

CHAPTER 7 • The Story of the Crystal Cup

1. Godfré Ray King, *Unveiled Mysteries* (Schaumburg, Ill.: Saint Germain Press, 1982), pp. 236–42.
2. Matt. 26:27.
3. Gen. 5:22, 24.
4. See Elizabeth Clare Prophet, *Predict Your Future: Understand the Cycles of the Cosmic Clock,* chapter 10.
5. Rom. 13:10.

CHAPTER 8 • From Glory unto Glory, Even as by the Spirit of God

1. See II Kings 2:11.
2. Matt. 24:40–41; Luke 17:34–36.
3. II Cor. 3:18.
4. Rev. 1:16.
5. See Matt. 17:1–13; Mark 9:2–8; Luke 9:28–36.
6. See Rev. 22:5.
7. See Luke 6:38.

CHAPTER 10 • The Flame in the Heart of the Great Pyramid

1. On December 29, 1978, Serapis Bey announced the inauguration at winter solstice, December 21, 1978, of a fourteen-month cycle of initiation whereby we could increase the white sphere of our causal body. Since that time, every fourteen months has marked the start of another fourteen-month cycle through the successive spheres of the causal body from the center outward. Each fourteen-month cycle is an opportunity to increase one sphere of our causal body. The messenger called

it "the opening of the window of heaven whereby God says all of the hosts of the LORD will assist you to increase that causal body ring through your words and deeds on earth." For the messenger's teachings on the fourteen-month cycles, see *Pearls of Wisdom,* vol. 27, no. 56b.

2. In announcing the fourteen-month cycle of initiation, Serapis said, "The goal of these fourteen months is the passing through of your lifestream on the fourteen stations of the cross of the Woman and her seed. . . . " The fourteen stations of the cross are fourteen events in the last hours of Jesus' life, from the time of his judgment and trial to when he was laid in the sepulchre. They represent his mastery and sacrifice on behalf of mankind. This Piscean cross is given to us for the balancing of karma and for the preparation of the initiation of the crucifixion on the cosmic cross of white fire. Answering the call of the ascended masters El Morya and Jesus, the messenger Elizabeth Clare Prophet and chelas began walking the fourteen stations of the Aquarian cross on June 27, 1972, seven years prior to this dictation. The fourteen stations of the Aquarian cross is a path of initiation that we walk today with the Divine Mother charted on the cosmic clock. A new cycle of that walk begins each year on June 27. At the time of this dictation, we were walking the seventh station of the cross—The Woman and her seed fall the second time. Charted on the cosmic clock, the seventh station is the seven o'clock line under the hierarchy of Leo. For teaching on the cosmic clock, see Elizabeth Clare Prophet, *Predict Your Future.*
3. See the Decree to Beloved Mighty Astrea—"The Starry Mother," pp. 131–32.
4. Prov. 16:18.
5. Ps. 46:10.
6. The fifth labor of Hercules was to clean the Augean stables in a single day. Augeas had thousands of cattle and their stalls had not been cleared out for years. Hercules diverted the courses of two rivers and made them flow through the stables in a great flood that washed out the filth in no time at all.
7. See chapter 13.

CHAPTER 11 • Meditation on the Crystal of the Self

1. The first chapter of the Book of Genesis describes the creation of the heavens and the earth (the entire matter universe) over a period of six "days," corresponding to the first six rays. The seventh day of creation, corresponding to the seventh ray, is described in chapter 2: "And on the seventh day God ended his work which he had made; and he rested on the seventh day from all his work which he had made."
2. Rev. 12:1–6.
3. Isa. 9:6.
4. Mal. 3:10.
5. *Prayers, Meditations and Dynamic Decrees for Personal and World Transformation,* available at http://Store.SummitLighthouse.org.

CHAPTER 12 • Surya: A Being from the God Star, Sirius

1. Sirius is the brightest star in the heavens and is the seat of God-government for this sector of the galaxy. Sirius is known as the Dog Star, a binary star of the constellation Canis Major. In a spiritual sense, all have come from Sirius. It is our point of origin and our home at the deepest level of our being.
2. John 14:12.

CHAPTER 13 • I AM Maximus, I Drop a Sound, I Maximize Light

1. The ascended master Serapis Bey writes of the Solar-El in his *Dossier on the Ascension:* "The real meaning of the soul is 'Solar-El,' which refers to the latent power of the divine angel within man. (I do not expect that all of my words will be interpreted correctly nor that they will be understood by all, but I must state the law in order that those who have been initiated to a level of comprehension suitable for the revelation inherent within this mystery may then comprehend it.) The Solar-El is the infinite idea of God projected by the divine light through the so-called seven densities of creation, including the angelic realm, and evolving within man as the evolution of divine energy intended in the beginning." (*Dossier on the Ascension,* pp. 6–7)

2. Luke 19:13.
3. Students of the ascended masters are encouraged before going to sleep to ask to be taken by the angels directly to the spiritual retreats. For a prayer for this purpose, see Mark L. Prophet and Elizabeth Clare Prophet, *The Masters and Their Retreats,* p. 414.

CHAPTER 14 • **The Initiation of the Eighth Ray**

1. The eighth ray is the ray of integration, where we integrate the mastery of the seven rays through the flame of the Christ, the threefold flame. The eighth ray corresponds to the secret chamber of the heart, an eight-petaled chakra behind the heart chakra, where the threefold flame is sealed. Uzziel is the archangel of the eighth ray. For a profile of Archangel Uzziel and additional teaching on the eighth ray, see *The Masters and Their Retreats,* pp. 375–77.
2. The cosmic cross of white fire is the symbol of the *man*ifestation of God, or man. It is the place where God and man meet. The vertical line of the cosmic cross of white fire is the fire descending from God and the horizontal bar is your extension of that light into the physical octave. It is the cross that divides the circle of Being into the four quadrants that are given unto man that he might take dominion over earth, air, fire and water. And the cross is the sign of the path of initiation. To pass initiations you must be centered in the heart of the cross, the sacred heart, the spiritual heart center of your temple where your heart is a flaming sun center of devotion unto God. For additional teaching, see *Opening of the Seventh Seal,* chapters 4, 19, and 36.
3. Rev. 22:1.
4. Matt. 21:12; Mark 11:15.
5. Rev. 21:6.
6. Rev. 7:4.
7. Rev. 5:1.
8. Rev. 20:11.
9. Rev. 5:6–8.

10. The causal body is made up of the seven concentric spheres of pulsating color and consciousness surrounding the I AM Presence in the planes of Spirit. Within these interpenetrating forcefields of your spiritual attainment are the recordings and the momentums of all the good that you have ever magnetized from the heart of God and then "caused" to be sent forth to other parts of life. Hence, it is your body of causative good. Herein are the records of your good works and your virtuous thoughts, feelings and motives.
11. In a June 1993 lecture, the messenger revealed the meaning of Excalibur as "the sword out of the white light, or the steely white light, of the Mother.... And if El Morya finds you worthy, he may wield his sword Excalibur in your defense."
12. Rev. 11:1.
13. The deathless solar body is the ascended master light body, the wedding garment that the soul must weave through devotion to God if she is to enter into the alchemical marriage of the soul's permanent bonding to the Holy Christ Self and the ritual of the ascension. See *Dossier on the Ascension,* pp. 151–59.
14. In a dictation in 1973, the ascended lady master Portia announced that the Great White Brotherhood vested the authority of the Vicar of Christ in the Mother of the Flame, the messenger Elizabeth Clare Prophet. See "Coronation of the Vicar of Christ," *Pearls of Wisdom,* vol. 16, no. 51, December 23, 1973.
15. The Jupiter Effect was a very popular prediction that there would be a major cataclysm in 1982 when the planets were in alignment in Libra, coinciding with peak activity in the sunspot cycle.
16. Rev. 14:6.
17. Rev. 4:7.
18. Dan. 11:31; 12:11; Matt. 24:15; Mark 13:14.
19. Rev. 2:17.
20. Isa. 6:8.

CHAPTER 15 • The Opening of the Door to the Octaves of Light

1. Rev. 14:4.
2. Matt. 13:33; Luke 13:21.
3. During the late 1960s and early 70s, the city of Berkeley, California, became a center for anti-establishment and socio-political activism. It was a haven for anarchists, civil unrest, and the hippie movement, including the proliferation of drugs and street living. Beginning with the Free Speech Movement in 1964, the city became a hub of protests and demonstrations. Continued riots and protests have occurred in 2011, 2014, 2017 (for a period of eight months), and 2019.
4. See chapter 6 n. 25, pp. 277–78.
5. In a dictation given through the messenger Elizabeth Clare Prophet on December 28, 1975, Chananda stated that "the Indian Council of the Great White Brotherhood summons the messenger . . . to project the blueprint for the teaching center in India. So let it come to pass, for there must be the restoration of the original teaching of the Mother brought forth upon that continent." (*Pearls of Wisdom,* vol. 59, no. 23) For information on the current activities of chelas of the ascended masters in India, go to https://chananda.org/.
6. According to the legends and histories of King Arthur of Britain, Excalibur was the name of the sword given to Arthur by the Lady of the Lake. The ascended master Lanello, in a dictation entitled "The Sign of Excalibur," explains that "the gleaming, silver-white sword Excalibur, blinding in its presence, signifies the fire of the Mother complete and raised. Thus, it is in truth the appearance of the ascension flame." (*Pearls of Wisdom,* vol. 28, no. 4)
7. In answer to this call, chelas established the Ashram of the World Mother in New Delhi, India, in 1980. See also note 5.
8. See chapter 4 n. 2, p. 275.
9. See Judg. 6:25–32.
10. Isa. 11:9.
11. Joel 2:27.
12. See Mark 14:44.

13. I Sam. 15:22–23.
14. Matt. 5:18.
15. Matt. 3:2.
16. James 2:23.
17. Luke 1:19.
18. John 8:32.

CHAPTER 16 • **The Spirit Cup and the Matter Cup**

1. John 14:15.
2. The Watchers were a band of angels who left off from their service to God, abandoned their God-estate, and fell to earth through lust. Their story is told in the book of Enoch. See Elizabeth Clare Prophet, *Fallen Angels and the Origins of Evil: Why Church Fathers Suppressed the Book of Enoch and Its Startling Revelations.*
3. The following "Confidential File" albums are available from AscendedMasterLibrary.org (search by title or product code):
   - A78090 *Confidential File 10017: Psychotronics: "The Only Way to Go is Up!"*
   - A78096 *Confidential File 10019: The Religious Philosophy of Karl Marx / The Economic Philosophy of Jesus Christ*
   - A78092 *Confidential File 10033: The Psychology of Socialism: The Religion of Hatred, the Cult of Death / The KGB: Organized Terror*
   - A79028 *Confidential File 10045: The Right to Live in the New Age—Marijuana: The Death Drug*
4. *The Manipulators of Capitalism and Communism* is available on DVD from store.SummitLighthouse.org.
5. See note 3. This lecture is also available as a paperback book from store.SummitLighthouse.org.
6. Rev. 12:6, 14.
7. Ralph Dickson Yaney, *10,001: The Birth of the Avatars, the Battle of Armageddon, and the Future of Planet Earth,* 2nd ed. (Emigrant, Mont.: Darjeeling Press, 2011).
8. Lord Maitreya, October 14, 1973, "Opportunity to Bring Forth Christed Children," *Pearls of Wisdom,* vol. 27, no. 45, September 9, 1984.

9. Jesus, December 25, 1978, "Dedicate Yourself to the Issue of Abortion for upon This Issue Hang All Others," *Pearls of Wisdom,* vol. 55, no. 23, December 1, 2012.
10. Mother Mary, "Something Must Be Done," *Pearls of Wisdom,* vol. 12, no. 24, June 15, 1969.
11. Rev. 11:7; 12; 13; 16:13; 17; 19:2, 19, 20; 20:2, 10.

CHAPTER 17 • **Light!**

1. Matt. 6:23.
2. Mark 8:12; Luke 11:29.
3. To receive current *Pearls of Wisdom* (free delivery by email, $5.95 per month for print), go to www.SummitLighthouse.org/Pearls-Wisdom.
4. Rev. 3:11.

Picture Credits

p. 20 Colossi of Memnon / Wikimedia creativecommons.org/licenses/by-sa/4.0/ MusikAnimal.

p. 21 Grand Colonnade, Temple of Luxor / Wikimedia creativecommons.org/licenses/by-sa/4.0/ Mahmoud Mostafa Ashour.

p. 24 Courtyard of Amenhotep III, Temple of Luxor / Wikimedia creativecommons.org/licenses/by-sa/3.0/ Abdullah .Nassar100.

p. 31 Parthenon / Flickr creativecommons.org/licenses/by/2.0/ Steve Swayne.

p. 33 Great Pyramid / Wikimedia creativecommons.org/licenses/by-sa/3.0/ Nina Aldin Thune.

p. 35 Head of Serapis / Wikimedia Jastrow.

p. 36 Catacombs beneath the Serapeum / Flickr creativecommons.org/licenses/by/2.0/ Institute for the Study of the Ancient World.

p. 162 Sunflower / Flickr creativecommons.org/licenses/by-nc-nd/2.0/ lucapost.

p. 192 Surya statue / Flickr creativecommons.org/licenses/by-sa/2.0/ Raveesh Vyas.

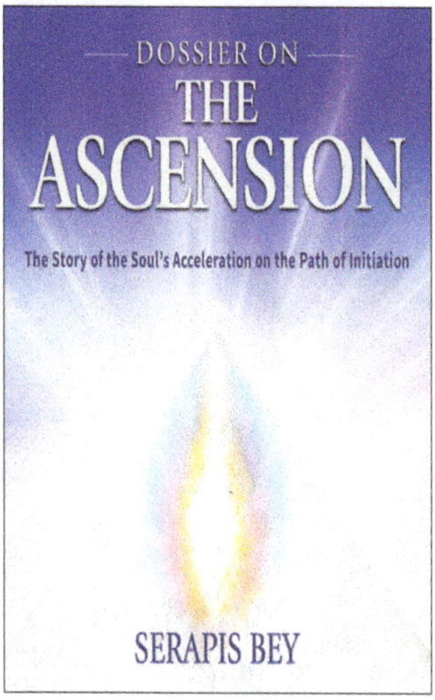

212 pp ISBN 978-0-916766-21-4

Dossier on the Ascension

The Story of the Soul's Acceleration
into Higher Consciousness on the Path of Initiation

SERAPIS BEY

Breaking the wheel of rebirth... Union with God... The ascension...

Throughout the ages, those of all faiths have sought to go beyond the limits of the mind, to attain immortality. History leaves the record of a few who reached that goal—Zarathustra, who ascended back to God in "the great flame"; Elijah, who was carried up into heaven in a "chariot of fire"; Jesus, who was taken up into a cloud from Bethany's hill.

Now, Serapis Bey and the Brotherhood of Luxor reveal inner secrets of the path to the ascension. They open the door to their mystery school, sharing keys to immortality. And they show how you can apply their spiritual techniques to find the answers to life's ultimate questions.

- Journey to the Central Sun through the meditations of the seraphim.
- Learn the meaning of the Deathless Solar Body as the vehicle of the soul beyond the veil.
- Find your ultimate freedom to be your Real Self.

The flame of the ascension is the key which
unlocks the door to immortality for every man.

—Serapis Bey

432 pp. ISBN 978-0-922729-27-2

Reincarnation

The Missing Link in Christianity

BY ELIZABETH CLARE PROPHET

"This is an extremely important book, a book providing profound insight and truth, a book which will open minds and remove fears."

—Brian Weiss, M.D., author of *Many Lives, Many Masters*

"Imaginative and provocative. . . . Elizabeth Clare Prophet's assertion that not only mystical Gnostics but also a Jewish wisdom teacher like Jesus taught reincarnation is sure to rattle your karmic chain."

—Marvin Meyer, author of *The Gospel of Thomas: The Hidden Sayings of Jesus*

This groundbreaking work makes the case that Jesus taught reincarnation and traces the history of reincarnation in Christianity—from Jesus and early Christians through church councils and the persecution of so-called heretics. Using the latest scholarship and evidence from the Dead Sea Scrolls and Gnostic texts, it also argues persuasively that Jesus was a mystic who taught that our destiny is to unite with the God within. Your view of Jesus—and of Christianity—will never be the same.

312 pp ISBN 978-0-922729-35-7

Kabbalah

Key to Your Inner Power

BY ELIZABETH CLARE PROPHET

"A masterpiece. The rich tradition of the Kabbalah comes to life in a language that is accessible even to those unfamiliar with this ancient and classic tradition."

—Caroline Myss, Ph.D.,
New York Times bestselling author of *Anatomy of the Spirit*

"A clear and eloquent presentation of the Kabbalah, at once spiritual and practical."

—Daniel C. Matt, author of *The Essential Kabbalah*

Mystics are adventurers of the spirit who dare to push beyond the boundaries of orthodox tradition to pursue a common goal—the direct experience of God. *Kabbalah: Key to Your Inner Power* explores the once-secret Jewish mystical tradition known as Kabbalah.

With intriguing new perspectives, it shows how we can use Kabbalah's extraordinary revelations about the creation of the universe, our relationship to God and our purpose in life to unlock our own spiritual power. It brings to life the path of the Jewish mystics—their joys and ecstasies, their sacred visions, and their practical techniques for experiencing the sacred in everyday life.

About The Summit Lighthouse

The Summit Lighthouse is an internationally recognized spiritual center for the advancement of inner awakening. Our international organization is a global family that is inspired, guided, and sponsored by those known as the ascended masters.

The ascended masters are the most beloved and trusted transcendent beings guiding our planet's material and spiritual evolution. Most of the world's religions are currently based on the revelations of one or more of these masters before their ascension. We openly embrace spiritual seekers from all paths of light including the mystical traditions of the world's religions.

The ascended masters and their messengers have given us over fifteen thousand hours of invaluable inner wisdom and insightful instruction, and they have provided the means for our direct initiation into higher consciousness.

For the ascended masters . . . no subject is off limits! Their teachings contain amazing truths and awesome answers on spirituality, alchemy, astrology, sacred geometry, spiritual science, karma, reincarnation, ascension, archangels (and fallen angels), and even those issues that are considered taboo or "out of this world."

Primary Goals of the Teachings of the Ascended Masters

The ascended masters challenge us daily to be bold, to dare to be who we truly are, and to face adversity with courage, patience, perseverance, honesty, integrity, inner love, discipline, and discernment—all for a greater sense of inner peace, fearlessness, stillness and silence, harmony, self-mastery, compassion, and wisdom.

These teachings help our souls get back to the origin of their individualized inner source of True Self Love—the Higher Self, or I AM Presence. Our point of contact with our Higher Self is the "Spark of Life" or "Sacred Fire of the Heart," the place where our consciousness expresses its true divine nature of unconditional love and happiness, universal oneness, and an authentic desire to serve others.

How Our Teachings Came into Being

Our teachings were all released through highly trained and trusted messengers, Mark L. Prophet and Elizabeth Clare Prophet. Mark was contacted by the Ascended Master El Morya at the age of eighteen and received training from him for many years before he was instructed to establish The Summit Lighthouse in 1958 in Washington, D.C.

With his ascension in 1973, Mark passed the torch for the mission to his gifted wife, Elizabeth Clare Prophet, who continued her service until her retirement in 1999.

The dictations of the ascended masters were regularly given in public. The ascended masters also inspired thousands of lectures delivered by the messengers. The content of the dictations are, by most human standards, beyond the mind's ability to construct in real time. They carry very powerful frequencies of light, awakening us to the highest truths we've ever experienced.

We leave it up to you to decide the value for yourself.

Moving toward Your Victory

No matter what path of light you are on, spiritual freedom is attained using tools that have been passed down in wisdom teachings through the millennia: meditation, selfless service, devotional music, prayer, mantra, and the science of the spoken Word. The masters bring an accelerated understanding of these principles, especially suited for the challenges of the modern world, including dynamic decree work and the use of the violet flame.

Next Steps

We are genuinely excited to meet you on the path . . . and hope you are too. We extend a warm welcome from everyone at The Summit Lighthouse, and we invite you to explore the teachings of the ascended masters at our website https://wwwSummitLighthouse.org. Check out our free online lessons and hundreds of articles on a wide range of spiritual subjects. Browse through our online bookstore. And if you would rather talk to someone in person, please feel free to contact us today!

The Summit Lighthouse®
63 Summit Way
Gardiner, Montana 59030 USA
1-800-245-5445 / 406-848-9500

Se habla español.

info@SummitUniversityPress.com
SummitLighthouse.org

Elizabeth Clare Prophet is a world-renowned author, spiritual teacher, and pioneer in practical spirituality. Her groundbreaking books have been published in more than thirty languages and over three million copies have been sold worldwide.

Among her best-selling titles are *The Human Aura; The Science of the Spoken Word; Your Seven Energy Centers; The Lost Years of Jesus; The Art of Practical Spirituality;* and her best-selling Pocket Guides to Practical Spirituality series.

CPSIA information can be obtained
at www.ICGtesting.com
Printed in the USA
JSHW030934030722
27529JS00003B/6

9 781609 884000